Would Democratic Socialism Be Better?

LANE KENWORTHY

OXFORD
UNIVERSITY PRESS

OXFORD
UNIVERSITY PRESS

Oxford University Press is a department of the University of Oxford. It furthers
the University's objective of excellence in research, scholarship, and education
by publishing worldwide. Oxford is a registered trade mark of Oxford University
Press in the UK and certain other countries.

Published in the United States of America by Oxford University Press
198 Madison Avenue, New York, NY 10016, United States of America.

Library of Congress Control Number: 2022900096
ISBN 978-0-19-763681-7 (pbk.)
ISBN 978-0-19-763680-0 (hbk.)

DOI: 10.1093/oso/9780197636800.001.0001

1 3 5 7 9 8 6 4 2

Paperback printed by LSC Communications, United States of America
Hardback printed by Bridgeport National Bindery, Inc., United States of America

Would Democratic Socialism Be Better?

Contents

1. Is Capitalism Not Good Enough?   1

2. An End to Poverty in Rich Countries   15

3. An End to Poverty Everywhere   24

4. More Jobs   36

5. Decent Jobs   44

6. Faster Economic Growth   56

7. Inclusive Growth   64

8. More Public Goods and Services   75

9. Affordable Healthcare for All   82

10. Helpful Finance   91

11. Truly Democratic Politics   97

12. Economic Democracy   108

13. Less Economic Inequality   120

14. Gender and Racial Equality   131

15. More Community   144

16. A Livable Planet   155

17. Would Democratic Socialism Be Better Than Social
    Democratic Capitalism?   163

Acknowledgments   171
Notes   173
References   191
Index   215

1

Is Capitalism Not Good Enough?

Socialism is back in the conversation. In the United States, of all places, recent polls suggest the share of young people who have a favorable impression of socialism is about the same as the share that have a favorable view of capitalism.[1] A self-described democratic socialist, Bernie Sanders, was runner-up in the Democratic Party's presidential primary in 2016 and 2020. Think tanks and magazines devising plans for socialist policies and institutions have sprouted up.[2] The *New York Times* and the *Washington Post* have each had an avowed socialist among their op-ed writers in recent years.[3] Since 2016, membership in the Democratic Socialists of America (DSA) has jumped from a few thousand to nearly 100,000.[4]

Is there a compelling case for socialism? Should we aspire to shift, in the reasonably near future, from a basically capitalist economy to a socialist one?

Let's stipulate that socialism refers to an economy in which two-thirds or more of employment and output (GDP) is in firms that are owned by the government, citizens, or workers. Two-thirds is an arbitrary cutoff, but it's as sensible as any other. It connotes a subsidiary role for the private non-worker-owned sector.

Since the Bolshevik revolution in Russia in 1917, much of the debate about socialism has focused on lessons that can be drawn from the experience of the former Soviet Union, Cuba, and other actually existing self-styled socialist countries.[5] I will ignore this almost entirely. Because each of those cases featured an autocratic political system, they are of little or no relevance to most modern proposals for socialism. Similarly, while the contemporary Chinese model is attractive to some,[6] my focus is on the kind of socialism currently desired by proponents in the world's affluent democratic nations. That socialism presupposes a democratic political system. That socialism would be a democratic socialism.

Some of the debate over democratic socialism concerns goals. The case for democratic socialism typically is motivated by goals such as freedom, opportunity, democracy, equality, and solidarity, among others. While I have some quibbles—as I explain in later chapters, I think some attach too high a priority to economic equality and to a particular form of economic democracy—for the most part I endorse the outcomes democratic socialists say they want. The aim of this book isn't to question those goals.

Would Democratic Socialism Be Better?. Lane Kenworthy, Oxford University Press. © Lane Kenworthy 2022.
DOI: 10.1093/oso/9780197636800.003.0001

To offer a realistic alternative, socialism must be workable. Socialism's proponents have put a good bit of effort into designing institutions and policies that might make a democratic socialist economy function effectively. I will draw on these proposals. In doing so I'll assume they are in fact workable, though I'll also emphasize that there is considerable uncertainty, since evidence is thin or nonexistent.

A potentially significant consideration in evaluating democratic socialism is the possibility of a "transition trough"—a steep and lengthy downturn in economic well-being during the shift from capitalism to socialism.[7] There might indeed be a significant economic cost to transitioning if opponents stop investing or shift their assets to other countries. But maybe not. Perhaps the transition trough would be like an ordinary economic recession—painful but temporary. This too I will set aside.

My focus is on what has tended to be the centerpiece of the case for democratic socialism: the notion that capitalism is bad, or at least not very good. In reaching this conclusion, most have either analyzed a theoretical ideal-type of capitalism, as Karl Marx famously did in *Capital*, or used a single country, often the United States, as a stand-in for capitalism.[8] To fully and fairly assess democratic socialism's desirability, we need to compare it to the best version of capitalism that humans have devised: social democratic capitalism, or what is often called the Nordic model.[9] I try in this book to offer such an assessment. My conclusion is that capitalism, and particularly social democratic capitalism, is better than many democratic socialists seem to think.

The Reference Point: Social Democratic Capitalism

Social democratic capitalism features a capitalist economy, a democratic political system, good elementary and secondary (K-12) schooling, a big welfare state, employment-conducive public services (childcare, job training, and others), and moderate regulation of product and labor markets. This set of institutions and policies improves living standards for the least well-off, enhances economic security, and boosts equality of opportunity. It does so without sacrificing the many other things we want in a good society, from liberty to economic growth to happiness and much more.[10]

Figures 1.1 through 1.5 give a flavor of social democratic capitalism's success. On the horizontal axis in each of the charts is a social democratic capitalism index. Every affluent longstanding-democratic country has a welfare state, but their expansiveness and generosity differ significantly. Employment-oriented public services and moderate (rather than stringent) product and labor market regulations aim to boost employment, and these too vary widely across the

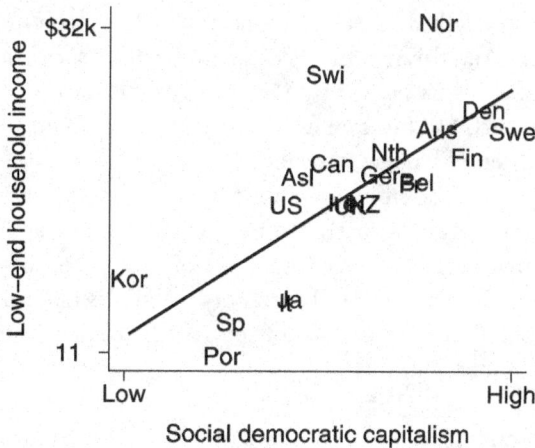

Figure 1.1 Social democratic capitalism and living standards of the least well-off

Low-end household income: posttransfer-posttax income at the 10th percentile of the income distribution. 2010–2016. The incomes are adjusted for household size and then rescaled to reflect a three-person household, adjusted for inflation, and converted to US dollars using purchasing power parities. "k" = thousand. Data sources: Luxembourg Income Study; OECD. Social democratic capitalism: average standard deviation score on four indicators: public expenditures on social programs as a share of GDP, replacement rates for major public transfer programs, public expenditures on employment-oriented services, and modest regulation of product and labor markets. The data cover the period 1980–2015. Data source: Lane Kenworthy, *Social Democratic Capitalism*, Oxford University Press, 2020, pp. 39–40. "Asl" is Australia; "Aus" is Austria. The line is a linear regression line. The correlation is +.73.

world's rich democratic nations. The social democratic capitalism index captures these country differences.[11]

The country ranking is consistent with what we would expect. The Nordic countries score highest (they are to the right on the horizontal axis). They are followed by five continental European nations that have big welfare states but less public spending on employment-promoting services and heavier regulation of product and labor markets: Austria, Belgium, France, the Netherlands, and Germany. In the lower half of scores are Switzerland, Japan, and six English-speaking countries, which have smaller welfare states and limited public spending on employment-oriented services. They are joined by three southern European nations and South Korea, which have medium-sized or small welfare states, comparatively little employment-promoting service spending, and heavy product and labor market regulation.[12]

On the vertical axis in Figure 1.1 is a measure of the living standards of the least well-off: the income of a household at the tenth percentile of the income distribution (90 percent of households have larger incomes, and 10 percent have smaller ones).[13] The incomes are adjusted for inflation over time and for cost-of-living differences across countries. The chart shows that the incomes of low-end households tend to be higher in nations that make greater use of social democratic capitalism. And this income measure understates social democratic capitalism's benefits, because it doesn't take into account the monetary value of government services such as childcare and eldercare, which tend to be more plentiful under social democratic capitalism.[14]

In Figure 1.2 we see that the employment rate tends to be higher with social democratic capitalism. This owes partly to its extensive use of employment-promoting government services: active labor market programs such as retraining and job placement and family-friendly programs like early education and paid parental leave. These kinds of services encourage more people, particularly women and parents, to enter employment, they help persons who lose a job to prepare for and find another one, and they serve as a direct source of jobs for teachers, trainers, caseworkers, and others. High employment rates also owe to social democratic capitalism's use of moderate, rather than heavy, regulation of product and labor markets. The easier it is to start up, operate, and shut down a business, and the more flexible firms can be in hiring and firing workers, the more private businesses are likely to be able and willing to boost employment.[15]

The vertical axis in Figure 1.3 shows a measure of economic insecurity: the share of households that experience a large income decline from one year to the next. The share tends to be smaller in nations with more of a social democratic capitalist orientation. This is partly because public insurance programs

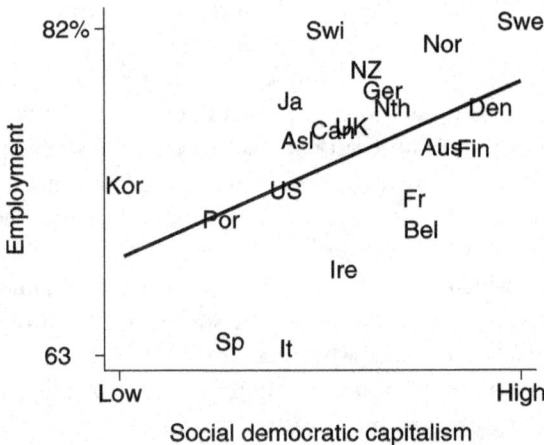

Figure 1.2 Social democratic capitalism and employment

Employment: employed persons age 25–64 as a share of all persons age 25–64. 2010–2016. Data source: OECD. Social democratic capitalism: see Figure 1.1. "Asl" is Australia; "Aus" is Austria. The line is a linear regression line. The correlation is +.47.

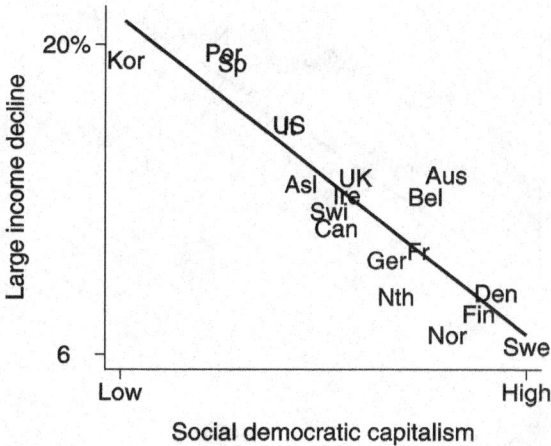

Figure 1.3 Social democratic capitalism and economic insecurity

Large income decline: Share of households experiencing a year-to-year income decrease of 25 percent or more. Average over the 2-year periods between 1985 and 2015. Excludes households that enter retirement between one year and the next. Data source: Jacob S. Hacker, "Economic Security," in *For Good Measure: Advancing Research on Well-Being Metrics beyond GDP*, edited by Joseph E. Stiglitz, Jean-Paul Fitoussi, and Martine Durand, OECD, 2018, table 8.4, using data from the ECHP, EU-SILC, CPS, and CNEF (BHPS, SOEP, HILDA, KLIPS, SHP, SLID). Social democratic capitalism: see Figure 1.1. "Asl" is Australia; "Aus" is Austria. The line is a linear regression line. The correlation is -.88.

compensate for lost earnings. It's also because social democratic capitalism boosts employment, so if a household member loses his or her job, it's easier for another member of the household to become employed, increase work hours, or take on a second job.

Figure 1.4 shows a strong positive association between social democratic capitalism and opportunity. We can think of opportunity as individuals' capability to choose, act, and accomplish—what Isaiah Berlin called "positive liberty" and Amartya Sen has labeled "real freedom."[16] While critics of big government tend to assume that public social programs reduce freedom, many of these programs are capability-enhancing. They boost people's cognitive and noncognitive skills, increase their employment options, ensure that hard times do minimal damage, and reduce dependence on family and friends. More than a century ago, John Stuart Mill recognized that true freedom to lead the kind of life we want requires education, health, and economic security.[17] More recently, Anu Partanen has highlighted this point in a comparison of her native Finland with her adopted country, the United States. Observing that many Americans don't have access to high-quality, affordable health insurance, childcare, housing in good school districts, college, and eldercare, Partanen notes that this diminishes not only Americans' economic security but also their freedom:

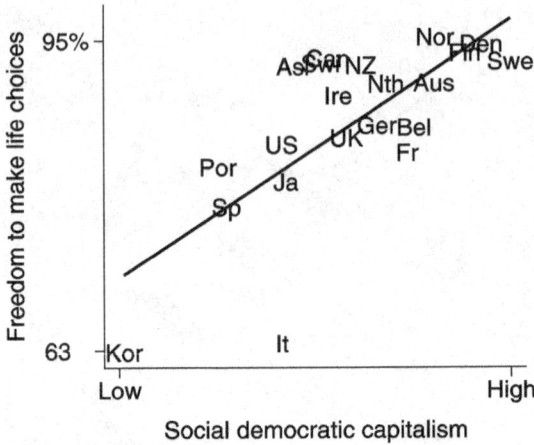

Figure 1.4 Social democratic capitalism and opportunity

Freedom to make life choices: share responding "satisfied" to the question "Are you satisfied or dissatisfied with your freedom to choose what you do with your life?" 2005–2019. Data source: Gallup World Poll, via the *World Happiness Report 2020*, online appendix. Social democratic capitalism: see Figure 1.1. "Asl" is Australia; "Aus" is Austria. The line is a linear regression line. The correlation is +.72.

Most people, including myself, assumed that part of what made the United States a great country, and such an exceptional one, was that you could live your life relatively unencumbered by the downside of a traditional, old-fashioned society: dependency on the people you happened to be stuck with. In America you had the liberty to express your individuality and choose your own community. This would allow you to interact with family, neighbors, and fellow citizens on the basis of who you were, rather than on what you were obligated to do or expected to be according to old-fashioned thinking. The longer I lived in America . . . the more puzzled I grew. For it was exactly those key benefits of modernity—freedom, personal independence, and opportunity—that seemed, from my outsider's perspective, in a thousand small ways to be surprisingly missing from American life today. . . . In order to compete and to survive, the Americans I encountered and read about were . . . beholden to their spouses, parents, children, colleagues, and bosses in ways that constrained their own liberty.[18]

We have no direct measure of opportunity, but a useful indirect measure comes from a question asked by the Gallup World Poll: "Are you satisfied or dissatisfied with your freedom to choose what you do with your life?" We can treat the share responding "satisfied" as an indicator of opportunity, of the degree to which capabilities extend widely across the population. This share is on the vertical axis of Figure 1.4. The pattern across countries is consistent with the hypothesis that social democratic capitalism enhances opportunity.[19]

Figure 1.5 looks at happiness, which some consider the ultimate prize.[20] The Gallup World Poll regularly asks the following question: "Please imagine a ladder, with steps numbered from 0 at the bottom to 10 at the top. The top of the ladder represents the best possible life for you and the bottom of the ladder represents the worst possible life for you. On which step of the ladder would you say you personally feel you stand at this time?" Across the rich democratic countries, we see a strong positive association between social democratic capitalism and life satisfaction.

Social democratic capitalism's chief practitioners have been Denmark, Finland, Norway, and Sweden. Skeptics on the left sometimes suggest that the model peaked in the 1970s, retreating since then in the face of a business offensive and economic globalization.[21] This is true when it comes to income inequality, as we will see in a later chapter.[22] But inequality is the exception rather than the rule. Among the five outcomes shown on the vertical axes in Figures 1.1 to 1.5, we have over-time data for three. Figure 1.6 shows that incomes of households at the low end of the socioeconomic ladder have continued to rise rapidly in all four Nordic countries since the 1970s, both in absolute terms and relative to what's happened in the United States.[23] Figure 1.7 shows that the Nordics have

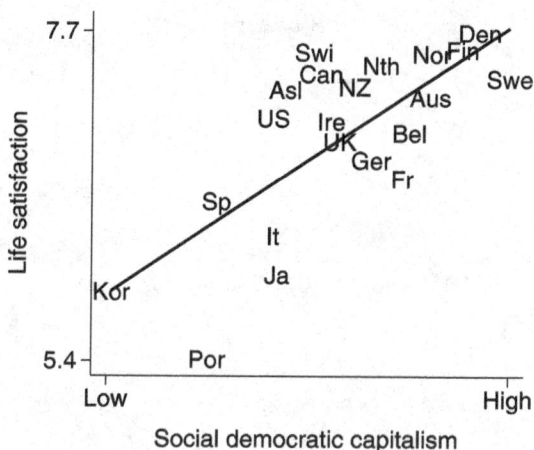

Figure 1.5 Social democratic capitalism and happiness

Life satisfaction: average response to the question "Please imagine a ladder, with steps numbered from 0 at the bottom to 10 at the top. The top of the ladder represents the best possible life for you and the bottom of the ladder represents the worst possible life for you. On which step of the ladder would you say you personally feel you stand at this time?" 2005–2019. Data source: Gallup World Poll, via the *World Happiness Report 2020*, online appendix. Social democratic capitalism: see Figure 1.1. "Asl" is Australia; "Aus" is Austria. The line is a linear regression line. The correlation is +.72.

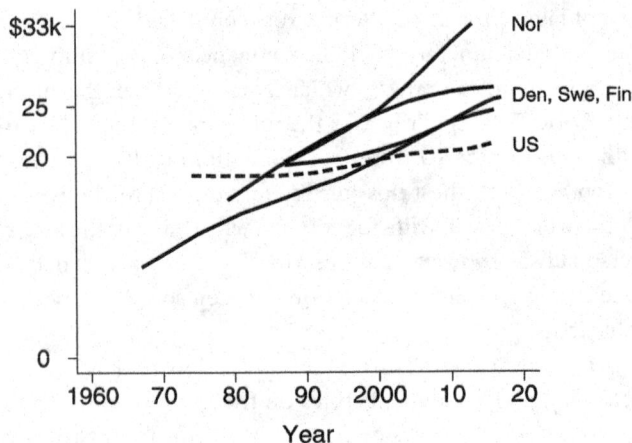

Figure 1.6 Living standards of the least well-off

Tenth-percentile household income. Posttransfer-posttax income. The incomes are adjusted for household size and then rescaled to reflect a three-person household, adjusted for inflation, and converted to US dollars using purchasing power parities. "k" = thousand. Data sources: Luxembourg Income Study; OECD. The lines are loess curves.

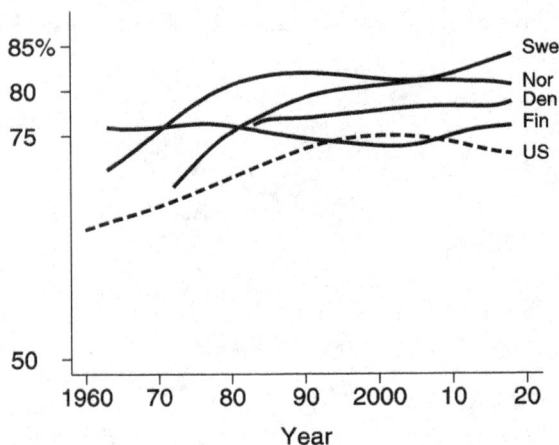

Figure 1.7 Employment

Employed persons age 25–64 as a share of all persons age 25–64. The vertical axis doesn't begin at zero. Data source: OECD. The lines are loess curves.

maintained or improved their high employment rates.[24] And in Figure 1.8 we see that life satisfaction has increased slightly in Norway and Finland while falling slightly in Denmark and Sweden. Here, too, all of the Nordics have performed a good bit better than the United States.[25]

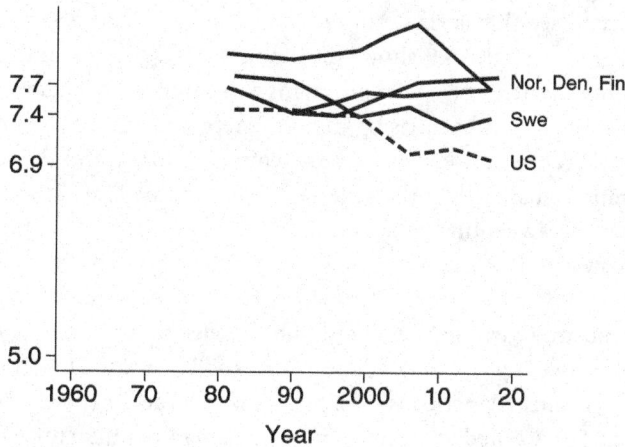

Figure 1.8 Life satisfaction

Average response to the question "All things considered, how satisfied are you with your life as a whole these days?" Scale of 0 to 10. The vertical axis doesn't begin at zero. Data source: World Values Survey.

Some observers believe the Nordic nations have unique features—culture, good government, small size, among others—that allow them, and only them, to achieve the good outcomes produced by social democratic capitalism without suffering tradeoffs. But a careful look at the evidence suggests this isn't true.[26] The model's success almost certainly is transferable to other affluent democratic nations. Indeed, all of those nations already are partial adopters of social democratic capitalism, and they've benefited from that.

While the Nordic nations are, to this point, the only ones to have fully embraced social democratic capitalism, other countries have been moving in that direction.[27] Many of the continental European nations have long had expansive and generous public social programs. Over the past two decades, some of them—most notably Germany, the Netherlands, and Austria—have added early education, lifelong learning, active labor market policy, and other employment-conducive public services, and some have loosened their product and labor market regulations. Both steps bring these countries into closer alignment with the social democratic capitalist model. The United Kingdom also moved in this direction under the New Labour governments headed by Tony Blair and Gordon Brown from 1997 to 2010, though the Conservative governments since then have pulled back somewhat. Even the United States, long seen as the welfare state laggard among the affluent democracies, has continued its slow but fairly steady long-run movement toward social democratic capitalism.[28]

One way to see this is via an indicator of the scope and generosity of public social programs. Figure 1.9 shows the amount governments in the rich democratic countries spend on social programs as a share of gross domestic product (GDP). The share has been rising in all of these nations for roughly a century. And the difference between the Nordic countries today and the United States today is much smaller than the difference between the United States today and the United States a century ago.

So when we ask "Would democratic socialism be better?" we should be asking not whether it would be better than capitalism per se, or better than American-style capitalism. Our question should be: In what ways would democratic socialism improve upon social democratic capitalism?[29] How would Danes, Swedes, Germans, Americans, Koreans, and people in other countries have better lives if they opted for democratic socialism rather than the Nordic model?

Before moving on, let me emphasize that the label "social democratic capitalism," which I'll use throughout the book, is shorthand for a set of policies and institutions: a capitalist economy, a democratic political system, good K-12 schooling, a big welfare state, employment-conducive public services, and moderate regulation of product and labor markets. It *isn't* intended to be shorthand for the policy preferences of particular Social Democratic parties, nor for the electoral success of those parties.

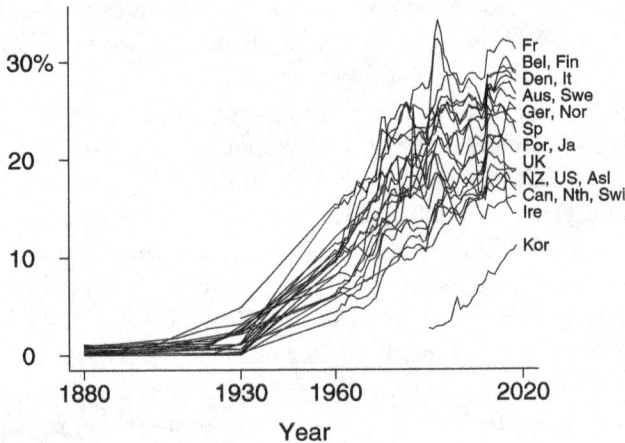

Figure 1.9 Public social expenditures

Share of GDP. Gross public social expenditures. Data source: Esteban Ortiz-Ospina and Max Roser, "Public Spending," *Our World in Data*, using data for 1880–1930 from Peter Lindert, *Growing Public*, volume 1, Cambridge University Press, 2004, data for 1960–1979 from OECD, "Social Expenditure 1960–1990: Problems of Growth and Control," OECD Social Policy Studies, 1985, and data for 1980ff from OECD, Social Expenditures Database. "Asl" is Australia; "Aus" is Austria.

What Is Democratic Socialism?

What might democratic socialism look like? Some advocates envision it, vaguely, as a society in which everyone has access to what they need, there is little inequality of income or wealth or power, and behavior is cooperative.[30] Most proponents, however, think of democratic socialism mainly as a different way of structuring the economy. For socialists in prior eras this meant government economic planning, but today nearly all socialist proposals rely heavily on markets.[31] The core distinguishing features of contemporary democratic socialist ideas are public ownership of firms and economic democracy.[32]

Ownership of companies in democratic socialism would be mainly public rather than private. One straightforward version of this would involve government taking ownership of ("nationalizing") firms in a variety of industries. Jeremy Corbyn, the Labour Party candidate for prime minister in the United Kingdom in 2017 and 2019 and a self-described socialist, proposed to nationalize rail, water, electricity distribution companies, and mail, as well as some steel firms.[33] Getting two-thirds or more of the economy in government hands would require far more. Here, for example, is the current distribution of employment by industry in the United States:[34]

13.9%	Government
13.0	Professional and business services
12.4	Healthcare
10.2	Leisure and hospitality
9.8	Retail trade
7.9	Manufacturing
5.5	Self-employed
5.3	Finance
4.5	Construction
4.1	Other services
3.6	Wholesale trade
3.4	Transportation and warehousing
2.3	Education
1.8	Information
1.4	Agriculture
0.4	Mining
0.3	Utilities

Government (federal, state, and local) currently accounts for about 14 percent of employment. If all of healthcare, manufacturing, finance, transportation, education, and utilities were nationalized, that would bring public employment to only about 45 percent of the total. An additional 20 percent or so would be needed to get to two-thirds.

Another way to think about this is by size of firm. Here is the current breakdown in the United States:[35]

13.9%	Government
8.6	Private: 1 to 9 employees
21.7	Private: 10 to 99 employees
20.9	Private: 100 to 999 employees
35.0	Private: 1,000 or more employees

Nationalizing all currently private firms that have more than 1,000 employees and most that have more than 100 would bring two-thirds into the public sector.

Nationalization isn't the only approach to public ownership. Another is to change the nature or the distribution of stock shares. For example, employees could own a large number of firms collectively. One way to do this would be to gradually transfer stock shares in large companies to a fund controlled by labor unions or by some other worker-elected representative body.[36]

Another proposal for how to change stock ownership is John Roemer's "coupon socialism" plan.[37] Mid-sized and large companies would issue stock shares, just as they do today in capitalist economies. At age 18, each person is given a certain number of coupons, equal to a per capita share of the total value of the economy's stock shares, which she can use to purchase shares in particular firms (or in a mutual fund or index fund). Coupons can be used for this purpose only; they can't be sold for cash. Firms pay dividends, yielding an income flow to their owners. And ownership confers the right to vote as a shareholder in electing a firm's board of directors. If a person sells some or all of his shares in a particular company, he receives coupons, which can be used only to purchase shares in other firms. Share ownership can't be inherited or gifted; at death, a person's coupons go back to the common pool, to be redistributed among living citizens.

Because stock shares can be traded, the price (in coupons) of successful firms will increase. Thus, over the course of a lifetime, people who invest in more successful companies will end up with a larger ownership share than others. This may also yield them more income via the dividend payments of the companies (or mutual funds) whose shares they own. But this type of income inequality will be minor relative to what exists in contemporary capitalist economies, where a small share of the population own lots of stock shares and most people own few or none.

Firms in the Roemer plan can raise money by issuing new shares and selling them on the stock market for coupons. The government (central bank) determines the value of new stock shares, which gives it some influence over the direction of economic activity. If the government wants to encourage investment in, say, clean energy, it can increase the value of new shares of firms in that line of business. But otherwise a Roemer "coupon socialism" economy would operate similarly to existing affluent capitalist economies.

If one common vision of democratic socialism revolves around shifting from private to public ownership of firms, another sees it as the expansion of democracy to the economic sphere, within firms and/or in the broader economy. Tom Malleson lays out a version of this:

> *Democratic workplaces.* Firms are run as worker cooperatives (except for those run by a single individual, or those of large capital-intensity or national importance, which are co-managed between worker representatives and state representatives). The majority of the workforce of each co-op must be full members with equal rights to participate in the governance of the firm, elect managers, and receive a share of the profits. Temporary workers could be permitted, but after a probationary period they must enjoy full rights to become members should they wish to do so. Each firm is free to remunerate as it sees fit. . . .
>
> A *democratized market system.* Co-ops and consumers interact with each other and are coordinated by way of a market system. This is the second component of the economy—a cooperative market system regulated by an interventionist state. The market system is regulated to improve consumer democracy by reducing inequality. . . .
>
> *Democratic finance and investment.* Citizen democracy over economic development is protected by capital controls and promoted through public institutions that are both accountable and well-equipped to deal with market failures (such as externalities, public goods, etc.) These public institutions exist at different levels: accountable investment at the highest level is achieved through a National Investment Fund, while meaningful involvement occurs at the local level through Public Community Banks (ideal for dealing with local externalities) and participatory budgeting (ideal for dealing with local public goods). Public funds are allocated by the government to regions based on the share of their population; then municipalities direct funds to public community banks and participatory budgeting. Participatory budgeting decides on local investment priorities and the public community banks disperse their funds as loans to co-ops (and individuals) on the basis of criteria decided by the elected municipal government.[38]

While there are other conceptualizations of democratic socialism, public ownership and economic democracy are the key features for most contemporary proponents.[39]

Here I need to clear up a terminological confusion. The confusion stems mainly from Bernie Sanders, who came close to being the Democratic Party's presidential nominee in the United States in both 2016 and 2020. Sanders favors the Nordic model, but he labels it democratic socialism. It isn't only Sanders; some on the center left in Europe over the past century have called themselves socialists even though what they desire is essentially the Nordic model.[40] Throughout the book I'll stick to the more conventional usage: I'll refer to the Nordic model as social democratic capitalism, and I'll use the terms "socialism" and "democratic socialism" to refer the kinds of economic system I've described in this section.[41]

What's Wrong with Social Democratic Capitalism? Would Democratic Socialism Be Better?

My aim in this book is to advance our thinking about what kind of economic system we want, and about whether democratic socialism should be a prominent part of the discussion. I hope to push this discussion in the direction of comparison, concreteness, and evidence.

The case for a modern democratic humane socialism typically has two parts. The first is that capitalism is bad, at or least not especially good. Is that correct? The bits of evidence I've shown you in this chapter suggest that the social democratic version of capitalism actually has done rather well. The rest of the book looks into this in much greater detail. Each chapter examines one of the things that we should want in a good society, that contemporary democratic socialists typically say they want, and that socialism might, conceivably, improve our ability to achieve: an end to poverty in rich countries, an end to poverty everywhere, more jobs, decent jobs, faster economic growth, inclusive growth, more public goods and services, affordable healthcare for all, helpful finance, truly democratic politics, economic democracy, less economic inequality, gender and racial equality, more community, and a livable planet. I offer a close look at the evidence about how capitalist economies have performed on these outcomes, with particular attention to the performance of social democratic capitalism.

The second part of the case for democratic socialism is the notion that it would be an improvement. For each of these outcomes, I consider what, if anything, we can conclude about whether democratic socialism would do better than social democratic capitalism. There is no existing democratic socialism along the lines of what present-day advocates envision, so it's impossible to conduct an evidence-based comparison between democratic socialism and social democratic capitalism. Instead, we have to consider a hypothetical democratic socialism. But that shouldn't stop us from being as systematic and detailed as we can.

2

An End to Poverty in Rich Countries

In proportion as capital accumulates, the situation of the worker, be his payment high or low, must grow worse.

— Karl Marx[1]

This system [capitalism] creates enormous wealth but also great misery for the majority.

— Vivek Chibber[2]

To me democratic socialism is the value that in a modern, moral, and wealthy society no person should be too poor to live.

— Alexandria Ocasio-Cortez[3]

The eradication of poverty will only happen when the socioeconomic system has been seriously overhauled and founded upon economic democracy.

— Gregg Olsen[4]

Capitalism has been effective at achieving economic growth—a steady and significant increase in the quantity of goods and services. Figure 2.1 tells the story. Economic historians have estimates of gross domestic product (GDP) per person back to the year AD 1 for France and back a few centuries or more for some other countries. For most of the past two thousand years—and by extension, for virtually all of human history—the quantity of goods and services we produced barely budged.[5] Then, with the advent of capitalism around the middle of the 1800s, economic productivity surged and output grew rapidly in nations such as the United States, Germany, France, and a handful of others. Capitalism isn't the whole story; government provision of property rights and public goods has been key, as has the scientific method. But capitalism has been central.[6]

It could have turned out that owners (capitalists) grabbed all of the gains from rising productivity and output. Owners have more power than workers, because there usually are fewer firms looking for workers than workers looking for an employer.

Would Democratic Socialism Be Better?. Lane Kenworthy, Oxford University Press. © Lane Kenworthy 2022.
DOI: 10.1093/oso/9780197636800.003.0002

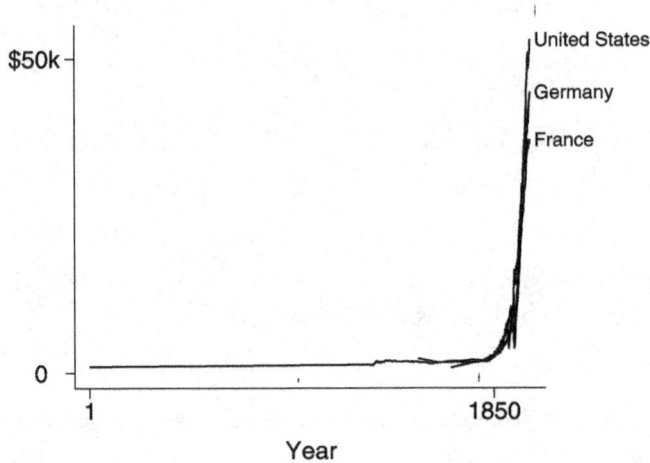

Figure 2.1 GDP per capita

Adjusted for inflation and converted to 2011 US dollars using purchasing power parities.
"k" = thousand. The data begin in AD 1 for France, in 1500 for Germany, and in 1650 for the United
States. Data source: Maddison Project Database 2018, rug.nl/ggdc.

In practice, the gains have been shared to a nontrivial degree. Ordinary
workers have gotten steadily higher wages, incomes, and living standards. One
reason is that firms sometimes find it difficult to locate available workers, or ones
with needed skills or experience. This gives workers enough leverage to secure
a wage increase. A second is labor unions, which negotiate on behalf of large
groups of workers and have the ability to strike, giving them considerably more
power than individual employees have. A third is government minimum wages,
which have tended to rise over time, along with regulation of hiring and firing
procedures, work hours, working conditions, and more. In addition, in the period from 1945 through the 1970s, many employers were willing to acquiesce to
steady wage increases in order to stave off a repeat of the decade-long depression
of the 1930s and to discourage workers from embracing communism.

As a result, it isn't only the rich who have experienced rising living standards.
Nor is it just the rich and the middle class. There has been very significant improvement for the working class and even the poor. People at the low end
have higher incomes, better housing, longer lives, more education, shorter
workweeks, and more retirement years than did their counterparts from a century or two ago. And if we look across the world's countries today, those with
larger per capita GDP have less poverty and longer life expectancy.[7]

But has this come to an end? Since the 1970s, globalization, reduced barriers
to entry, and the rise of low-cost behemoths such as Walmart and Amazon have
increased the competitive pressure many firms face. Falling transportation and
communication costs have made it easier for companies to move jobs to lower-cost

parts of the world, or to threaten to do so. Computers and robots have created new possibilities for automating tasks. The "shareholder value" revolution in corporate governance has encouraged managers to prioritize a rising stock price ahead of the well-being of workers. Labor unions have weakened. Consequently, a growing share of firms have felt compelled or incentivized to pursue a "low road" approach to jobs—to minimize labor costs above all else, to treat workers simply as commodities.[8] Has this development ended, or perhaps even reversed, the steady rise in incomes and living standards for people at the low end in the world's affluent democratic nations? Is capitalism no longer good for the poor?

Incomes and Material Well-Being

In the early 1960s, the US government formulated the world's first official poverty line, set at about three times what it cost a household to meet minimal nutritional requirements. The poverty rate for the country—the share of Americans in households with an income below the line—was 22 percent as of 1959. Over the next decade and a half, the rate fell steadily, reaching 11 percent in 1973. Some poverty analysts predicted we would see the end of the poverty in America within a decade.[9]

That didn't happen. There has been continued progress, but it has been slow. Figure 2.2 shows household income at the 10th percentile of the distribution in the United States and other affluent democratic nations. This is a better indicator than the poverty rate because it doesn't rely on a crude binary (either you're poor or you aren't) classification.[10] Since the late 1970s, incomes of low-end American households have increased, but quite slowly.[11]

What about other rich countries? In a few, low-end incomes have been stagnant, but in most they have risen, and more rapidly than in the United States. The Nordic countries in particular have been successful at achieving significant income increases for their least well-off.[12]

Figure 2.3 offers another way to assess the degree of progress. On the vertical axis is change in 10th-percentile household incomes since the late 1970s. On the horizontal axis is economic growth, measured as growth of GDP per capita, over the same period. In most of the countries, the incomes of low-end households have grown more or less in proportion to growth of the economy. Notable exceptions include Germany and the United States, where low-end incomes have increased much more slowly than economic growth allowed. In Germany, this was partly a function of reunification with the former East Germany in 1990 and policy makers' choice to create a low-wage ("mini-jobs") segment of the labor market beginning in the early 2000s. The US story is a more complicated one, to which I'll return.

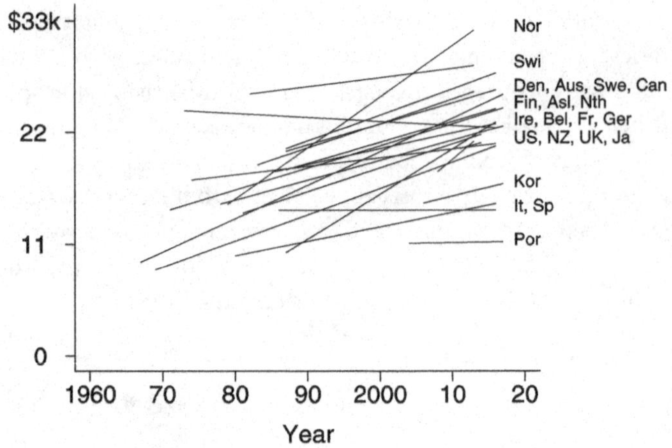

Figure 2.2 Tenth-percentile household income

Posttransfer-posttax household income. The incomes are adjusted for household size and then rescaled to reflect a three-person household, adjusted for inflation, and converted to US dollars using purchasing power parities. "k" = thousand. Data sources: Luxembourg Income Study; OECD. "Asl" is Australia; "Aus" is Austria. The lines are linear regression lines.

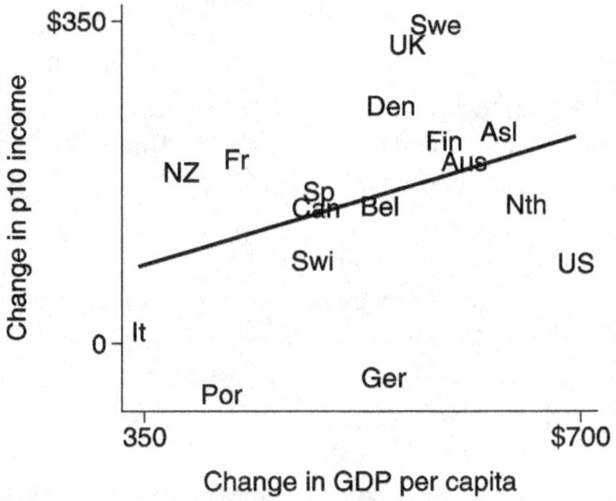

Figure 2.3 Tenth-percentile household income growth by economic growth

Per year change, 1979–2015. Because the actual years vary somewhat depending on the country, change is calculated by regressing household income or GDP per capita on year. Household incomes are posttransfer-posttax, adjusted for household size (the amounts shown are for a household with three persons). Household incomes and GDP per capita are adjusted for inflation and converted to US dollars using purchasing power parities. Data sources: OECD; Luxembourg Income Study. Ireland and Norway are omitted; both would be far off the plot in the upper-right corner. "Asl" is Australia; "Aus" is Austria. The line is a linear regression line.

A more direct indicator of material well-being is people's responses to questions about their living conditions. Since 2007, the Gallup World Poll has asked a representative sample of adults in each country whether there has been a time in the past year when they didn't have enough money to (1) buy food that they or their family needed or (2) provide adequate shelter or housing. The share of households responding yes to these two questions ranges from 5 percent in Denmark to 15 percent in the United States and 20 percent in South Korea. Other indicators of material deprivation tell a similar story.[13] Unfortunately, we have no measure of material hardship that is available more than a decade or two back in time, so we can't tell whether progress at reducing it has continued or faltered.

What about longevity? In the United States, average life expectancy increased from 39 years in 1880 to just shy of 80 years today. The rise in other rich democratic countries has been equally dramatic. In the late 1800s and the first half of the 20th century, this increase owed mainly to progress in preventing and curing infectious diseases, especially among newborns and children. Since then, progress has come mainly from extending the lives of those who make it to middle age, by reducing the incidence of and boosting the survival rate from heart disease, cancer, accidents, lung disease, liver disease, suicides, and homicides. This latter form of progress is more difficult, so the rise in life expectancy has been slower. But it has continued.[14]

If that's true for the average person in these countries, is it also true for the poor? In the United States, the answer, at least since 1980, is no. Life expectancy for Americans in the top 60 percent of incomes has increased, but for those in the lower 40 percent it has been stagnant.[15] Why? The rate of smoking has fallen less rapidly among lower-income Americans than among those with higher incomes. Opioid addiction and overdose have increased more rapidly among Americans with less education and income. The income disparity in medical care very likely has increased; between 1980 and 2010 the share of Americans without health insurance increased, and most who lack insurance have low to moderate income. Differences in healthcare provision between more-affluent urban areas and poorer rural areas appear to have widened. And the gap in income itself has grown, albeit mainly between those at the very top and everyone else. On the other hand, some health determinants haven't diverged according to income: for instance, while lower-income Americans are more likely to be overweight or obese than those with higher incomes, the income gap in obesity actually has shrunk in recent decades.[16]

It appears that, with respect to health developments among the poor, the American experience may be unique. In eight European countries for which data are available since 1990—Finland, France, Italy, Norway, Spain, Sweden, Switzerland, and the United Kingdom—mortality decreased (longevity increased) over the period from 1990–94 to 2005–09 among persons with less than a high school education. In fact, it decreased more for persons with low education than for those with a college degree. Other findings suggest the same is true in Canada.[17]

To sum up: Since the mid-1800s, when sustained economic growth commenced in the world's twenty or so rich longstanding-democratic nations, incomes and broader well-being of people at the low end of the socioeconomic ladder have tended to improve. Beginning in the 1970s, automation, globalization, shifts in corporate culture, union decline, and other developments have led some observers to conclude that this progress has ended. Indeed, since the 2008–09 financial crisis, stories of economic decline and frustration among the working class, and the way this has contributed to the rise of "populist" and anti-immigrant political parties, have been increasingly prominent. Yet the data suggest that incomes and longevity among the least well-off have continued to rise in nearly all of these countries. The United States is more the exception than the rule.

Government Transfers Are Now the Key Source of Income Growth for Poor Households

Let's return to incomes and consider the mechanism through which economic growth boosts the income of the poor. We tend to think of this process as centered on earnings: as the economy grows, more of the poor are able to get a job, work more hours, and see their hourly wage increase.

Since the late 1970s, however, in many of the rich democratic countries the earnings of low-end households have increased very little, if at all. The main reason for this is that many households don't have any earners. Figure 2.4 shows the share of households with no earner in the United States, a country in which paid work has long been central to the national ethos and in which the employment rate has tended to be comparatively high. Throughout this period about 20 to 25 percent of American households have had no earners, and this share has risen a bit in recent decades.

This shouldn't be too surprising. Among US households, 26 percent are "headed" by a person age 65 or older, a share that has been increasing as people live longer and as the large baby boom generation reaches retirement age. At any given moment, around 2 to 7 percent of American adults are unemployed, meaning they would like to have a paying job but can't find one. Others live in places where job opportunities are so scarce that they have given up searching for work. About 20 percent are disabled, and approximately 30 percent will at some point in their career experience a disability significant enough to cause them to miss 90 or more days of work.[18] Other people are constrained by family circumstances.

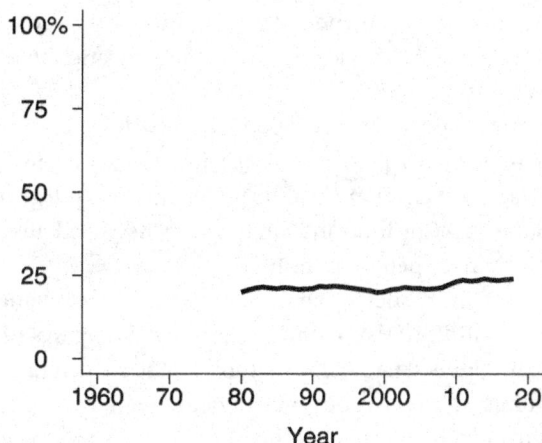

Figure 2.4 US households with zero earners
Share of all households. Data source: US Census Bureau, Historical Income Tables: Households, census.gov, table H-12.

As a result, a significant share of the income of households at the low end of the socioeconomic ladder comes from government transfers. And increasingly, those transfers have become their chief source of income growth. Since the late 1970s, in most of the rich longstanding-democratic nations, when the incomes of households in the lower fifth have increased it typically has owed to increases in government transfers.[19] Government transfers have become the core mechanism through which economic growth reaches the least well-off.

Some government transfers are designed to automatically rise over time as the economy grows. This happens when, for instance, pensions or unemployment compensation are indexed to average wages. Other transfers increase only when policy makers explicitly decide they should. A key reason why the incomes of low-end households in the United States have risen so little in recent decades is that only one of America's main government transfer programs, Social Security, is structured so that benefit levels automatically increase in sync with economic growth. The rest require intentional action by policy makers, and proposals to raise benefit levels have often gotten blocked.

Would Democratic Socialism Be Better at Ending Poverty in Rich Countries?

Incomes of Americans on the lower rungs of the socioeconomic ladder are too low, and they've increased too little since the late 1970s. Too many Americans have trouble meeting their housing and food bills. And for a large number, life expectancy has stalled. Some interpret these facts as an indication that capitalism has outlived its usefulness.

For people at the low end in the Nordic countries, however, incomes are higher than in the United States, public services pay for many things Americans are forced to purchase on their own (healthcare, childcare, college, eldercare), few people have trouble meeting food and housing expenses, and life expectancy has been rising faster than for people at the top.

How would a switch from social democratic capitalism to democratic socialism help the least well-off in the Nordic nations? And why would America's poor be better off if the United States chose democratic socialism rather than social democratic capitalism? The main argument would seem to be that socialism has a simple, straightforward mechanism for solving poverty: everyone gets a share of the proceeds from the country's wealth or its companies. This could take the form of dividends from stock "coupons," a direct payout from the nation's sovereign wealth fund, or something else.

But step back and think about what this means. It means the government has decided to pay out part of the economy's proceeds to low-income citizens, rather than only to private holders of stocks, bonds, or land. An alternative, and equally straightforward, way to do this is to tax incomes and assets and distribute the revenue to the poor.

One strategy for getting the money to people is to increase the scope and generosity of existing social assistance programs.

Another could be via a universal basic income (UBI).[20] A basic income would give individuals a regular cash payment. Eligibility wouldn't be conditional on need or employment status. A generous version, proposed recently by Philippe Van Parijs and Yannick Vanderborght, would give each permanent fiscal resident of a country, including children, an amount equal to one-fourth of the nation's per capita GDP, which in the contemporary United States would be about $15,000 per year. With a basic income of this size, the poverty rate would drop to zero.

Or we could adopt a "negative income tax." Unlike a basic income, this would go only to people (or households) with low income, but it would guarantee them enough government cash assistance to bring them above the poverty line.

There is no clear reason why we need socialism in order to get a more generous social assistance program, a universal basic income, or a negative income tax. These programs are no more incompatible with capitalism than are existing welfare state programs, statutory minimum wages, and laws that say firms must recognize and negotiate with labor unions. They wouldn't prevent people from starting up a business, hiring and firing workers, and making a profit.

It's true that in a nation with a capitalist economy many employers will oppose a basic income or a negative income tax or increased social assistance generosity. Each would require an increase in taxes, and they would improve people's
ability to leave crummy, low-paying jobs, and employers may not be pleased with
this. But employers have opposed lots of social programs and regulations over
the past hundred years. Despite that opposition, quite a few such programs and
regulations have been enacted, implemented, and subsequently expanded. As we
saw in chapter 1, the share of GDP spent on public social programs in rich democratic countries has jumped from essentially zero a century ago to about 25 percent today.

Even a UBI no longer seems out of the realm of possibility. There have been a
number of small-scale experiments with UBIs, including recent ones in Finland,
Canada, and the United States. The state of Alaska has had a UBI for decades,
though the amount is quite small.

Center-left governments have had plenty of opportunity to increase government transfers to a level where those transfers would eliminate poverty, but
they've chosen not to do so. Citizens of Switzerland were able in 2016 to vote in
a national referendum on a proposal to create a generous UBI, but they overwhelmingly voted no. The core reason no rich democratic nation has enacted
poverty-eliminating social assistance or a negative income tax or a generous universal basic income is that this would sharply increase the incentive for people
with limited labor market prospects to live off the benefit rather than seek employment. Encouraging employment is popular because it fosters a sense of
reciprocity and community and because it helps to generate tax revenues that
finance government programs.[21]

There may come a point when a majority of the citizenry in these countries
believes everyone should have the freedom to choose not to work. But that time
hasn't yet arrived. This is a problem for those who favor a transition to from capitalism to socialism. If you can't convince a majority of people to support an extension of the welfare state, which most are already familiar with and fond of, are
you likely to succeed in convincing them to shift from an economic system with
mostly private property to one with mostly public property?

3

An End to Poverty Everywhere

The tremendous suffering in the world today demands a response. Capitalist development has created mass abundance, but it hasn't met the basic needs of the most vulnerable. Millions still die every year of preventable diseases. Many more spend their lives mired in poverty.

—Bhaskar Sunkara[1]

We should want to improve the lives of the least well-off in rich nations. Their struggles are worthy of our concern.[2] But we should worry even more about how to make things better for the billions of people around the world who live in much more meager conditions. Would democratic socialism improve our ability to do that?

Most of the World's Poorest People Are Poor Because They Live in a Poor Country

Much of the world's population is poorer than even the least well-off in the affluent nations. Figure 3.1 offers one way to see this. It shows that the income of the poorest Americans (1 on the horizontal axis) situates them at the 68th percentile of the world's income distribution (vertical axis), meaning their income is higher than that of approximately two-thirds of the world's population. In Brazil, a person in the middle of the distribution (50 on the horizontal axis) has an income similar to an American at the bottom. In China and even more so in India, the bulk of the population have incomes below those of the lowest-income Americans.

To a significant degree, people who are poor are those who live in poor countries. One measure of poverty, for which the World Bank has data, is a household income of less than $2,000 a year ($5.50 per day). Figure 3.2 shows that the share of a country's population that has an income below this amount is predicted quite well by the country's per capita GDP. The same is true for life expectancy, as we see in Figure 3.3.[3]

Would Democratic Socialism Be Better?. Lane Kenworthy, Oxford University Press. © Lane Kenworthy 2022.
DOI: 10.1093/oso/9780197636800.003.0003

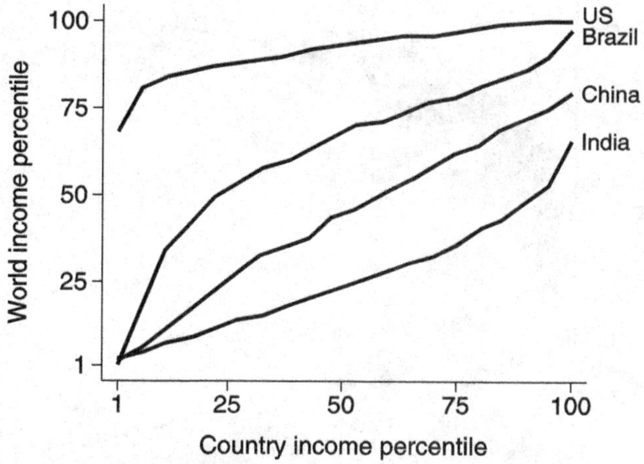

Figure 3.1 Household incomes in the United States and three poorer countries

Data source: Branko Milanovic, *The Haves and the Have-Nots*, Basic Books, 2011, figure 3.

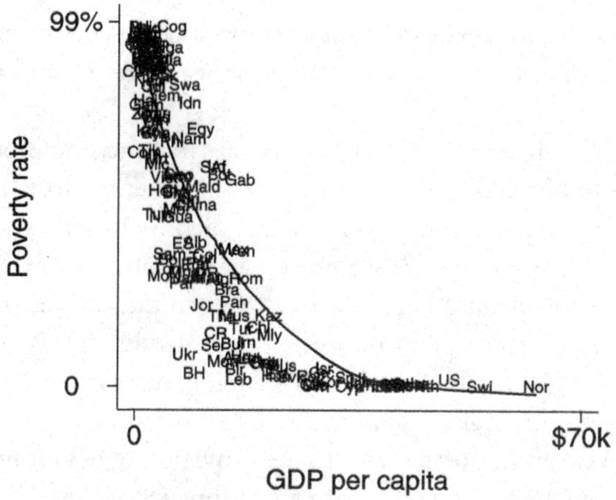

Figure 3.2 Country poverty rate by country GDP per capita

Poverty rate: share of persons living in a household with an income less than $5.50 per day. Incomes adjusted for inflation and converted to 2011 US dollars using purchasing power parities. Average over 2004–2015. Data source: World Bank. GDP per capita: converted to 2011 US dollars using purchasing power parities. 2010. Data source: UNDP, "Human Development Data." Three small, rich city-states (Andorra, Luxembourg, and Singapore) are omitted. The line is a loess curve.

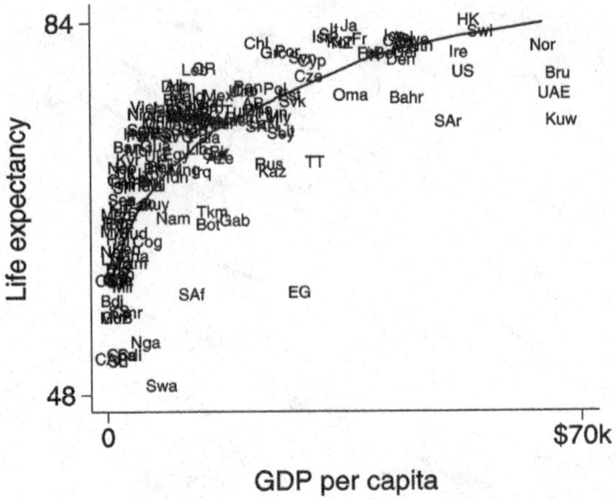

Figure 3.3 Country life expectancy by country GDP per capita
Life expectancy: years at birth. 2015. Data source: United Nations Development Program (UNDP), "Human Development Data." GDP per capita: converted to 2011 US dollars using purchasing power parities. 2015. Data source: UNDP, "Human Development Data." Three small, rich city-states (Andorra, Luxembourg, and Singapore) are omitted. The line is a loess curve, calculated with eight oil-rich nations excluded.

It isn't just incomes and longevity that improve as societies get richer. What people want and what they prioritize also tend to change. Three such changes are particularly important.

First, people tend to dislike loss.[4] The higher our income, the more insurance we are willing to purchase in order to minimize potential loss. For some types of insurance, such as insurance against low income in old age, government is the most effective provider. Germany created a public old-age pension program in the late 1800s, and other industrializing countries began to do so in the first half of the twentieth century, with many introducing or expanding them during the Great Depression in the 1930s. While many nations now have this type of public program, richer countries tend to have more expansive ones. Government also plays an important role in the provision of health insurance; public spending on healthcare tends to rise as nations get richer. The same is true for education.

A second change in people's desires as they get richer is to want more fairness in their society.[5] Drawing on several decades of public opinion survey data from multiple countries, Ronald Inglehart and Christian Welzel have found that once people can be confident of survival and of a decent standard of living, they tend to shift away from a worldview that emphasizes traditional sources of authority, religious dictates, traditional social roles, and the well-being of the group or community rather than that of the individual. A "postmaterialist" or "emancipative" worldview replaces a scarcity orientation.[6] One element of postmaterialism is a desire for basic political rights. Another element is universalistic humanism, which deems all persons, including members of outgroups, as equally worthy of rights, opportunities, and respect. In the world's rich democratic nations, the shift from a traditional orientation to a postmaterialist one emerged in the generation that grew up after the Great Depression and World War II.[7] As the rest of the world gets richer, we're beginning to observe it there too.[8]

A third shift that comes with affluence is a growing emphasis on personal liberty. Most of us want the freedom to choose what to believe, how to behave, with whom to live, and so on. As material well-being increases, this desire for freedom comes to the fore.[9]

Together, affluence, its causes (markets, stable and supportive government, and science), and its consequences (desire for more insurance, fairness, and personal freedom) have produced societies—and individuals in them—that are not only richer but also more secure, better educated, healthier, fairer, and freer.[10]

So when a poor country gets richer, life tends to improve for its citizens. Is capitalism preventing poor nations from getting richer?

Is the Modern Global Economy Good or Bad for the Poor?

Modern capitalism is, to a significant degree, global capitalism.[11] Since the middle of the twentieth century, exchange of goods and services between nations has increased sharply. It now accounts for about one-third of total world economic output, as we see in Figure 3.4.

An influential view holds that rich countries tend to make poor countries poorer. They are said to do by taking poor nations' raw materials and by directing poor nations' economies toward production of commodities that bring in little income, that discourage investments in education, and that offer limited opportunity for significant productivity gains. History offers plenty of examples.[12]

Today, it is less often the governments of affluent countries that dictate the economic direction of poor nations. The key players are global corporations and their supply chains. Some of these firms are engaged in extractive operations in developing nations, but most focus on manufacturing or services.

Trade between poor nations and rich ones can help the incomes of people in poor countries grow faster. If producers in poor countries are able to sell their goods and services in rich countries, the size of the market expands enormously. There are more customers, and those customers are, on average, able to pay more than customers in the poor nation. This enables increased production in the poor country, which can lead to more jobs and rising wages. Virtually every successful economic development story of the past half century—including South Korea,

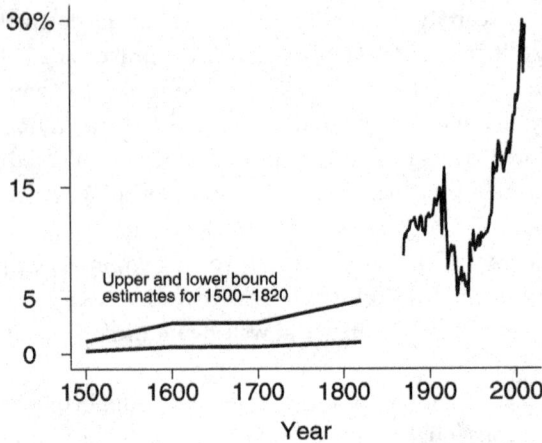

Figure 3.4 Trade

Average of exports and imports as a share of GDP. Includes all countries. Data sources: Esteban Ortiz-Ospina and Max Roser, "International Trade," *Our World in Data*, using data from Antoni Estevadeordal, Brian Frantz, and Alan M. Taylor, "The Rise and Fall of World Trade, 1870–1939," *Quarterly Journal of Economics*, 2003 for 1500–1820, Mariko J. Klasing and Petros Milionis, "Quantifying the Evolution of World Trade, 1870–1949," *Journal of International Economics*, 2014 for 1870–1949, and Penn World Tables for 1950ff.

Taiwan, Hong Kong, Singapore, China, Brazil, Botswana, and Mauritius—has relied heavily on exports to rich countries.[13]

When economic growth increases in poor nations, some of the added income goes to wealthy owners in those countries or to executives and shareholders of multinational corporations. But some of it goes to ordinary workers in the poor nations. Between 2000 and 2012, China's share of world manufacturing exports increased from 5 percent to 17 percent, and during that decade more than 200 million Chinese moved up into the global middle class.[14] More broadly, as we see in Figures 3.5 and 3.6, the period of rising trade since 1970 has coincided with, and almost certainly has been a key contributor to, the most rapid decrease in extreme poverty in human history.

Do these data paint too rosy a picture? They might, in three respects. First, the dramatic reduction in extreme poverty may cause us to overlook the fact that its level remains disturbingly high. Approximately 700 million people still live with an income of less than $1.90 per day.[15]

Second, while the number or share of people in poverty is a useful indicator of well-being, it can mislead. It's a binary measure: a household with an income below the poverty line is counted as poor, and a household with an income above the line is counted as not poor. Suppose a lot of people are slightly below the line at time 1 and then experience a small increase in income, putting them above the

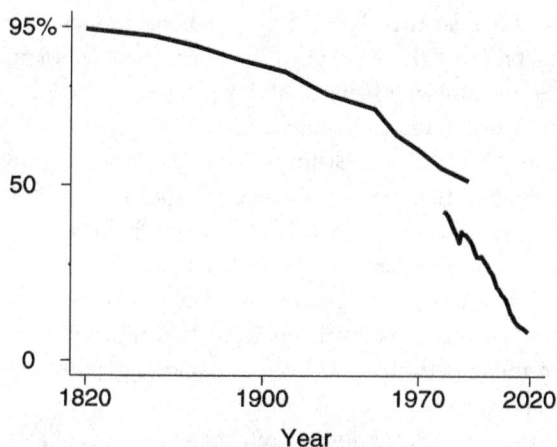

Figure 3.5 Share of people in extreme poverty worldwide

Share of persons living in a household with income less than $2 per day (upper line) or $1.90 per day (lower line). Data source for upper line: Max Roser, "Extreme Poverty," *Our World in Data*, using data from Bourguignon and Morrisson, "Inequality among World Citizens: 1820–1992," *American Economic Review*, 2002. Data source for lower line: World Bank.

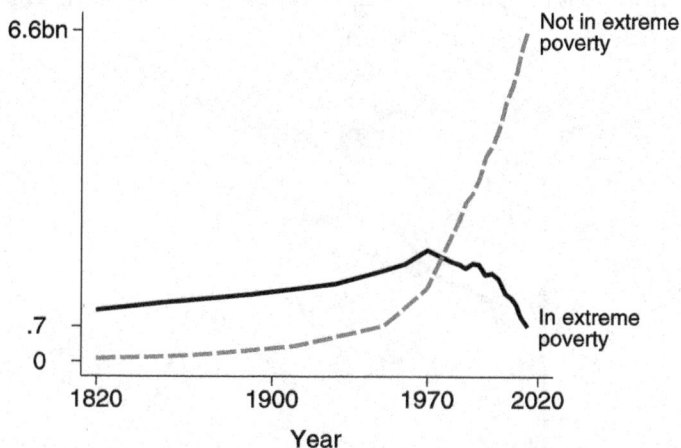

Figure 3.6 Number of people in extreme poverty and not in extreme poverty worldwide

Persons in households with an income of less than $1.90 per day. 2011 dollars. "bn" = billion. Data source: Max Roser and Esteban Ortiz-Ospina, "Global Extreme Poverty," *Our World in Data*, using data for 1820–1970 from Bourguignon and Morrisson, "Inequality among World Citizens: 1820–1992," *American Economic Review*, 2002 and data for 1981ff from World Bank Povcal Net.

line at time 2. It will appear that there's been a massive reduction in (extreme) poverty when in fact most of these people have experienced only a modest rise in living standards. Some observers believe this is exactly what has happened, especially in China and India, in recent decades.[16]

But the best available data suggest that's probably wrong. Figure 3.7 shows estimates of the growth rate of household income from 1988 to 2011 at various points along the worldwide income distribution. Households at the low end saw their incomes rise about 30 percent during these two decades. While that isn't as fast as we'd like, it's a significant improvement. And households from the 10th percentile to the 75th—a group comprising nearly two-thirds of the world's population, including most of those who live in developing countries—saw their incomes rise by 50 percent or more.

A third way in which the world poverty rate data might overstate actual progress has to do with China. Since 1990, China's rate of economic growth and of poverty reduction have been among the world's best. China has nearly a fifth of the world's population, so a decrease in its poverty rate has a sizable impact on the worldwide poverty rate. And in fact that is a key part of the story of poverty's decline in recent decades.[17]

But while this tells us that a free market or small-government version of capitalism hasn't been the key to poverty reduction, it doesn't gainsay the real progress that has been made. Nor does it suggest that the global economy hasn't

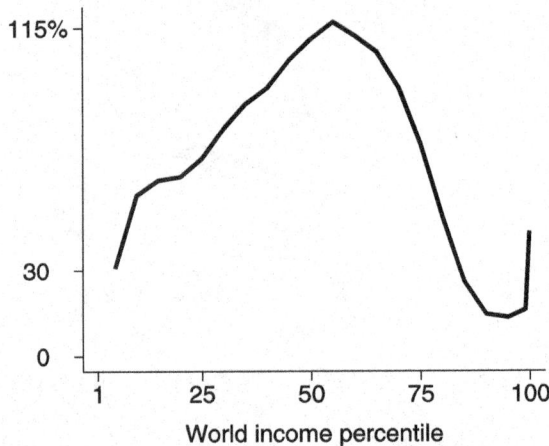

Figure 3.7 Income growth for people at various points along the worldwide distribution of income, 1988–2011

Cumulative percentage income growth per person. Incomes adjusted for inflation and converted to 2011 US dollars using purchasing power parities. Data source: Branko Milanovic, "Changes in the Global Income Distribution and Their Political Consequences," 2018.

played a role in reducing poverty. Exports to rich countries have been crucial to China's progress.[18]

Paul Krugman puts the point in the following way:

> Globalization really did deliver big time. . . . I was a grad student in the 1970s and I asked myself, "What should I specialize in?" I said "Well, what is the most important thing?" The answer was clearly development economics. Nothing was more important than making poor countries less poor. I didn't do it because it was too depressing. In the 1970s, development economics was a very depressing field. It was basically nondevelopment economics. It was all about the reasons why poor countries didn't seem to be able to get rich.
>
> Then all of that changed. Since then, we've seen, in terms of numbers of people, the rise of China, but then a little bit later, the rise of India. You see an enormous expansion of the quality of life for literally billions of people. All of that is clearly closely linked to globalization. All of these are export-oriented success stories.[19]

Would Democratic Socialism Be Better at Ending Poverty Everywhere?

In theory, socialism could be better. There is a lot of room for further progress, and it's certainly conceivable that a different economic system in rich countries or in poor countries, or both, would speed up the progress. But how, exactly?

Many proposals focus on reforming global rules that structurally disadvantage poor nations. Examples include ending "structural adjustment" programs that force poor countries to reduce government spending in order to qualify for loans, ending trade laws and agreements that prevent poor countries from helping their domestic firms and industries, instituting a global minimum wage, giving poor countries an equal voice at the World Trade Organization (WTO), the International Monetary Fund (IMF), and the World Bank, and canceling the existing debt of poor nations.[20]

Another approach is simply to give more money. In the mid-2000s, Jeffrey Sachs suggested that if rich nations increased their foreign aid to poor nations to just 0.7 percent of their GDP, we could end poverty worldwide within two decades.[21] A more direct strategy would be to transfer money to households— rather than governments, firms, or nonprofits—in poor countries. If we use a poverty line of $7.40 per day, about 58 percent of the world's population lived in poverty as of 2013. By one calculation, a fund generated by a 4 percent tax on the incomes of people with an income more than double that poverty line would be sufficient to move the incomes of those 58 percent above the line.[22]

The question is whether socialism would make it easier to pursue these or related strategies. Many of the rich capitalist nations have adjusted their trade strategies, foreign aid efforts, and taxation and redistribution programs over time, frequently in a progressive direction. That's especially true in the nations with more of a social democratic capitalist orientation.[23] In other words, there already has been significant movement in the right direction. Larger-scale or more direct efforts to boost incomes among the world's poor will require new political struggles, but that would be no less true with a socialist economy.

More pessimistically, some observers have concluded that we know too little about how to generate sustained improvement in living conditions in poor countries to be confident about particular strategies. According to Michael Clemens,

> Events of economic conception—growth takeoffs—tend to occur in small enclaves that get things right for extremely complex reasons, never homogeneously across large areas. In countries so small that the enclave was the entire country—Botswana, Hong Kong, Mauritius, Singapore, Taiwan—growth has been astounding. In countries where the national boundaries include places where it happened and places where it did not—Brazil, India—growth has been good. In places where the national boundaries happen to include no place where the right cocktail of factors has come together, there has been little or no growth. All of the bottom-billion countries fall into the last category. . . . Helping the bottom billion will be a very slow job for generations, not the product of media- or summit-friendly plans to end poverty in ten or 20 years. It will require long-term, opportunistic, and humble engagement, much of it through public action—built on a willingness to let ineffective interventions die and on a sophisticated appreciation of the stupendous complexity of functioning economies. The grievous truth is that although a range of public actions can and should help many people, most of the bottom billion will not, and cannot, be freed from poverty in our lifetimes.[24]

If this is correct, we have no basis for concluding that either capitalism or socialism would be better for poverty reduction in poor nations going forward. Our knowledge is too limited to permit any kind of informed judgment.

The Most Effective Poverty-Reduction Strategy: Open Borders

The quickest and most effective way to help the world's least well-off is to allow them to migrate to richer countries.[25] The pay of an unskilled worker who moves from Mexico to the United States goes up by 150 percent on average.

For an unskilled worker who migrates from Nigeria to the United States, the pay rise is more than 1,000 percent.[26] This is partly because schools and other skill-development institutions are more widely available and more effective in rich countries, but the main reason is that the economy is more productive.

The moral argument in favor of open borders is straightforward: birth country is no less accidental than is birth location *within* a country, and the former tends to be far more consequential. Freedom and equality of opportunity require the ability to choose where one lives. Democratic nations allow citizens to move freely within their borders. Even nondemocratic countries frequently do so; think of the massive movement of Chinese from rural areas in the western part of the country to cities in the east since the late 1970s. The same should be true between countries.

Opponents warn this could lead to an unmanageable number of people moving from poor or violent or politically repressive nations to rich democratic ones. We have two pieces of information to help us gauge the likely magnitude of the flow. One is responses to a Gallup World Poll question that has been asked in nearly all of the world's countries since 2007. The question is "Ideally, if you had the opportunity, would you like to move permanently to another country, or would you prefer to continue living in this country?" Figure 3.8 shows that about

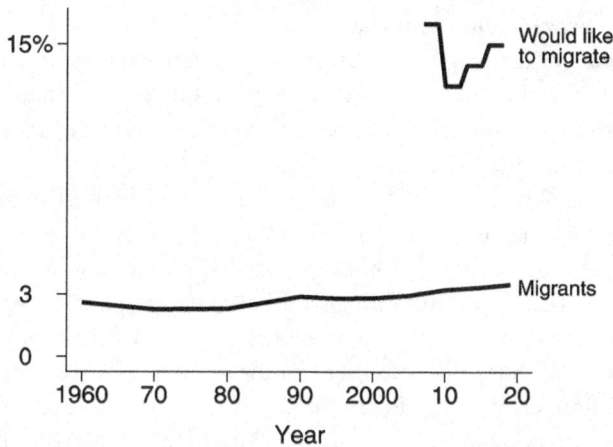

Figure 3.8 Migrants: actual and desired

Share of the world's population. Migrants: share of the world's population living in a country different from their country of birth. Data source: Michael Dimock, "Leaving Home," Pew Research Center, 2016, using United Nations data. Would like to migrate: share of the world's population saying they would like to move permanently to another country. Question: "Ideally, if you had the opportunity, would you like to move permanently to another country, or would you prefer to continue living in this country?" Data source: Gallup World Poll, reported in Neli Esipova, Anita Pugliese, and Julie Ray, "More Than 750 Million Worldwide Would Migrate If They Could," Gallup, 2018.

15 percent of people in the world say they would like to migrate, whereas only 3.5 percent have actually done so. This suggests that migration would indeed rise by a significant amount. Instead of 250 million migrants, there would be about 1.2 billion.

Many would go to the rich democratic nations. About 70 percent of current migrants go to those countries, and an even larger share would like to. The United States is home to the largest number. That number currently is about 45 million, which is 13 percent of the US population. It's conceivable that with open borders that number might rise to perhaps 300 million, doubling the US population.[27] That would be a big change, but it would be neither unprecedented nor unmanageable. The United States has a huge land mass, so space isn't an obstacle. America's population doubled in the periods 1850–1875, 1875–1905, 1905–1955, and 1955–2020. While a doubling due to open borders would happen relatively rapidly, it wouldn't be instantaneous. And there's a good chance it would be beneficial. The movement inside China since the late 1970s has been larger, and it has yielded a massive net gain in human well-being (apart from the increase in urban smog).[28]

A second piece of evidence on how open borders would play out comes from the European Union's experience since full implementation of the "Schengen Agreement" beginning in 1999. Skeptics feared an unmanageable flood of migrants from Romania, Poland, and other poor member countries to Germany, France, the United Kingdom, and other affluent ones. But it didn't happen. The actual flows proved quite manageable.[29]

Proponents of democratic socialism might offer two responses. One is that focusing on migration as a solution to poverty sidesteps the need to help improve economic conditions in the poorest countries. Indeed, by encouraging departure of the most capable, it could make things worse for some poor nations. Yet as Brian Caplan and Vipul Naik point out, "this is no more tragic than poor villagers exiting the backwaters of China and India. Development is ultimately about people, not places. And nonmigrants benefit, too. Remittances—which already far exceed the flow of foreign aid—start coming home almost immediately. Before long, successful immigrants start using their newfound business connections to develop their mother countries. Puerto Rico provides an excellent illustration. Over half of Puerto Ricans live abroad, but Puerto Ricans who stayed behind now enjoy a First World standard of living."[30]

A second potential argument by democratic socialism advocates is that open borders will never be politically feasible with a capitalist economic system, because the hefty political influence of the rich will allow them to block it, just as they do many other progressive policy proposals. We'll consider the issue of unequal political influence in chapter 11. But it's worth emphasizing that at the moment, at least in the United States, people who say they are working class or lower class are more likely than those who are middle or upper class to oppose increased immigration.[31] A society in which political influence is more equally distributed across income groups might therefore be one in which it is politically harder, not easier, to open the borders to the world's poor.

4

More Jobs

The hopes which accompanied the Keynesian revolution, of reforming capitalism so as to ensure continuous prosperity with full employment, are now all but extinguished.

—Joan Robinson and Frank Wilkinson[1]

With the end of post-war reconstruction in the 1960s, a grinding process of gradual institutional change set in that insensibly undermined and eventually removed most of the safeguards once devised to make capitalism compatible with then powerful collective demands for security, stability, equal opportunity, shared prosperity, and the like. Forty years later, we are beholding the results of an extraordinary historical development: a newly liberated capitalism having successfully extricated itself, Houdini-like, from the social fetters it had temporarily had to pretend to be willing and able to live with. Among the collective safety provisions that have fallen victim to capitalism's remarkable escape act is politically guaranteed full employment.

—Wolfgang Streeck[2]

The forms of automation in the digital age, which are now penetrating deep into the service sector, including sectors of professional services, makes it much less likely that future economic growth will provide adequate employment opportunities through the capitalist market. The magnitude of this problem is further intensified by the globalization of capitalist production. . . . Full employment through capitalist labor markets seems increasingly implausible.

—Erik Olin Wright[3]

A persistent failing of capitalism has been its inability to employ everyone who wants paid work. Some of this is "frictional": a type of job is automated out of existence, or a person's employer goes out of business and she needs some new training or education in order to find a job in her town that pays similarly. But some of it likely is "structural," inherent to the system—a function of the fact that

Would Democratic Socialism Be Better?. Lane Kenworthy, Oxford University Press. © Lane Kenworthy 2022.
DOI: 10.1093/oso/9780197636800.003.0004

employment decisions are decentralized and based on imperfect information. Indeed, companies may benefit from the existence of a "reserve army of labor," the nonemployed, because this allows them to pay a lower wage.[4]

Is capitalism incompatible with full employment? Would democratic socialism do better?

High Employment

The most widely recognized indicator of insufficient employment is the unemployment rate, which is the share of people who want to be employed but aren't. While this measure is helpful in judging the severity of the employment problem during an economic recession, it's less useful at other times. A better indicator is the employment rate: the share of the working-age population that is employed.[5] Figure 4.1 shows the employment rate among persons aged 25 to 64 in the rich democratic nations.

The employment rate in the top-performing countries is 80 percent or more, and in Sweden it is 85 percent. (These are pre-pandemic numbers.) Is that below "full employment"? It is if we think full employment means that 90 or 95 percent of persons aged 25–64 are in paid work. But I doubt that's what we want. Some working-aged persons prefer to stay home with children or an elderly family member, or to do volunteer work, or are in education or training, or are disabled, or have retired "early." Others have an alternative source of income—a partner

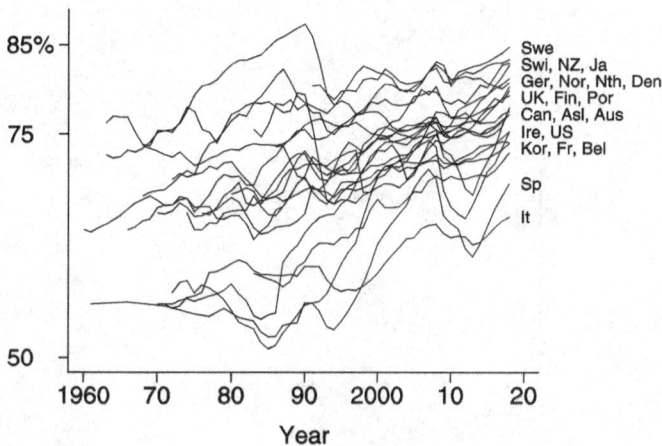

Figure 4.1 Employment rate

Employed persons age 25–64 as a share of all persons age 25–64. The vertical axis doesn't begin at zero. Data source: OECD. "Asl" is Australia; "Aus" is Austria.

or spouse, savings, a trust fund, lottery winnings—and prefer to paint or do volunteer work or play chess or golf or video games. Is 80 percent of working-aged
persons in paid work too low? Perhaps, but I suspect not.

It's worth thinking here about the merits and drawbacks of paid work. On the
one hand, employment has significant virtues.[6] It imposes regularity and disci-
pline on people's lives. It can be a source of mental stimulation. It helps to fulfill
the widespread desire to contribute to, and be integrated in, the larger society. It
shapes identity and can boost self-esteem. With neighborhood and family ties
weakening, the office or factory can be a key site of social interaction. Lack of
employment tends to be associated with feelings of social exclusion, discourage-
ment, boredom, and unhappiness. In addition, employment may help to achieve
desirable societal outcomes such as economic security and opportunity.

On the other hand, the need for a paycheck can trap people in careers that
divert them from more productive or rewarding pursuits. Work can be phys-
ically or emotionally taxing. It can be monotonous, boring, alienating. Some
jobs require a degree of indifference, meanness, or dishonesty toward customers
or subordinates that eats away at one's humanity. And work can interfere with
family life. We shouldn't be too surprised if a nontrivial share of people opt out.
I see little reason to expect they would choose differently under democratic
socialism.

Figure 4.2 shows employment rates for working-aged women, and Figure 4.3
shows the rates for working-aged men. While female employment rates have
been rising over the past half century, the rates among men have been falling.

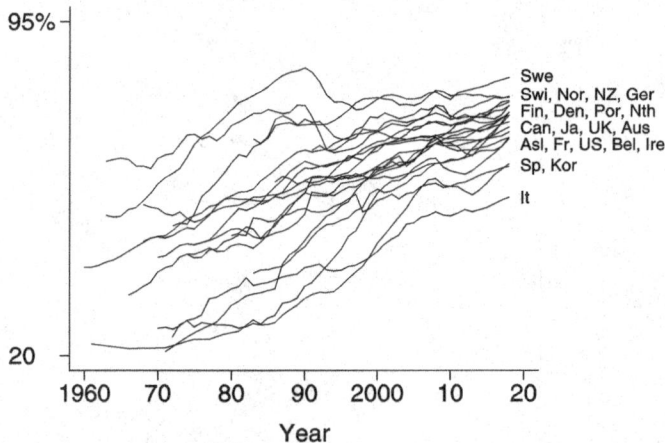

Figure 4.2 Women's employment rate
Employed women age 25–64 as a share of all women age 25–64. The vertical axis doesn't begin at
zero. Data source: OECD. "Asl" is Australia; "Aus" is Austria.

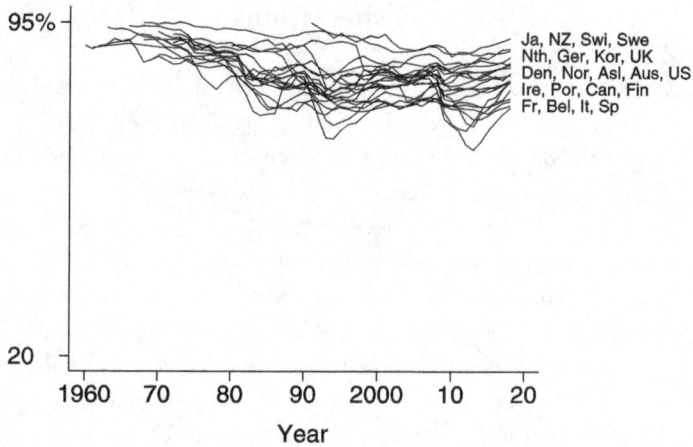

Figure 4.3 Men's employment rate

Employed men age 25–64 as a share of all men age 25–64. The vertical axis doesn't begin at zero.
Data source: OECD. "Asl" is Australia; "Aus" is Austria.

Some of this decline for men owes to the slow but steady shift from manufacturing to services. Another contributor is changes in family finances and in gender role norms; more working-aged men are financially able to choose something other than paid work, and more feel free of stigma in making such a choice.

Even if we believe an employment rate of 80 percent among working-aged persons is sufficiently high, we might worry that employment will decline going forward, because capitalism tends to eliminate jobs. Many commentators seem to believe this is already happening. However, they're likely misled by a focus on manufacturing jobs. Manufacturing employment has been decreasing in the affluent democracies since around 1970, and this trend has been quite steady.[7] As just noted, it is a key part of the reason why employment rates among working-aged men have declined. A focus on manufacturing and men misses the fact that the rich democratic nations have generated a large number of new service jobs over the past half century, and that the decline in employment among men has been more than offset by the rise in paid work among women. The overall employment rate in these countries (Figure 4.1) averaged 68.2 percent in the 1980s, 70.4 percent in the 1990s, 74.1 percent in the 2000s, and 75.2 percent in the 2010s.

Employment could decrease going forward. If artificial intelligence advances to a point where robots can do complex in-person service tasks—teacher, nurse, yoga instructor—as effectively as humans, we may indeed see a significant fall in the availability of paid work. But there is no sign that we are near this point yet.[8]

Recessions

Even if capitalism hasn't failed at providing jobs for a large share of working-aged persons, it surely hasn't done well enough at avoiding temporary job loss for large numbers of people during economic downturns. Is this an endemic failing, or can societies with a capitalist economy do better?

Prior to the 2008–09 "Great Recession," some prominent economists believed that our knowledge about how to steer the economy had advanced to a point where, in the words of Nobel laureate Robert Lucas, "the central problem of depression-prevention has been solved."[9] There would, in other words, be no more sustained economic downturns. That now looks quite unlikely.

If we can't prevent recession-induced unemployment, can we minimize its extent and duration? Here the answer seems to be yes. There is widespread agreement among experts that we can indeed do so, via monetary policy (lower interest rates, easier loan terms) and fiscal policy (increased government spending, reduced taxes).[10]

Implementation of this strategy faces two impediments. One is adherence to a belief that "austerity"—reducing government spending or increasing taxes—is the appropriate strategy in a recession.[11] There is no guarantee this view will dissipate. Mistaken notions can persist for quite a long time. One hopeful sign is that the US central bank, the Federal Reserve, has acted aggressively at four key junctures—at the end of the 1990s, in 2008–09, in 2018–19, and in response to the Covid-19-induced downturn in 2020—both to forestall the onset of a recession and to hasten its end. Fiscal policy is in the hands of elected policy makers, and their response may be dictated as much by partisan political strategy and the preferences of their voters or financial donors as by knowledge. But given that economic performance matters for election outcomes, even conservatives have some incentive to do the right thing. The fiscal policy response to the 2020 pandemic was encouraging. US policy makers passed emergency spending bills amounting to more than 15 percent of GDP. Even the German government, traditionally the most averse to government debt among the affluent democratic nations, committed to a huge injection of cash.[12]

The second barrier to effective fiscal policy expansion during a recession is high levels of public debt. Even policy makers who know that accepting a temporary increase in the government's deficit is the right thing to do during a recession may be reluctant if that means adding to an already-large public debt. However, there doesn't appear to be anything inherent in capitalism that forces governments to run up and maintain a large debt. As Figure 4.4 shows, the Nordic nations, in particular, have tended to balance their public budgets—and they've done this despite high levels of government spending. While Keynes prescribed deficit spending during economic recessions, in order to compensate

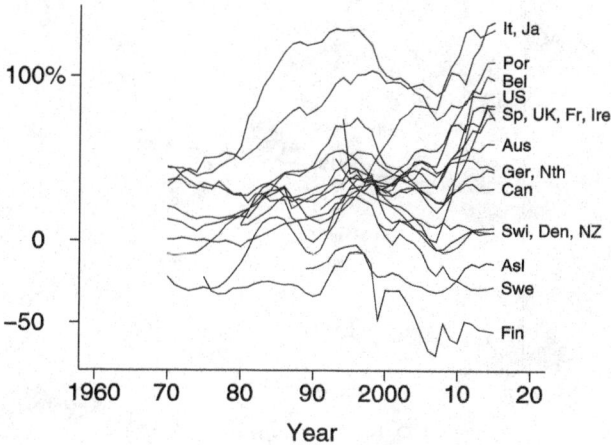

Figure 4.4 Government debt

Government net debt: government financial liabilities minus government financial assets, measured as a share of GDP. Higher on the vertical axis indicates larger debt. Data source: OECD. Norway, which has a surplus (negative net debt) of better than 200 percent of GDP, is omitted. "Asl" is Australia; "Aus" is Austria.

for a shortfall in private-sector demand, he favored running a surplus when the economy is growing in order the keep the budget in balance over the business cycle, and Nordic policy makers have adhered to that.[13]

Is Public Employment the Key to High Employment?

Among the affluent democratic nations, the Nordics—Denmark, Norway, Sweden, and Finland—have the highest levels of public employment. Government jobs account for 20 to 30 percent of all jobs in the Nordic nations. These countries also have relatively high overall employment rates. Are government jobs the key to boosting employment?

The large number of government jobs in the Nordic countries can mislead us. They are to a significant degree a product of the fact that most medical personnel (doctors, nurses, administrative staff) and most early education providers (teachers, staff) are employed by the government. In other countries their counterparts are more likely to be self-employed or in nonprofit or for-profit companies.

In any case, when we look across the full set of rich democratic nations, there is no noteworthy correlation between the public sector's share of employment and the overall employment rate. This is shown in Figure 4.5. A number of the nations with the highest overall employment rates—Switzerland, Japan,

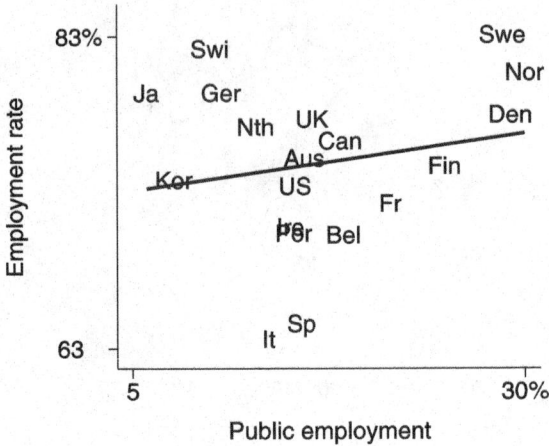

Figure 4.5 Public employment and the employment rate

2015. Public employment: persons employed by government as a share of all employed persons. Data aren't available for Australia and New Zealand. Data source: OECD, *Government at a Glance 2017*. Employment rate: employed persons age 25–64 as a share of all persons age 25–64. Data source: OECD. "Aus" is Austria. The line is a linear regression line.

Germany, and the Netherlands—are light on public employment. And some of the countries with a comparatively large public sector, such as France and Belgium, have a relatively low overall employment rate. So while government jobs can contribute to high employment, they are neither necessary nor sufficient.

Worker Control and High Employment

In one view of democratic socialism, a key element would be workers having control over decision making in their firm.[14] The appointment of top management in each firm would be via one-person-one-vote elections. Firms' corporate governance would approximate that of "worker cooperatives."

In cooperatives, workers typically adopt profit sharing as a key element of compensation. However, where workers have ultimate decision-making authority and their compensation is based to a significant degree on the ratio of profits to workers, they have an incentive to limit hiring. And when they do hire, they have an incentive to assign new workers to a separate tier that lacks voting rights and doesn't participate in the profit sharing.[15] If in a democratic socialist economy firms were required to give all employees equal voting rights and access to profit sharing, we might therefore expect those firms to resist expanding employment.

Worker cooperatives are few in number, so we don't know how pervasive this tendency is.[16] Nor can we be sure it would play out under socialism. But it's a potential worry.

Would Democratic Socialism Be Better at Achieving a Plentiful Supply of Jobs?

It might. But I don't see anything in the existing evidence that should lead us to conclude that social democratic capitalism is significantly underachieving, nor to be confident that democratic socialism would do better.

5

Decent Jobs

Along with capitalist growth comes . . . alienating and tedious work for the majority.

—Erik Olin Wright[1]

Job insecurity is the new norm.

—Guy Standing[2]

Once, I asked a liberal friend of mine to describe his dream world, to tell me what it would look like if everything he wanted had been accomplished. What did he see in the dream? "Full employment," he said. Now, I think everyone should have a job who wants one, but I have to say this is a pretty pitiful dream! It looks exactly like our current world, except we all have jobs. And jobs suck!

—Nathan Robinson[3]

Key incentive structures of capitalist economies contain biases toward long working hours.

—Juliet Schor[4]

The rich capitalist democratic countries have succeeded, as we saw in chapter 4, in increasing employment rates despite the challenges—globalization, competition, automation, shareholder value corporate governance, weakened labor unions—of the modern era. But have they done so mainly by creating a flood of bad jobs?

We'll look at pay in chapter 7. What about work conditions, the quality and security of jobs, and working time?

There are loads of undesirable jobs in every capitalist economy, as a lengthy collection of workplace studies and exposés attests.[5] The relevant questions are: Has there been improvement? If so, can improvement continue? And would democratic socialism do better?

Would Democratic Socialism Be Better?. Lane Kenworthy, Oxford University Press. © Lane Kenworthy 2022.
DOI: 10.1093/oso/9780197636800.003.0005

Conditions at Work

The available data, from public opinion surveys, don't suggest a significant deterioration in people's perception of their work conditions since the 1980s or 1990s.[6] In fact, most indicators suggest no worsening at all or even a trend toward improved conditions on the job. Figures 5.1 through 5.5 show that in recent decades there has been a reduction in most of the rich democratic countries in the share of employees who say their job isn't interesting, who say they rarely are able to make use of their skills and experience, who say they can't work independently, who say their opportunity for advancement isn't high, and who feel their job isn't useful.

One exception to the trend of constancy or improvement in perceived work conditions is the share who say their job is stressful. This is shown in Figure 5.6. On average about a third of respondents say their work is often or always stressful, and this share has increased in recent decades, albeit only a little. Is this peculiar to capitalism? We don't know. It's conceivable that democratic socialism would significantly reduce work stress. But if so, it should puzzle us that some of the countries in which labor unions are strongest, employee voice is most institutionalized, and public employment is highest—Sweden, France, Belgium, Norway—are also among those in which a comparatively large share of employees say work is always or often stressful.

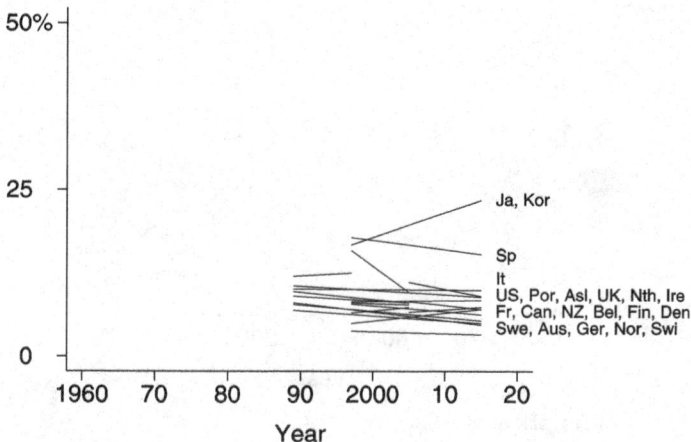

Figure 5.1 My job isn't interesting

Share of employed persons. The lines are linear regression lines. Question: "Please tick one box to show how much you agree or disagree that it applies to your job: My job is interesting." Response options: strongly agree, agree, neither, disagree, strongly disagree. The lines show the share responding disagree or strongly disagree. Data source: International Social Survey Programme (ISSP), zacat.gesis.org. "Asl" is Australia; "Aus" is Austria.

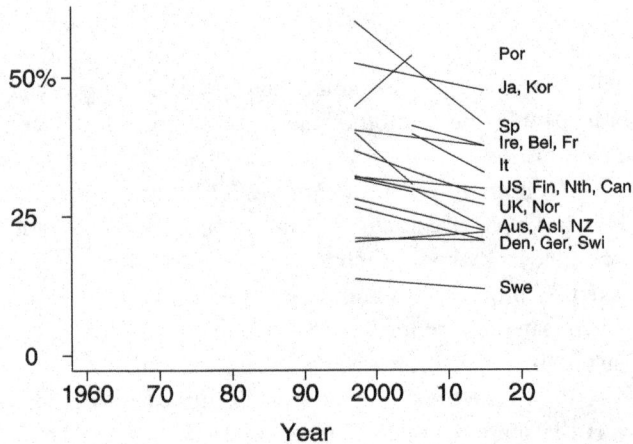

Figure 5.2 In my job I rarely use my skills and experience

Share of employed persons. The lines are linear regression lines. Question: "How much of your
past work experience and/or job skills can you make use of in your present job?" Response
options: almost none, a little, a lot, almost all. The lines show the share responding almost none or a
little. Data source: International Social Survey Programme (ISSP), zacat.gesis.org. "Asl" is Australia;
"Aus" is Austria.

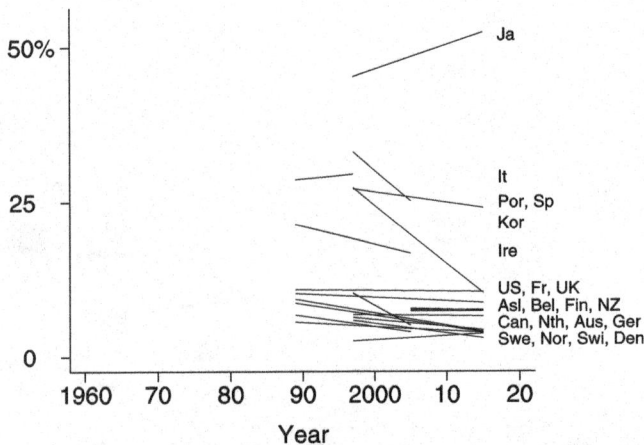

Figure 5.3 I can't work independently

Share of employed persons. The lines are linear regression lines. Question: "Please tick one box
to show how much you agree or disagree that it applies to your job: I can work independently."
Response options: strongly agree, agree, neither, disagree, strongly disagree. The lines show the share
responding disagree or strongly disagree. Data source: International Social Survey Programme
(ISSP), zacat.gesis.org. "Asl" is Australia; "Aus" is Austria.

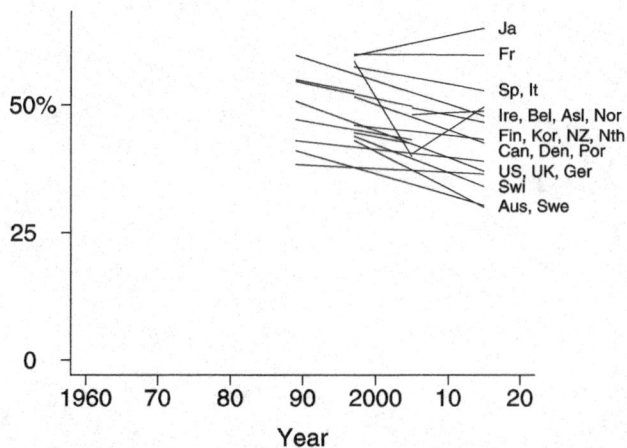

Figure 5.4 Disagree my opportunities for advancement are high

Share of employed persons. The lines are linear regression lines. Question: "Please tick one box to show how much you agree or disagree that it applies to your job: My opportunities for advancement are high." Response options: strongly agree, agree, neither, disagree, strongly disagree. The lines show the share responding disagree or strongly disagree. Data source: International Social Survey Programme (ISSP), zacat.gesis.org. "Asl" is Australia; "Aus" is Austria.

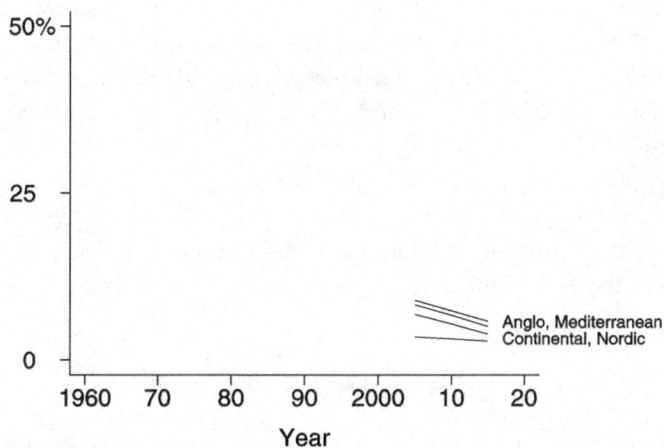

Figure 5.5 My job isn't useful

Share of employed persons. The lines are linear regression lines. Question: "Please select the response which best describes your work situation . . . you have the feeling of doing useful work." Response options: always, most of the time, sometimes, rarely, never. The lines show the share responding rarely or never, with don't know responses excluded. Data source: Magdalena Soffia et al., "Alienation Is Not 'Bullshit': An Empirical Critique of Graeber's Theory of BS Jobs," *Work, Employment, and Society*, 2021, using data from the European Working Conditions Survey.

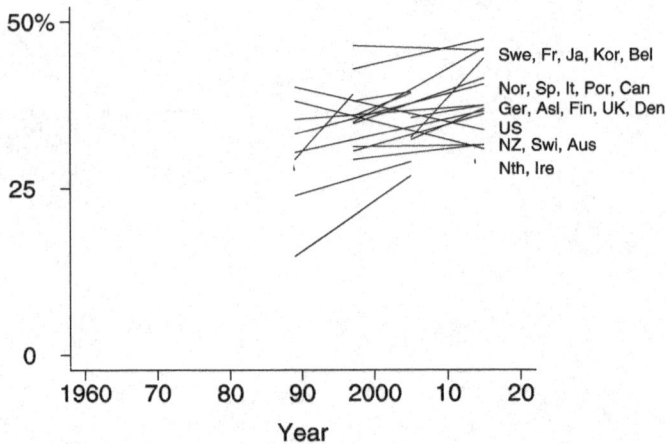

Figure 5.6 Work is always or often stressful

Share of employed persons. The lines are linear regression lines. Question: "Please tick one box to show how often it applies to your work: How often do you find your work stressful?" Response options: always, often, sometimes, hardly ever, never. The lines show the share responding always or often. Data source: International Social Survey Programme (ISSP), zacat.gesis.org. "Asl" is Australia; "Aus" is Austria.

It's possible that a high level of perceived stress is simply a condition of modern life. Arlie Hochschild, in her book *The Time Bind*, found that some Americans feel they have less control and more stress at home than in their workplace.[7] Recent studies of representative samples confirm that people tend to experience more stress at home than at work. And interestingly, the home-compared-to-work gap is largest for those with lower education and income.[8]

Are policy makers in a country with a capitalist economy incapable of addressing workplace stress? Given the long history of progress in regulating work conditions, from working time to safety to hiring and firing procedures and more, that seems unlikely.[9]

Job Regularity and Security

Seasonal jobs, work for temporary ("temp") agencies, gig or platform economy positions, independent contracting, freelancing, and some other types of work are outside what is considered the standard employment relationship. Many of these jobs come with irregular pay, which is fine for some households but problematic for others. Also, nonstandard workers may not be eligible for unemployment compensation or fringe benefits. And they may be more vulnerable to wage theft.

In the United States, recent studies estimate that 2.6 percent of employed persons are on-call workers, 1.5 percent are temp agency workers, 3.1 percent are workers provided by contract firms, and 0.5 percent are workers who provide services through online intermediaries such as Uber and Task Rabbit. Around 10 percent have irregular or on-call shifts. As many as 33 percent engage in freelance work of some kind.[10]

Have globalization, advances in automation, the rise of the gig economy, and union decline increased the prevalence of irregular jobs? We have over-time data only for two indicators: temporary employment and involuntary part-time employment. Figures 5.7 and 5.8 show that both have increased in a number of the rich democratic nations.

Have these shifts led to a decline in job security? A number of observers suggest that they have.[11] But data on job tenure—how long a worker has been with her current employer—suggest a different story. Comparable data for 15 European nations are available since the early 1990s. As we see in Figure 5.9, average tenure has decreased a bit in some countries but increased in just as many. In most there has been little change. In the United States, where we have data covering a longer period, there has been no decline since the 1960s.

Figure 5.10 shows employees' perceived job insecurity across the rich democratic nations. In most, the share who believe their job isn't secure has been flat or declining in recent decades.[12]

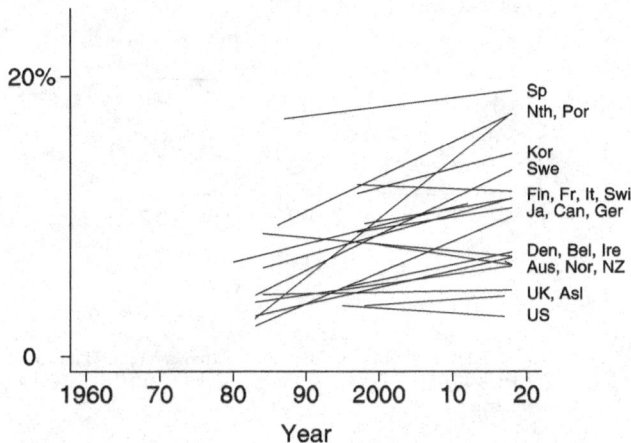

Figure 5.7 Temporary employment

Workers whose jobs have a predetermined termination date. Share of persons age 25–64. The lines are linear regression lines. Data source: OECD. "Asl" is Australia; "Aus" is Austria.

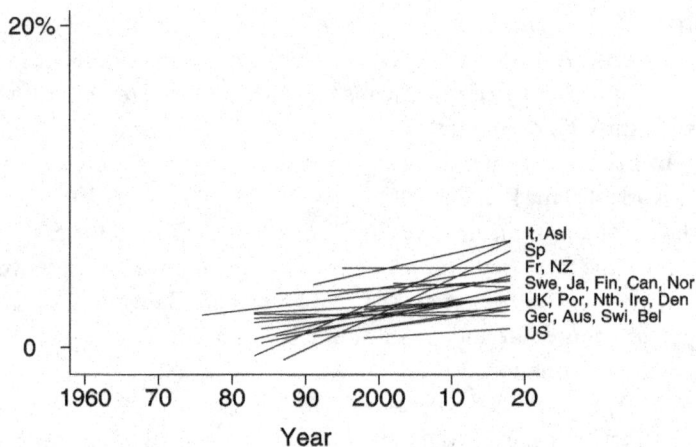

Figure 5.8 Involuntary part-time employment

Share of persons age 25–64. The lines are linear regression lines. Data source: OECD. "Asl" is Australia; "Aus" is Austria.

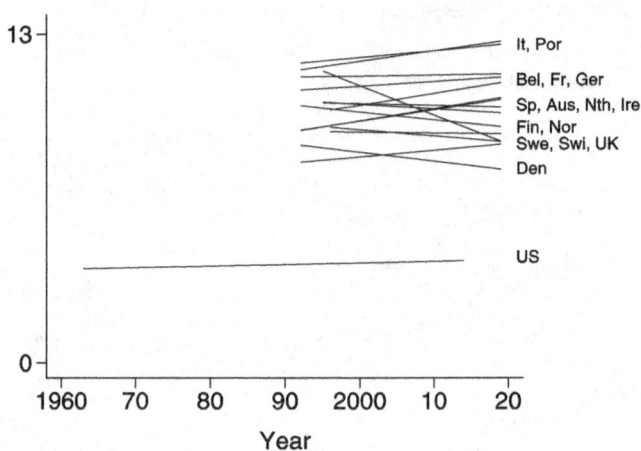

Figure 5.9 Average job tenure

Average number of years with current employer. The lines are linear regression lines. Data source: OECD. United States data are for the median, rather than average. Data source: Henry R. Hyatt and James R. Spletzer, "The Shifting Job Tenure Distribution," Discussion Paper 9776, IZA, 2016, figure 1. "Aus" is Austria.

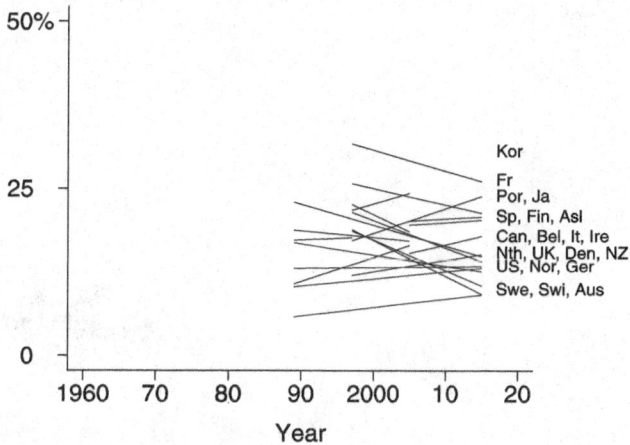

Figure 5.10 My job isn't secure

Share of employed persons. The lines are linear regression lines. Question: "Please tick one box to show how much you agree or disagree: My job is secure." Response options: strongly agree, agree, neither, disagree, strongly disagree. The lines show the share responding disagree or strongly disagree. Data source: International Social Survey Programme (ISSP), zacat.gesis.org. "Asl" is Australia; "Aus" is Austria.

Working Time

Another frequent worry about capitalism is that those who have jobs may be compelled to work more than they want.[13] It certainly is true that some people work very long hours. Figure 5.11 shows the share of employed persons who work more than 50 hours per week. In Japan and South Korea, more than 20 percent work very long hours. In the United States, 12 percent do. However, in a number of the rich democracies, the share is closer to 5 percent or even smaller.

On average, work hours have fallen dramatically over the past century and a half. Figure 5.12 shows the trends since 1870 in the 12 nations for which historical data are available. We have data for more countries beginning around 1970. Figure 5.13 shows a continued downward trend in nearly all of them.

A key source of declining work hours is paid vacation days and holidays, shown in Figure 5.14. Apart from the United States, an obvious outlier, the average number of mandated paid days off from work in the rich democracies is now 27.

Further reductions in working time are in the offing. France has moved to a 35-hour standard workweek (rather than 40), and other countries are likely to follow. We may add additional paid holidays and vacation days. Another proposal likely to gain traction is for periodic paid sabbaticals during one's work career.[14]

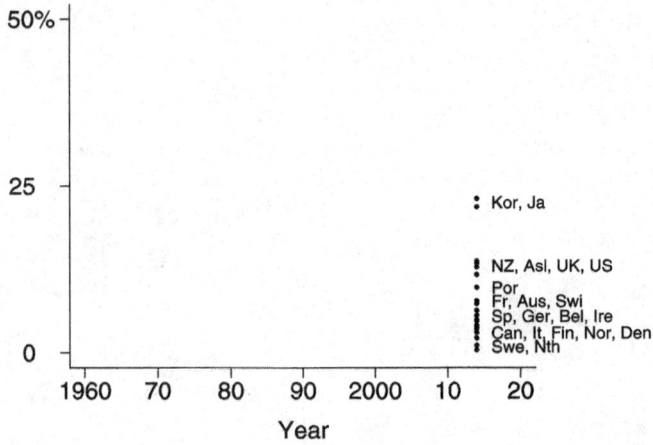

Figure 5.11 Long work hours

Share of employed persons whose usual hours of work per week are 50 or more. Data source: OECD. "Asl" is Australia; "Aus" is Austria.

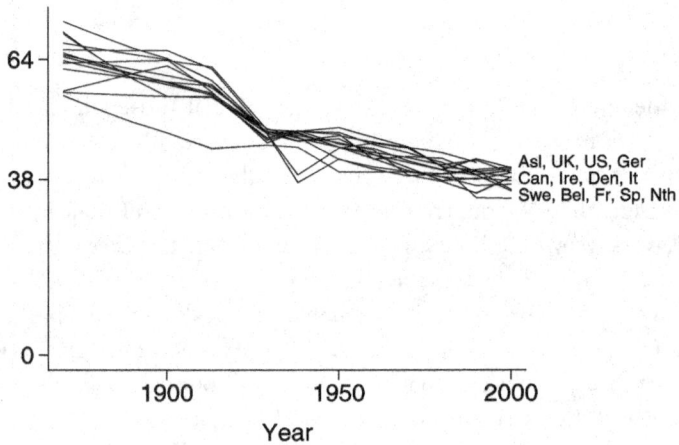

Figure 5.12 Work hours per week, 1870ff

Average weekly work hours per person engaged in nonagricultural activities. Data source: Max Roser, "Working Hours," *Our World in Data*, using data in Michael Huberman and Chris Minns, "The Times They Are Not Changin': Days and Hours of Work in Old and New Worlds, 1870–2000," *Explorations in Economic History*, 2007. "Asl" is Australia.

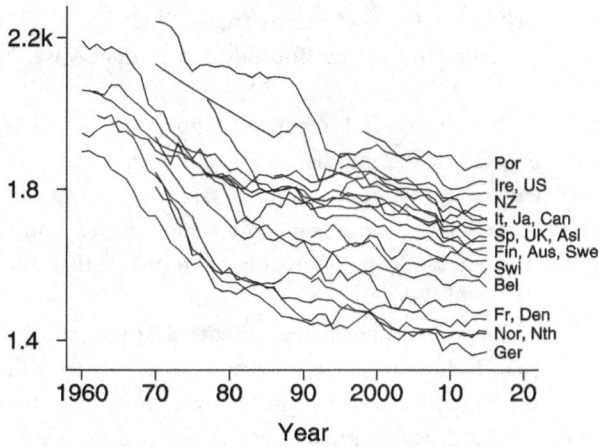

Figure 5.13 Work hours per year, 1960ff

Average annual hours worked per employed person. "k" = thousand. The vertical axis doesn't begin at zero. Data source: OECD. "Asl" is Australia; "Aus" is Austria.

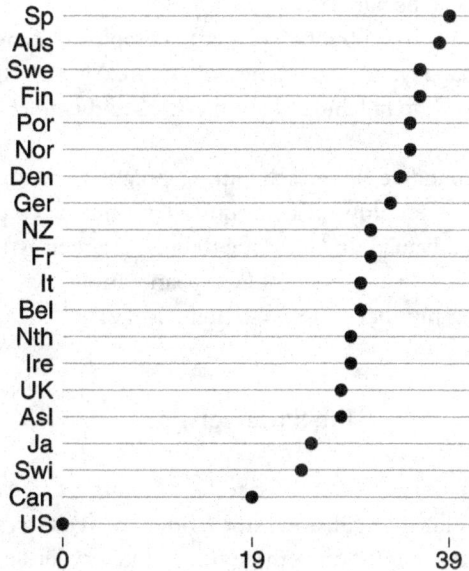

Figure 5.14 Mandated paid vacation days and holidays

Per year. Legally mandated paid vacation days and paid holidays. Data source: Adewale Maye, "No Vacation Nation, Revised," Center for Economic and Policy Research, 2019. "Asl" is Australia; "Aus" is Austria.

What about work predictability? Firms increasingly utilize "just-in-time" scheduling. This, according to Heather Boushey and Bridget Ansel,

> allows managers to adjust—and readjust—employees' schedules during the week, day, or even in the middle of a worker's shift. The software can break down schedules in 15-minute increments, meticulously paying attention to even the smallest fluctuations in store traffic, shaving minutes off an employee's shift if need be. In practice, this often means that managers do not post schedules until they are certain of the number of hours they have to give out (determined by upper management), and the managers' bosses seek to contain costs by holding them accountable for "staying within hours." It also leads managers to cut scheduled hours if they have gone over their allotted budget for labor costs earlier in the week. . . . Furthermore, some employers require workers to remain on-call, keeping their schedules free on the chance their employers may need them. Combined, these scheduling practices mean that many workers often have little or even no advance notice of their schedules.[15]

This flexibility allows firms to minimize labor costs without shortchanging customer service. But it can be hard on workers.

In 2014 and again in 2018, about 40 percent of employed Americans reported that they find out what days and hours they will be working less than one week in advance.[16] Studies of US retail and restaurant firms and employees yield similar estimates.[17]

It is possible to mandate better scheduling practices by employers. In San Francisco, large retail employers are required to notify employees of their schedule 2 weeks in advance. In Germany the requirement is 16 weeks, and in Denmark it is 26 weeks. In a number of European nations, firms must provide a guaranteed minimum number of hours to their workers.[18]

Job Satisfaction

The share of people in the rich capitalist democratic nations who think their work conditions are bad is fairly small, and aside from perceived stress on the job the share hasn't been rising. Temporary employment and involuntary part-time employment have become more common, but there has been no rise in job insecurity. Working time has been falling for more than a century, and it has continued to decrease. New just-in-time scheduling practices can make work schedules less predictable, but this appears to be mainly an American phenomenon, as other countries are restricting this practice.

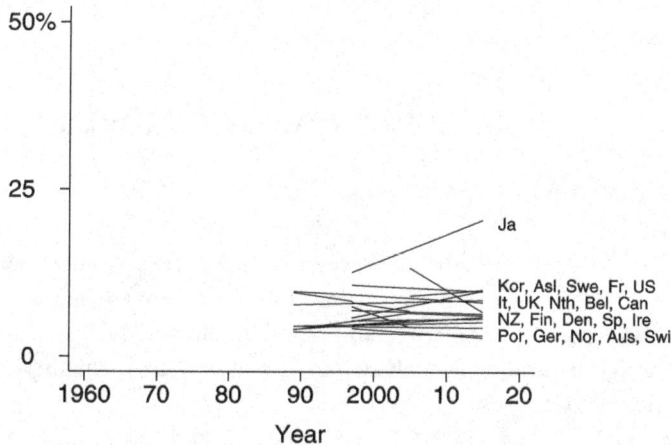

Figure 5.15 Dissatisfied with my job

Share of employed persons. The lines are linear regression lines. Question: "All things considered, how satisfied are you with your (main) job?" Response options: completely satisfied, very satisfied, fairly satisfied, neither, fairly dissatisfied, very dissatisfied, completely dissatisfied. The lines show the share responding fairly dissatisfied, very dissatisfied, or completely dissatisfied. Data source: International Social Survey Programme (ISSP), zacat.gesis.org. "Asl" is Australia; "Aus" is Austria.

What does all of this imply for job satisfaction? Figure 5.15 shows the share of people who say they are dissatisfied with their job. On average, that share is just 7 percent. And apart from in Japan, it hasn't increased over the past three decades.

Would Democratic Socialism Be Better at Providing Decent Jobs?

According to the best available data, trends in job quality, job security, working time, and job satisfaction over the long run and in recent decades have been better than capitalism's critics tend to suggest. It's also worth noting that workplace safety has increased markedly.[19]

There is plenty of room for further improvement. But I don't see a compelling rationale for concluding that we need democratic socialism in order to get that improvement. Progress will come partly via technological advances but to a significant degree through political struggle, just as it has over the past century and a half. Employers in a capitalist economy frequently resist regulation of work conditions, job security, working time, and other aspects of the employment relationship. Their ability to draw on a pool of unemployed persons looking for work, to replace people with machines, and to move to more profitable locations gives them a structural advantage. And their financial resources likely boost their political influence. Yet those advantages haven't, to this point, prevented long-run progress toward decent work.

6

Faster Economic Growth

This system, the American system, and every Western capitalist
system, is now in a period of low growth. . . . We are in a structural
crisis, not a cyclical crisis; and that structural crisis, I would argue,
derives from the very characteristics of a system which socializes
irresponsibly.

—Michael Harrington[1]

Economic growth might have problematic implications for our ability to preserve the earth's climate,[2] but in other respects it is an important goal for a good
society. It is valuable because it tends to boost living standards and because other
aims are more readily achieved in the context of an affluent, growing economy.[3]

Markets Are Helpful for Economic Growth

A capitalist economy features extensive private ownership of property and
markets in goods, services, and labor. Markets are helpful in two respects. The
first is resource allocation. The scale and complexity of a national economy make
effective planning and coordination via commands very difficult. Market prices
work better.[4] The second is innovation and improvement. Competition creates
incentives to develop new products and services, to improve existing ones, and
to increase efficiency.

Sustained growth requires more than markets. Daron Acemoglu and James
Robinson note that

> Secure property rights, the law, public services, and the freedom to contract
> and exchange all rely on the state, the institution with the coercive capacity to
> impose order, prevent theft and fraud, and enforce contracts between private
> parties. To function well, society also needs other public services: roads and a
> transport network so that goods can be transported, a public infrastructure so
> that economic activity can flourish, and some type of basic regulation to pre-
> vent fraud and malfeasance."[5]

Would Democratic Socialism Be Better?. Lane Kenworthy, Oxford University Press. © Lane Kenworthy 2022.
DOI: 10.1093/oso/9780197636800.003.0006

For the most part, it is governments that provide these things. Economic growth thus depends in part on effective government.

A third key is science—the application of the scientific method and the means needed to measure and analyze in order to improve products and the process of making them. Without science, market incentives are likely to yield some advance in productivity, but probably a limited amount.

Economic growth may also require a cultural shift. In *The Protestant Ethic and the Spirit of Capitalism*, Max Weber asked why early business owners would reinvest profits in order to accumulate wealth. At the time of his writing, around 1905, the capitalist economies in much of western Europe and the United States featured substantial competition, which encourages capitalists to reinvest profits in order to raise productivity and lower costs, in order to avoid being underbid and pushed out of business.[6] But why did early entrepreneurs continuously reinvest profits, especially in conditions of considerable uncertainty? As Weber noted, this orientation runs counter to "traditional" rational economic behavior: "A man does not 'by nature' wish to earn more and more money, but simply to live as he is accustomed to live and to earn as much as is necessary for that purpose." The reason early industrialists pursued growth, according to Weber, is that they felt there was no choice in the matter; they believed it their duty to reinvest and accumulate. A disproportionate number of these entrepreneurs were Protestant, affiliated with Calvinism or one of several related sects, and Calvinist doctrine viewed attainment of wealth through hard labor in pursuit of a calling—the calling of entrepreneur—as a sign of God's blessing.

We can see the impact of these institutions, policies, and attitudes in long-run economic growth patterns. Recall from chapter 2 (Figure 2.1) that there was little if any sustained economic advance prior to the mid-1800s. Then, once this configuration was in place in what are now the world's rich longstanding-democratic nations, economic growth took off.

Figure 6.1 highlights the importance of markets. It shows the available historical data on GDP per capita in the United Kingdom and China. In the United Kingdom this full configuration existed by the mid-1700s, and that's when economic growth began to surge. In China, by contrast, markets were severely constrained until economic reforms were introduced beginning in the late 1970s. China had hardly any economic growth prior to these reforms but very rapid growth thereafter.

Economic Growth in the Rich Capitalist Democracies

What do we know about the determinants of variation in economic growth within and between the world's affluent capitalist democracies? The surprising answer is: not very much.

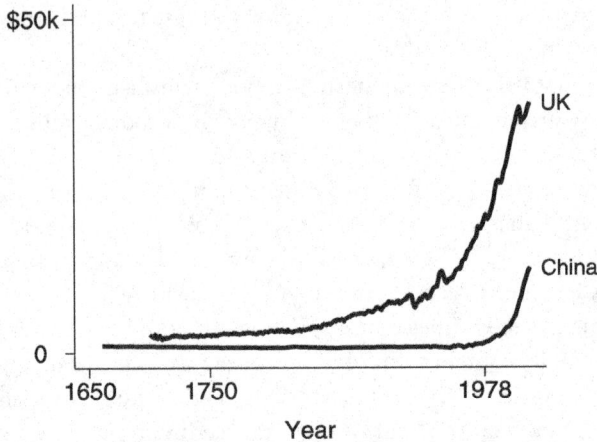

Figure 6.1 GDP per capita in the UK and China

Adjusted for inflation and converted to 2011 US dollars using purchasing power parities. "k" = thousand. Data source: Maddison Project Database 2018, rug.nl/ggdc.

Let's begin with patterns of economic growth in these countries over time. At any given moment, there typically is a country or two lauded as having unlocked the key to rapid growth. "Modell Deutschland" and "Japan Inc." in the 1970s and 1980s, the "great American jobs machine" in the 1980s and 1990s, the "Dutch miracle" in the 1990s, and the "Celtic tiger" in the 1990s and 2000s are among the more prominent recent examples. It turns out, however, that economic growth rates in many of the rich democratic nations have been remarkably constant over the past century or more. Countries that do especially well or poorly during a particular decade or business cycle often subsequently revert back to their long-run rate of growth.

Figure 6.2 shows GDP per capita in each nation since the early 1800s. The data are shown in logarithmic form, along with a regression line that begins in 1870. If GDP per capita grows at a constant rate, the data points will fall along this line. That's exactly what we see for a striking number of the countries. For a handful of others there is a clear break that occurs around World War II, with growth accelerating after the war. In those cases, two lines are shown in the figure.

What about cross-country differences in economic growth? Since the late 1970s, some of these countries have grown more rapidly than others.[7] This owes partly to "catch-up": countries that begin with a lower per capita GDP are able to grow more rapidly by borrowing technology from richer nations. Social scientists have offered up a slew of hypothesized determinants of post-1970s cross-national variation in economic growth that isn't due to catch-up, including education, research, modest economic regulation, international trade,

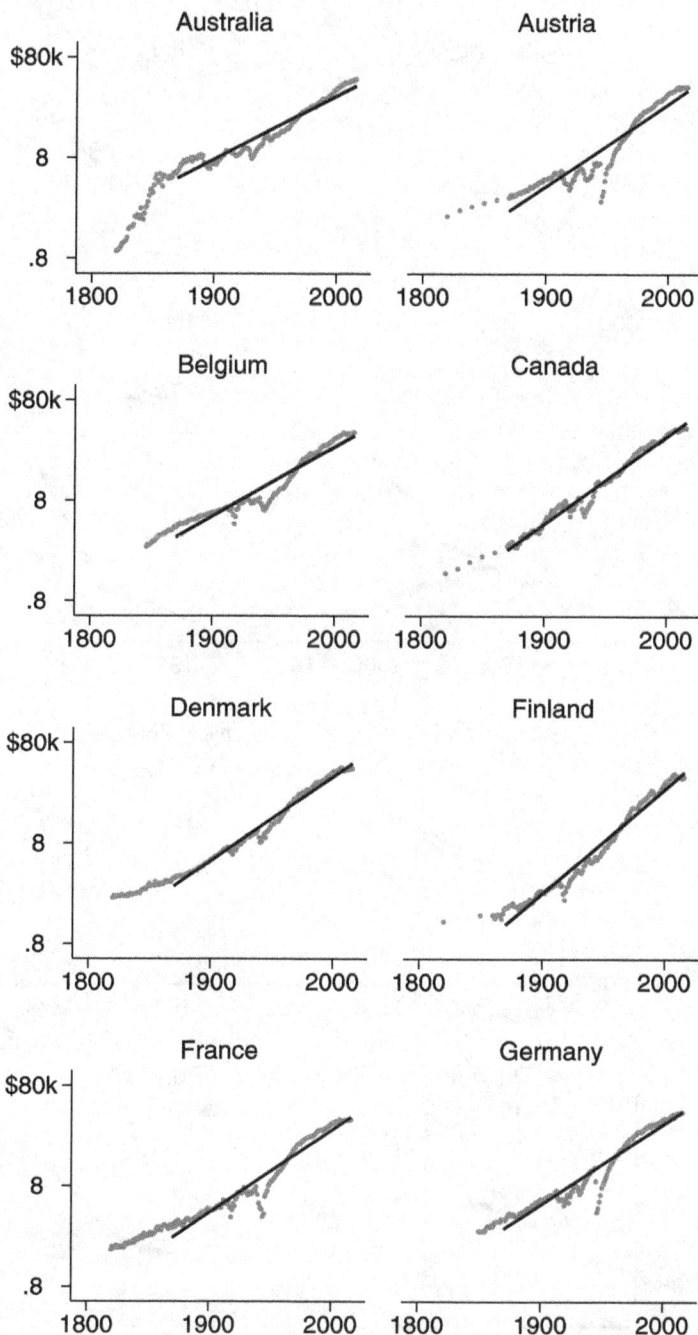

Figure 6.2 Trends in GDP per capita in 21 rich democracies

Natural log of inflation-adjusted GDP per capita. A log scale is used to focus on rates of change. "k" = thousand. The vertical axis does not begin at zero. The lines are linear regression lines; they represent a constant rate of economic growth since 1870. For Ireland, Italy, Japan, South Korea, Portugal, and Spain the data suggest a break in growth patterns, so there is one line for 1870–1945 and another for 1945–2016. Data source: Maddison Project Database 2018, rug.nl/ggdc.

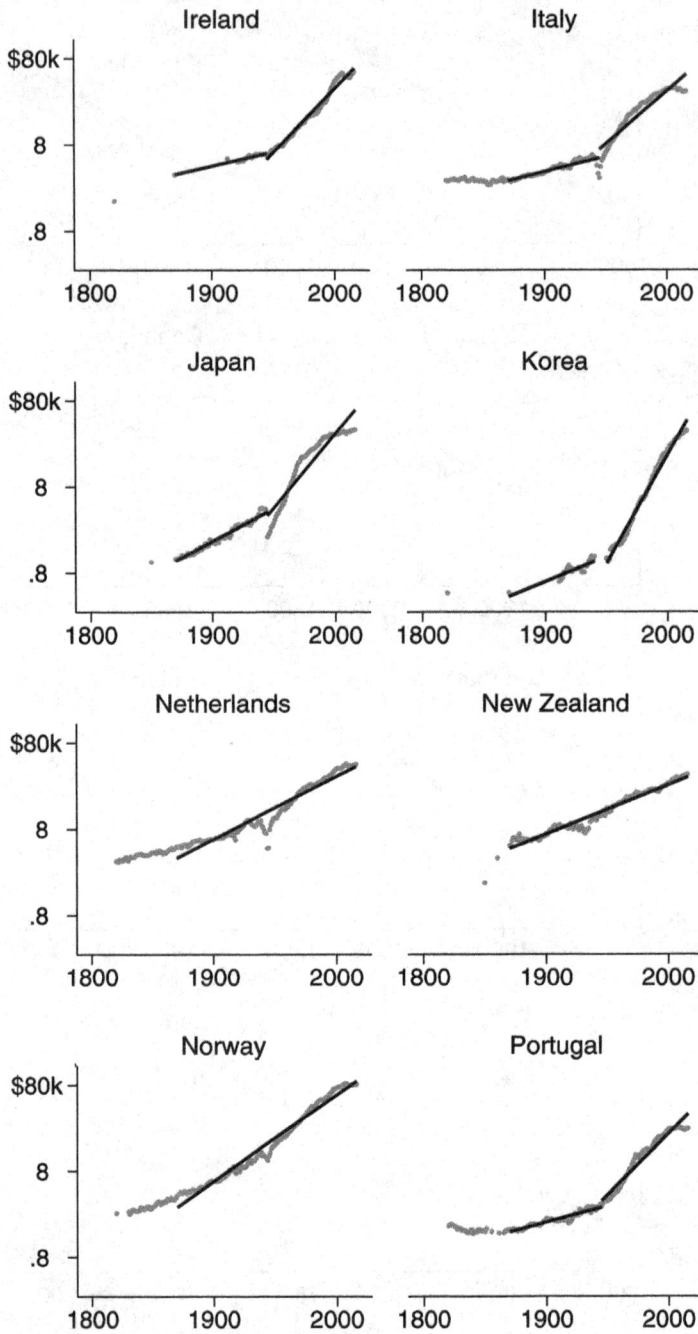

Figure 6.2 Continued.

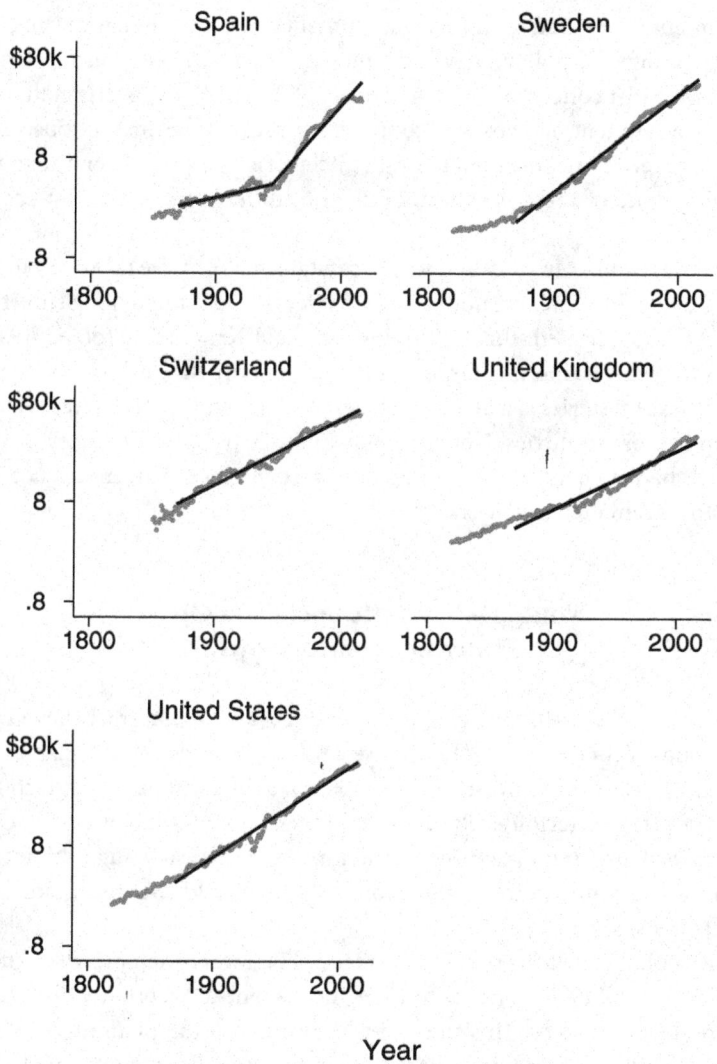

Figure 6.2 Continued.

government taxing and spending, government debt, state guidance (investment steering, industrial policy), government effectiveness, interest group organization, corporatist concertation ("corporatism"), left or right government, interest group–government coherence, cooperation-promoting institutions, institutional coherence, income inequality, financial crises, ethnic diversity, and trust. However, none of these is robustly linked to differences in rates of economic growth.[8]

So when it comes to rich democratic capitalist nations, we have very little clue about what yields faster economic growth over the medium to long run. Though not widely appreciated, this isn't unknown. Paul Krugman wrote in 1994 that "There are many economic puzzles, but there are only two really great mysteries. One of these mysteries is why economic growth takes place at different rates over time and across countries. Nobody really knows why." Two decades later his assessment hadn't changed: "The reasons some countries grow more successfully than others remain fairly mysterious."[9]

Would Democratic Socialism Give Us Faster Economic Growth?

For much of the twentieth century, proponents of socialism believed that it would boost economic growth because central planning would enable a more rational allocation of investment compared to the producer and consumer preferences that determine allocation in a market economy. However, most have long since given up on planning. Contemporary advocates suggest three main reasons why a democratic socialist economy might yield faster economic growth than capitalism.

First, with more of the economy under public rather than private ownership, government will be better able to steer investment to where it will yield long-run productive returns. This steering wouldn't be full-on planning; it would be guidance with a lighter touch. Private investors may have short time horizons, causing them to prioritize near-term profits over productivity, market share, export competitiveness, or long-term profits. Private investors may have limited information. They may be unconcerned about spillover benefits from particular firms and industries. They may lobby for policies that limit competition. In these ways, allocation of resources in a capitalist economy can inhibit economic growth. In theory, government can help to remedy these sorts of market failure via proactive steering of capital toward particular firms or sectors. It can do so via subsidies, favorable loan terms, assistance with coordination, export help, and protection against imports.[10]

Advocates of this type of state guidance point to numerous examples of its use in rich democratic capitalist economies, but we have no systematic evidence that it has improved long-run economic growth in these countries. The two nations that are most commonly referenced as success stories, Japan and France, haven't actually grown more rapidly than other affluent democracies.[11]

There is a strong case for increased government steering of funds toward "clean" (non-greenhouse-gas) energy sources.[12] But the aim here is to save the planet, not to boost economic growth. We don't know whether it will also achieve the latter.

A second reason proponents of socialism believe it would yield faster economic growth is that income inequality likely would be lower in a socialist economy. Income inequality may be bad for economic growth for a variety of reasons. The rich spend a smaller fraction of their income than the middle class and the poor, so greater inequality may reduce consumer demand. People might not work as hard if they perceive the distribution of pay and income to be unfair. More income inequality may increase the political influence of the rich, leading to less investment in growth-enhancing public goods such as schools and infrastructure.[13]

It turns out, however, that there is no empirical association between income inequality and rates of economic growth in existing rich democracies.[14]

Third, socialism might reduce the frequency and depth of financial crises. Finance lubricates an economy. Firms and individuals need to be able to borrow money to invest in skills, start up a new business, expand an existing one, research new product or process technology, and more. But providers of finance sometimes take on excessively risky investments, and when too many investments go bad, lenders may pull back, sending the economy into recession (or depression).

Putting more providers and users of finance under public ownership might reduce the likelihood of financial instability, though we don't know that for certain. In any case, the experience of the rich capitalist democracies offers no evidence that countries with less frequent or less lengthy financial crises tend to achieve faster long-run economic growth.[15]

So the specific arguments for why socialism will boost economic growth have no evidentiary backing in the experience of the world's affluent democratic capitalist nations. More broadly, we know very little about why, among these countries, economic growth has been faster in some periods than in others, or why it has been faster in some of these nations than in others. Given this ignorance, I see no justification for confidence that democratic socialism would give us faster growth.

7

Inclusive Growth

Rising inequality might be seen by some as a price worth paying if
it went together with robust growth for everyone. When it goes together with stagnating living standards across most of the distribution, though, it is now seen as representing a fundamental societal
challenge for the rich countries of the OECD. Indeed this combina-
tion, compounded by the impact of the Great Recession, is widely
seen as calling into question the sustainability of their long-standing
economic and social models—or at least their manifestations in the
neoliberal era from the early 1980s.

—Brian Nolan[1]

As for the middle class, it is the dinosaur in the room, set for
extinction.

—Yanis Varoufakis[2]

Capitalism has been the engine of unparalleled increases not only in economic
output but also in living standards for ordinary people. Even when the rich get
a disproportionate share of the proceeds of economic growth, there has tended
to be enough "trickle down" that households in the broad middle class and at
the bottom see their well-being rise significantly.[3] For those in the middle, this
happens partly via government transfers and services but primarily through
more jobs and rising wages.[4]

However, capitalism creates incentives for firms to try to minimize labor
costs.[5] And since the late 1970s, a variety of developments—computers and
robots, globalization, heightened product market competition, the turn to
a "shareholder value" orientation in corporate governance, and looser labor
markets—have increased firms' incentive to resist wage increases and enhanced
their leverage vis-à-vis workers. In some of the affluent democratic nations, especially the United States, the result has been stagnant wages and very limited
increases in household incomes despite healthy economic growth.[6]

Would Democratic Socialism Be Better?. Lane Kenworthy, Oxford University Press. © Lane Kenworthy 2022.
DOI: 10.1093/oso/9780197636800.003.0007

How big a problem is this? Can it be solved in a capitalist economy?[7] Would democratic socialism be more effective at delivering growth that's broadly shared?

Potential Solutions to the Wage Growth Problem in Capitalism

Figure 7.1 shows the best picture we currently have of wage developments in the rich democracies in recent decades. It covers the period from 1995 to 2013 (the earliest and latest years of available data). On the horizontal axis is each country's economic growth rate, and on the vertical axis is its growth rate of median compensation.[8] The line in the chart is a 45-degree line; a country will be on the line if median compensation has grown at the same pace as the economy.

That's roughly what we would hope for in a good economy: ordinary working people see their wages rise in sync with the economy's rate of growth. But it's what has actually happened only in some of them: Sweden, Finland, Denmark, France, Norway, the United Kingdom, the Netherlands, Belgium, and Italy. In the other nations, which lie well below the dashed line, compensation increases have lagged behind economic growth.

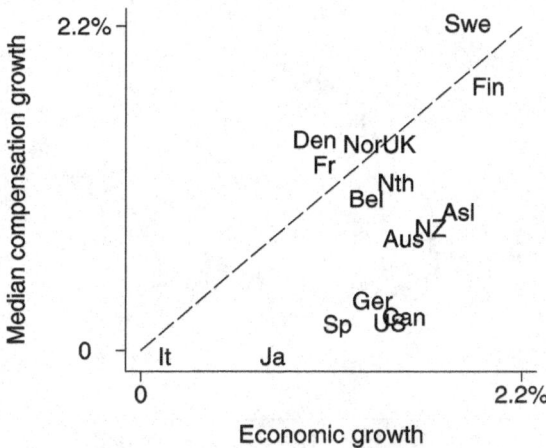

Figure 7.1 Economic growth and median compensation growth

1995–2013. Median compensation growth: average annual growth rate of median inflation-adjusted compensation (wages plus in-kind compensation plus employees' and employers' social contributions). Data source: Cyrille Schwellnus, Andreas Kappeler, and Pierre-Alain Pionnier, "The Decoupling of Median Wages from Productivity in OECD Countries," *International Productivity Monitor*, 2017, table 1. Economic growth: average annual growth rate of inflation-adjusted GDP per capita. Data source: OECD. "Asl" is Australia; "Aus" is Austria. The line is a 45-degree line; a country will lie on this line if its median compensation growth rate is equal to its economic growth rate.

Labor Unions and Collective Wage Bargaining

The degree to which compensation growth has kept up with economic growth is largely a function of labor unions and collective bargaining. The Nordic nations and Belgium have high unionization rates, so it isn't surprising to see them close to the line in Figure 7.1. France and the Netherlands also are close to the line. In France the unionization rate is low, but the law requires extension of collectively bargained wage agreements to nonunionized workers. In the Netherlands this kind of extension of collectively bargained agreements isn't legally mandated, but it is a strong norm. The countries with the lowest rates of unionization and no compensating mechanism, such as the United States, sit farthest below the line. According to one estimate, if US labor unions today had the same power as they had in the early 1980s, compensation for ordinary American workers would be about 25 percent higher than it actually is.[9]

The fact that labor unions have been critical for wage growth in contemporary rich democratic nations is a problem, because unions have weakened over the past half century.

In the United States and other rich democratic nations, labor unions arose with the industrial revolution in the mid-1800s. As we see in Figure 7.2, American unions grew in size and strength through the first several decades of the 20th century. In 1935, the National Labor Relations Act guaranteed the right

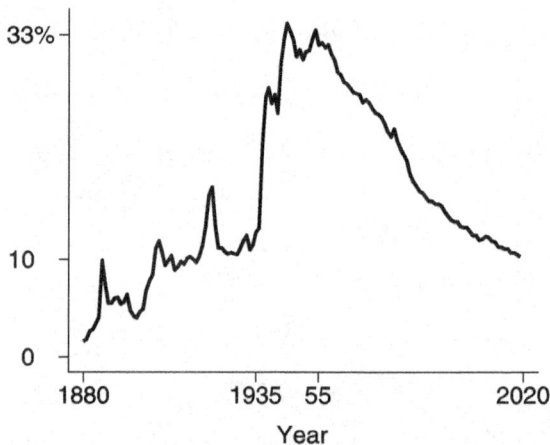

Figure 7.2 Unionization in the United States

Share of employees who are union members. Data sources: 1880–1982 are from Richard B. Freeman, "Spurts in Union Growth: Defining Moments and Social Processes," in *The Defining Moment: The Great Depression and the American Economy in the Twentieth Century*, edited by Michael D. Bordo et al., University of Chicago Press, 1998, table 8A.2. 1983ff are from Bureau of Labor Statistics, data. bls.gov, series LUU0204899600, using Current Population Survey data.

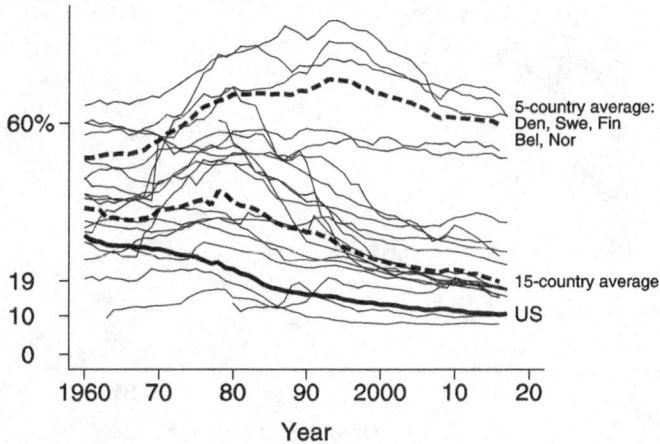

Figure 7.3 Unionization in 21 rich capitalist democracies

Share of employees who are union members. 5-country average: Bel, Den, Fin, Nor, Swe. 15-country average: Asl, Aus, Can, Fr, Ger, Ire, It, Ja, Kor, Nth, NZ, Por, Sp, Swi, UK. The thin lines are for individual countries. Data source: Jelle Visser, "ICTWSS: Database on Institutional Characteristics of Trade Unions, Wage Setting, State Intervention, and Social Pacts," Amsterdam Institute for Advanced Labour Studies, version 6.0, 2019, series ud, ud_s.

of workers in private-sector firms to form a union, required firms to negotiate with that union, and ensured protections for workers who go on strike. Over the ensuing twenty years union membership surged, reaching a peak of around 33 percent in the decade from 1945 to 1955. Since then, unionization in the United States has fallen steadily and sharply. Today, only 10 percent of employed Americans are union members.

In the 1970s and 1980s, America's union decline was widely viewed as exceptional.[10] But developments in recent decades suggest a different conclusion. As Figure 7.3 makes clear, unionization rates have been falling in most of the affluent democratic nations. Only five—Belgium, Denmark, Finland, Norway, and Sweden—still have a rate above 35 percent, and four of those five are helped by the fact that access to unemployment insurance is contingent on union membership. The average unionization rate in the other 15 countries dropped from 42 percent in the late 1970s to just 19 percent in the late 2010s.[11]

The situation isn't as dire when it comes to the share of workers whose pay is determined by collective bargaining, because, as I just noted, extension practices in some countries mean that pay developments for workers who aren't represented by a union are nevertheless determined by a collective agreement. Figure 7.4 shows that collective bargaining coverage (vertical axis) has remained relatively high in some rich democratic countries despite low unionization (horizontal axis). But in a third of these nations bargaining coverage is quite low, and

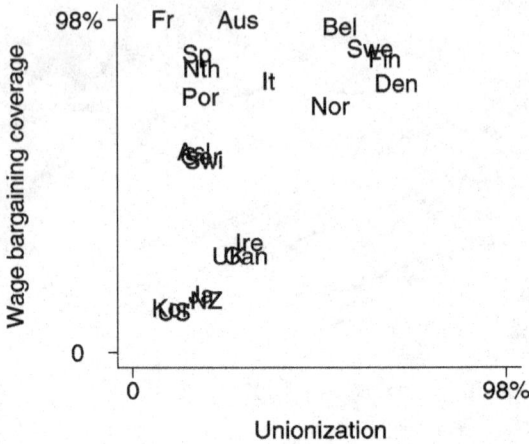

Figure 7.4 Unionization and wage bargaining coverage

Average for the years 2010–2017. Unionization: share of employees who are union members. Wage bargaining coverage: share of employees whose wages are determined by a collective agreement. Data source: Jelle Visser, "ICTWSS: Database on Institutional Characteristics of Trade Unions, Wage Setting, State Intervention, and Social Pacts," version 6.0, 2019, Amsterdam Institute for Advanced Labour Studies, series ud, ud_s, adjcov. "Asl" is Australia; "Aus" is Austria.

it may decline in others, as it already has to a significant degree in the United Kingdom and Germany.[12]

Are there alternative ways to ensure, in a capitalist economy, that economic growth yields steadily rising income for ordinary workers? I see four main possibilities: tight labor markets, statutory minimum wages, profit sharing, and earnings subsidies.

Tight Labor Markets

When employers can benefit from hiring more workers but find it difficult to do so, they are more likely to increase wages. The key indicator here is the unemployment rate. A low unemployment rate suggests there are relatively few people looking for jobs but unable to find one. In this situation, employers will be willing to offer a higher wage in order to attract additional workers and keep the ones they have. Wages will tend to rise.

The US experience bears this out. Over time, there is a strong association in the United States between the unemployment rate and the rate of wage increase. We see this for the country as a whole and within states.[13]

To create and sustain a tight labor market, the key policy lever is monetary policy. Central banks in the affluent democratic nations are charged with maintaining both price stability and low unemployment. The longer the labor market can remain tight, the stronger the pressure on employers to increase wages and salaries. To achieve this, the central bank needs to be willing to resist raising interest rates when the unemployment rate gets low enough to potentially cause a jump in inflation.

In the United States, the central bank's tendency since the inflationary period of the late 1970s and early 1980s has been to increase interest rates quickly and sharply when the unemployment rate falls to 5 or 6 percent. A notable exception was the late 1990s. With the unemployment rate at 4 percent, its lowest level since the 1960s, Federal Reserve chair Alan Greenspan held interest rates low despite opposition from other Fed board members who worried about potential inflationary consequences of rapid growth, rising wages, and the internet stock market bubble. Not coincidentally, the late 1990s is one of only two periods of nontrivial wage growth for American workers in the lower half in recent decades.

The other period of significant wage growth is in the late 2010s. The US unemployment rate was below 4 percent from 2017 through early 2020 (when the Covid-19 pandemic hit). While the Federal Reserve waffled a bit, it resisted significantly raising interest rates. This once again led to an increase in wages for Americans in the middle and lower parts of the distribution.[14]

There are two limits to the efficacy of tight labor markets as a driver of wage growth. First, periods of low unemployment tend to be brief. Even if the central bank does a good job of allowing a low jobless rate to persist, tight labor markets may obtain in perhaps one out of every three years, and that may not be enough to secure sizable pay increases over the long run.

Second, the association between low unemployment and wage increases appears to be more pronounced in the United States than in the United Kingdom.[15] So this approach might not work everywhere.

Statutory Minimum Wages

In the middle of the twentieth century, during the era of strong labor unions, few of the affluent democratic nations had a statutory minimum wage. Unions often didn't want one, fearing that this type of government intervention would weaken their position vis-à-vis employers. But this has begun to change, and 14 of the 21 rich democracies now have a minimum wage.

Figure 7.5 shows the inflation-adjusted value of the statutory minimum wage in these 14 countries. In most of them it currently sits at between $9 and $12 per hour.

A statutory minimum wage allows policy makers to push wages up via a simple political decision. In some of the rich democracies that's what they have

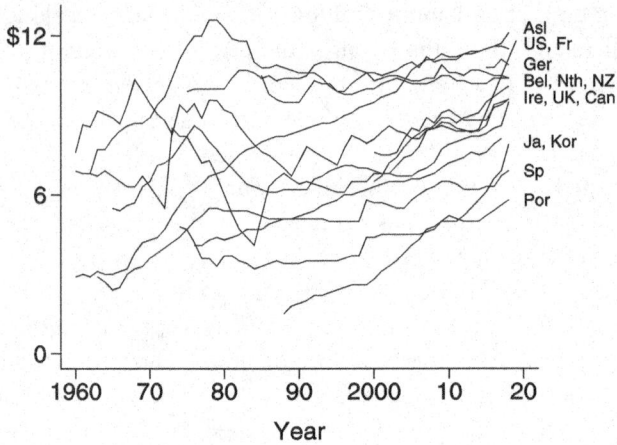

Figure 7.5 Statutory minimum wage

2018 US dollars. Currencies converted using purchasing power parities. The US data are a population-weighted average for the country, taking into account federal, state, and local minimums. Austria, Denmark, Finland, Italy, Norway, Sweden, and Switzerland don't have a statutory minimum wage. Data source: OECD. Data source for US 2000ff: Ernie Tedeschi, "Americans Are Seeing the Highest Minimum Wage in History (Without Federal Help)," *New York Times*, 2019. "Asl" is Australia.

tended to do in recent decades. In France, for example, the minimum wage was increased from $3 per hour in 1960 to $7 in 1980, and then to $11.50 as of 2018. The United Kingdom enacted a minimum wage in 2000 at $6.50 and by 2018 had raised it to $9.60. Ireland too instituted a statutory minimum in 2000, setting it at $7.50, and then increasing it steadily to $9.60. Canada's minimum wage also was $9.60 as of 2018, up from $7.60 in 1980. New Zealand's has jumped from $6 in 1980 to $10 in 2018.

In other nations, policy makers have decided to limit the degree of increase in the minimum wage, often in an attempt to bring wages more into line with competitor nations. In the Netherlands, the minimum wage was increased steadily from $6.80 in 1961 to $12.60 in 1979. But policy makers then allowed it to fall to $10.50 during the 1980s and have kept it at that level since.[16] Belgium, too, had a comparatively high minimum wage around 1980 but then held it flat in subsequent decades.

The same is true in the United States, at least at the federal government level. The US federal minimum wage was increased steadily and sharply from its inception in the late 1930s until the late 1960s. It then dropped a bit in the 1970s, due mainly to higher inflation. Since 1980 it has stayed essentially flat. In the late 1990s, however, some states and cities began adopting a statutory minimum wage above the level of the federal minimum, sometimes also indexing their minimum wage to prices or increasing it regularly. As a result, the average minimum wage across the country has risen, and the rise has been particularly sharp since 2014.

In all of the nations that have a minimum wage, its level is set by elected policy makers, though sometimes on the advice of a group of experts (such as the United Kingdom's Low Pay Commission).[17] In principle, this means it can be increased as much as the populace would like it to be. In practice, opponents of a high wage floor, such as business organizations, may be able to exert more influence on policy makers than ordinary citizens and thereby keep the minimum wage below what the majority wants.

Another constraint on the ability of a statutory minimum wage to ensure wage growth is the fact that it will tend to apply to a relatively small number of people. In the United States, for example, the federal minimum wage applies directly to around 2 percent of workers, and the effects of increasing it tend to fade out by around the 20th percentile of the wage ladder.[18] A rise in the minimum wage doesn't, therefore, guarantee that wages of most ordinary workers will increase.

A way to address this problem is via sector-specific or occupation-specific minimum wages. This enables policy makers to directly affect the wages of a much larger share of the workforce. Australia illustrates how this can work. Each year a Fair Work Commission sets minimum wages for more than 100 different sectors and occupations, from "Aboriginal Controlled Health Services" to "Wool Storage, Sampling, and Testing," as well as for various pay grades within these categories.[19] These minimum wages ("wage awards") are based on characteristics of the work and required skills. They directly determine the pay of about 20 percent of Australian employees, and indirectly of many more.[20]

The United States has experience with something similar. In the 1940s, "wage boards" determined pay levels for particular occupations and sectors. They exist today in a few states, including California and New York, though they play a small role in overall wage setting.[21]

The chief worry about a rising minimum wage is that it may reduce employment. However, the best available evidence suggests that modest increases in the statutory minimum in the past haven't done so. The best test, because it is closest to an experimental design, is a "difference in differences" approach.[22] The fact that many of the US states have set minimum wages higher than the federal minimum, in varying degrees and at different times, is helpful for analytical purposes. In the early 1990s David Card and Alan Krueger compared employment changes in fast food restaurants on either side of the New Jersey–Pennsylvania border after one state increased its minimum wage while the other didn't. Arindrajit Dube and colleagues pursued this strategy for every pair of adjacent counties straddling state borders in which one increased its minimum wage between 1990 and 2006. They, like Card and Krueger, found no adverse employment effect of minimum wage increases.[23]

Profit Sharing

Another way to boost earnings is profit sharing, whereby employees receive part of their compensation in the form of a portion of the firm's profit rather than as a guaranteed wage or salary. For owners, the advantage is that when the firm is struggling, for example during a recession, its labor costs will fall, because part of the reduction in profits will be absorbed by workers via reduced take-home pay. For workers, the advantage is that if profits rise, their pay automatically will too. Over time, their pay will be higher than it would have been without profit sharing.[24]

There is, as just noted, a risk for employees: they will bear part of the cost of falling profits during bad economic times. Then again, workers will tend to have greater employment security, as the enhanced flexibility in labor costs makes it less likely that firms will need to fire employees during rough times.[25]

Profit sharing isn't common in the rich democratic nations. But it probably could be if it were subsidized. Hillary Clinton's 2016 presidential campaign proposed to offer firms that implement profit sharing a 2-year tax credit equal to 15 percent of the amount they share (higher for small businesses). The credit would apply to shared profits up to 10 percent of a worker's salary or wage. For instance, if a new profit share program in a firm added $5,000 to the pay of someone making $50,000 a year, the firm would receive a subsidy of $750.[26]

Earnings Subsidy

Government transfers and tax credits to people in paid work but with low earnings are a fourth mechanism for boosting incomes in a context of weak labor unions. The United States and the United Kingdom began using employment-conditional earnings subsidies in the 1970s, and in recent decades many other rich democratic countries have adopted some version of them. These programs have proven effective at raising the incomes of households who struggle in the labor market while also encouraging employment.[27]

The dashed lines in Figure 7.6 show the structure of the US Earned Income Tax Credit (EITC). The EITC subsidizes earnings by as much as 45 percent, providing up to $6,300 per year for a household with three or more children, though the average amount recipient households get is $2,300. The benefit level increased sharply between 1987 and 1996, but since then it has been flat.

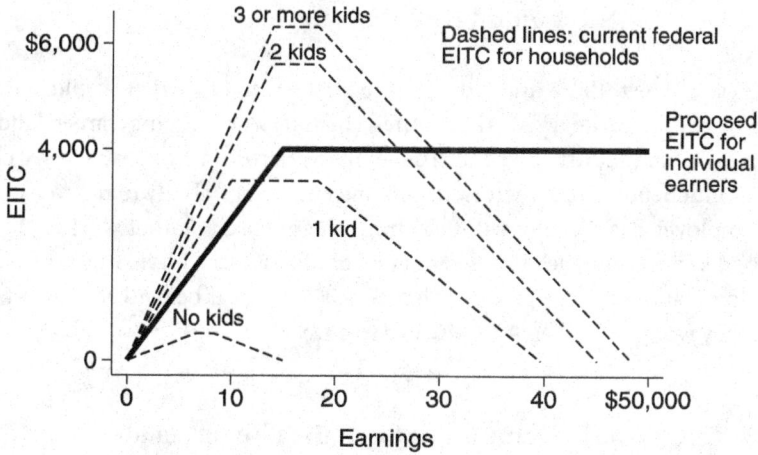

Figure 7.6 EITC benefit structure: actual and proposed
See the text for discussion. Data source for the current federal EITC: Tax Policy Center, "Earned Income Tax Credit Parameters."

The solid line in Figure 7.6 shows a possible alternative version of the EITC, modeled on Sweden's earnings subsidy.[28] The alternative version would be paid to individuals rather than households, thereby enhancing work incentives for second earners in households. It also would include workers further up the distribution. The current EITC starts to taper off once earnings reach a certain level and disappears altogether at household earnings of $55,000. The alternative version would give every person who earns at least $10,000 the same amount, say $4,000, and raise the earnings cutoff so that most employed persons qualify. These changes would enhance the degree to which the EITC boosts household incomes.

To enable the EITC to assist with not only income levels but also income *growth*, it could be indexed to GDP per capita (the current EITC is indexed to prices). This would allow the EITC to rise over time in sync with the economy.

Some worry that an employment-conditional earnings subsidy will cause wage levels to fall. In the presence of the earnings subsidy, employers may offer a lower wage than they otherwise would, and workers may be willing to accept a lower wage. Also, the earnings subsidy might increase the supply of less-educated people seeking jobs, and without an increase in employer demand for such workers, this rise in supply could push wages down. Studies suggest that the EITC may indeed reduce wages somewhat, but the evidence is thin and the effect is likely fairly small.[29] The best way to address this danger is with a moderate to high minimum wage.

Additional Ways to Help

In the US context, there are additional regulatory changes that would help to boost wages for ordinary workers. These include encouraging career ladders within firms and industries; protecting employees from being improperly classified as independent contractors; improving employees' ability to recover wages their employer has illegally withheld from them; ensuring that workers in retail, food service, and cleaning sectors be paid for at least 4 hours per shift; and requiring that all workers paid less than $50,000 per year be paid at an overtime rate if they work more than 40 hours in a week.[30]

Would Democratic Socialism Be Better at Delivering Inclusive Growth?

Proposals for socialism that emphasize economic democracy tend to favor pay based on profit sharing. That would be better than pay under capitalism for some workers, but worse for workers whose firm isn't successful. Socialist proposals such as John Roemer's "coupon socialism" (chapter 1) would boost incomes mainly via dividend payments to individuals. This very likely would ensure that incomes rise more in concert with the overall economic product than is the case in some capitalist economies. But it's also quite possible that things wouldn't turn out that way. The US stock market didn't rise much during the decades of strong economic growth in the middle of the twentieth century.

Would pay growth under democratic socialism be better than what we observe in the contemporary Nordic countries with their strong labor unions? As we saw in Figure 7.1, in these countries as well as a few others, median compensation has increased at approximately the same pace as the economy in recent decades. I doubt most proponents of socialism would expect it to rise faster than that.

In many of the rich democratic nations, union membership has fallen sharply. The share of workers covered by collective bargaining also has declined significantly in the United States, the United Kingdom, and Germany, and this may spread to other affluent democracies. These countries might have to turn to alternative mechanisms to ensure that pay rises in sync with the economy: periodic tight labor markets, steadily rising sector-specific and occupation-specific minimum wages, widespread profit sharing, and an employment-conditional earnings subsidy that is indexed to GDP per capita. Would pay growth under democratic socialism be better than under a capitalism with these institutions? I am skeptical.

8

More Public Goods and Services

> In a just society, all persons would have broadly equal access to the
> material and social means necessary to live a flourishing life.
> —Erik Olin Wright[1]

> Imagine the library model in other spheres of life. Say, for example,
> free medical clinics where anyone could go and get treatment. Free
> colleges, where people could go and take whatever classes they
> wanted, without being bankrupted by debt. Free bikes to borrow, a
> free water park.
> —Nathan Robinson[2]

Public goods and services make life better in a variety of ways.[3] They increase
freedom and opportunity, minimize economic insecurity, and help parents balance work and family. They also reduce inequality. The inequality reduction
doesn't show up in measures of income or wealth distribution, because access
to housing and transportation and healthcare and childcare doesn't get counted
as part of a household's income or assets. But while these don't alter inequality
of income or wealth, they clearly reduce inequality of living standards and
well-being.[4]

For many proponents of democratic socialism, expansive provision of free or
inexpensive public services and goods would be a core feature. Does capitalism
constrict such provision? Would democratic socialism do better?

What Does Expansive Public Goods and Services Look Like?

Imagine you live in a society with an extensive array of affordable high-quality
public goods, public services, and public insurance programs.

During pregnancy your parent or parents regularly visit a doctor who
monitors the pregnancy, listens to concerns, and dispenses advice about optimal diet, things to avoid, how to deal with stress, and related matters. The birth
occurs in a hospital or perhaps at home but with access to physician assistance
and appropriate technology. Throughout the first year of life, a nurse checks in

Would Democratic Socialism Be Better?. Lane Kenworthy, Oxford University Press. © Lane Kenworthy 2022.
DOI: 10.1093/oso/9780197636800.003.0008

with you and your parents to promote well-being and supply information about breast-feeding, your sleep patterns, illnesses, eating, and more. All of this is provided free or with a small copayment.

A universal parental leave program provides your parent(s) with 14 months of leave from paid work, replacing about 80 percent of their former salary. Parents can split these months however they like, though if your father (or other second parent) doesn't take at least two of them they get a total of 12 instead of 14.

After your first birthday, your parents can enroll you in a high-quality "early education" (childcare) center either part-time or full-time, depending on how they want to balance their paying jobs with caring for you. The staff in these centers are required to have the same qualifications as elementary school teachers. Many of these centers are run by the government; they are, in effect, extensions of public elementary schools, though they focus on social activities and play rather than education. Others are privately run—some for profit, some not. They may be formed by groups of parents or by companies. They must meet the same quality standards as the public centers. Your parents pay for early education, but the total amount they owe is capped at less than 10 percent of their income.

Throughout your childhood your parents receive a "child allowance" of about $300 per month per child from the government to help defray the cost of childrearing.

Around age 6 you enter the public school system, where you attend elementary and secondary school up to age 18. This costs your parents nothing. There may be some fees for participation in sports or band or the arts, but they are small and families with low income pay less. School provides free, nutritious lunches and, depending on family income, also free breakfasts. It also offers free or low-cost after-school activities. If your parents prefer to pay to put you in a private school, they are welcome to do that.

If you have a physical, mental, or emotional disability, you receive support services. When you are young, an aide may come to your home regularly. Once you enter elementary school, much of the service provision may be through the school system. There is no cost to your parents. If your needs persist beyond school age or throughout your life, you will continue to receive appropriate services.

After graduating from high school, you may attend college. If you choose a public university in your state or region, there is no tuition charge. Unless you live at home with your parents, you will owe for the room and board at college, which is about $10,000 a year. To pay for this, you can take out a government guaranteed loan. This loan will have a low monthly payment because the interest rate is low and because it can be paid back over 20 (or perhaps 30) years. And if your wage or salary turns out to be below average, your payments are further reduced.

When you finish college, you may decide to get additional education. Post-graduate schooling isn't free, but again you are eligible for low-interest long-term loans with an income-based repayment plan.

If you aren't interested in college, you may choose, around age 16, to enroll in an apprenticeship program that combines schooling with on-the-job vocational training. These programs run for three or four years and are tightly integrated with local firms and employer organizations to ensure that the skills being produced are needed ones rather than simply ones schools feel competent to provide. The apprenticeship programs are paid for by companies with a subsidy from the government.

Following school or an apprenticeship, most adults will get a paying job. If you struggle to find employment, you are eligible for government help. That will be true throughout your life if your company downsizes or goes out of business. Firms must notify a local labor market board when they plan to lay off employees and when they have job openings that have lasted more than a few weeks. Workers who are displaced or who leave their job by choice can receive subsidized training. Staff in the labor market boards keep in close communication with firms and with boards in other areas regarding trends in skill needs. The training programs are full-time and range in duration from a few weeks to more than a year. The service then helps to place workers in new jobs. If necessary, a subsidy may be used to encourage a private-sector employer to hire, or a public-sector job may be created.

Throughout your working career you'll receive about 80 percent of your former pay if you can't work due to sickness, injury, or unemployment.

Each year you get 30 paid days (six weeks) of vacation or holiday.

Housing typically is the largest expense for a household. Some people in your society own a home, but many rent. Government policy ensures that there are few barriers to construction of new rental properties, particularly in cities and near them. This increases the likelihood that the supply of rental housing meets or exceeds demand, which helps to keep housing affordable. A housing assistance program provides a subsidy to low- and middle-income renters so they pay no more than 30 percent of their income in rent. Landlords aren't permitted to discriminate against prospective tenants who receive this assistance. In addition to ensuring that housing is affordable, this gives families genuine choice about where to live, allowing them to escape from problematic neighborhoods if they wish to. Government also provides some rental housing directly ("public housing") and subsidizes additional affordable rental housing owned by nonprofits and communities ("social housing").

Public transportation, in the form of rail lines, subways, buses, trolleys, and bike- and scooter-sharing, is extensive and affordable for all. And government provides additional incentives for construction of housing within walking distance of core public transport routes.

Government at all levels is attentive to the provision and maintenance of public spaces and infrastructure—roads, bridges, bike lanes, walking paths, sidewalks, stoplights, enforcement of speed limits, air traffic control, museums, parks, sports fields, public restrooms, forests, campgrounds, beaches, oceans, lakes, swimming pools, zoos, phone lines, broadband, the internet, public television and radio programming, subsidization of free private TV and radio networks, libraries, festivals, and more.

You, like every citizen, are eligible for a free public bank account. In-person banking services are provided by post office branches, and you can use any public or private ATM machine multiple times per month at no charge. The government also provides free tax preparation services for the 80 percent or so of the population who have an uncomplicated tax return. Each person receives a postcard or short letter explaining the government's calculation of the tax they owe or refund they are to receive. If the information is correct, you send a text or email to confirm. These financial services save people hundreds or thousands of dollars each year in fees charged by tax preparation services and payday lenders. They also reduce stress and frustration and free up time.

You are eligible for basic legal services. If you are accused of a crime or your landlord is attempting to evict you, you will receive legal representation at no cost.

During your working years you have access to the same family-friendly policies used by your parents—paid parental leave, early education, a child allowance, and so on.

You have full health insurance coverage from cradle to grave. There may be copayments, and some elective procedures aren't covered, or are covered only partially, but you are never in danger of dying or suffering a significant deterioration in your quality of life because you don't have access to the funds needed to pay for medical care.

Your safety and health also are aided by effective policing. There is both more and less policing than the current norm in the United States. In high-crime areas, police create a large and highly visible presence, as this tends to reduce violence.[5] At the same time, other matters that currently are under police purview, such as emergency mental health calls, are handled initially by mental health specialists, with police called in only if there is an identifiable threat of violence.

When you reach retirement age, you are guaranteed a basic government pension. It's relatively small, but it's enough, when coupled with other public goods and services, to ensure that you can get by. There is a more generous public pension funded by dedicated tax payments throughout your working life, with benefits roughly proportional to your earnings. And many firms offer an additional defined-contribution pension to their employees.

You also are eligible to receive public long-term care assistance. You may choose to live in an eldercare institution or to receive eldercare services in your home. In-home assistance can be for several hours, throughout the day, or round-the-clock if needed. There is a copayment, but it is modest—a few hundred dollars per month.

This description of public goods, services, and insurance programs isn't hypothetical. Much of it currently exists in contemporary rich capitalist nations, especially the Nordic countries.[6] Perhaps there is a particular service, good, or income support that a government would never be willing or able to offer under capitalism, but I'm not sure what that would be.

Should Public Goods and Services Be Provided by Government?

To say that goods and services are "public" means that government pays for them, through general tax revenue or sometimes via an earmarked tax or fee.[7] Should government also be the provider?

Not so long ago, many political parties on the left believed government should produce key manufactured goods such as steel, cars, and chemicals. But it's now widely agreed that private ownership and market competition tend to be more effective at delivering innovation, good quality, and low cost in manufacturing.

Services and certain goods are different in that that we often want not only innovation, quality, and low cost but also universal access. It isn't necessary that all citizens have a car. But everyone should have safety, schooling, healthcare, basic transportation (roads, buses, subways), clean water, sewage, electricity, and internet access.

That doesn't mean government must be the provider, however. We could rely on private providers and regulate them to ensure that they extend service to all. Broadly speaking, we have three options for provision: fully public, a mix of public and private, and fully private with regulation.[8] Which should we choose for services where universal access is critical? That will depend on particularities of the service and on national or local circumstances. The world's affluent democratic nations vary widely in provision of education, healthcare (as we'll see in the next chapter), transportation, policing, mail delivery, utilities, and other services. There is no reason to presume fully public or fully private provision will always be the best option. The choice should be dictated by the goals—universal access, quality provision, cost control, and innovation.

In some instances this requires embracing competition from private providers. That doesn't mean taxpayers must bear the full cost of a private provider if it exceeds that of a public one. What it means is users should be allowed to choose between public and private providers.

There are two potential drawbacks. The first is that if enough users switch to private providers, the public provider may no longer be able to offer high quality at low cost. If too many students in an area choose private schools (or public schools across town), the local public school may not be able to serve its remaining students very effectively. But this shouldn't cause us to shy away from allowing private alternatives. It simply requires extra effort, and perhaps extra resources, to ensure that public provision to the remaining students is as good as possible or to help those students shift to other schools.

The second (related) problem is social division. When people with greater means choose private service providers and those with less use public providers, inequality of income and assets spills over into other realms of life. Economic inequality becomes social inequality. Arguably, societies function better—they achieve a greater sense of common purpose—when there are elements of life in which the rich, middle, and poor share the same space or experience.[9]

But forced togetherness is not an optimal solution here. We don't limit the number of grocery stores in a town in order to force people to come together. By the same token, we shouldn't try to achieve this end by limiting choice of schools or hospitals. A better path is to strive for excellence in public service provision so that middle-income and wealthy users—a sizable share of them, at any rate—voluntarily select the public option. In addition, we might consider an alternative mechanism for achieving social mixing, such as a mandatory year of national service after secondary school.[10]

At the same time, we shouldn't go overboard on choice. For instance, in elementary and secondary schooling there is no need to offer parents a menu of "education plans" with various combinations of subject coverage or different options for sequencing math classes. We should simply allow them to choose which school their child will attend. In healthcare, we should allow people to choose their provider, but it isn't necessary to offer dozens of health insurance plans to choose among. A few options is likely to be enough.

Can we get good outcomes with *only* private service providers? In some instances, yes; think of mobile phones or rental cars. But in others, such as schools, healthcare, transportation, water, sewage, electricity, and internet, private providers have tended to be unwilling or unable to ensure to everyone at an affordable price, so government needs to play a role, potentially a large one, in provision.

Would Democratic Socialism Be Better at Achieving Expansive Public Goods and Services?

Governments in existing rich capitalist democratic nations, particularly the Nordics, fund an array of public goods, services, and insurance programs. Most are available and affordable to everyone. The choice about whether providers are public, private, or both should be pragmatic, based on which can achieve the goals of universal access, quality provision, cost control, and innovation. I'm not aware of a convincing case for why democratic socialism would do better.

9

Affordable Healthcare for All

> If our goal is to provide high-quality healthcare in a cost-effective way, what should we be doing? Clearly, we must move toward a single-payer system.
>
> —Bernie Sanders[1]

A good healthcare system will feature universal coverage, good quality, cost control, and patient choice.

In a rich nation, everyone should have health insurance and access to affordable healthcare. That's partly because healthcare improves health outcomes and partly because without health insurance a person can get hit with massive, life-altering medical expenses.[2]

Improvements in the quality of medical care since the mid-1800s have been one of the most important sources of advancement in human well-being. In 1880, life expectancy in the United States and much of western Europe was around 35 years. The discovery of ways to prevent and treat infections dramatically reduced deaths, especially of newborns and other children. Since the mid-twentieth century, new techniques and medicines to treat chronic diseases have yielded additional gains in longevity. There is more to come, from improved understanding of diet, addiction, and mental illness to cures for cancer and beyond.

The care available to people should include effective prevention, diagnosis, and treatment. This doesn't mean everyone should have immediate access to every treatment or every type of medication for as long as they want. It's reasonable to set limits on the types of care that are covered. It's reasonable to impose waits for nonemergency diagnosis and treatment. It's appropriate to ask people to pay out of pocket or to purchase separate insurance if they wish to have extras covered or if they want to minimize wait times or maximize choice of provider.

All rich democratic countries have been spending a rising portion of their national income on healthcare, as we will see later in this chapter. The main reason is that rapidly rising productivity in production of food and other goods allows us to spend more on services, and most of us consider healthcare a very important service, so we're willing to pay a good bit of our income to get it.[3] No rich nation will go bankrupt spending 10 percent or 20 percent or even 30 percent of

Would Democratic Socialism Be Better?. Lane Kenworthy, Oxford University Press. © Lane Kenworthy 2022.
DOI: 10.1093/oso/9780197636800.003.0009

its GDP on healthcare. At the same time, there is no need to tolerate unnecessary waste in a system that accounts for such a large share of the economy.[4] Where large and rapidly rising expenditures are a result of conscious, informed choice by consumers or policy makers, we can rest at ease. Where they are a product of inefficiency or rent seeking by providers, insurers, or other actors, we should strive to do better.

Patient choice of physicians, hospitals, and clinics is, arguably, the least critical of the four desiderata. But to many people it does matter, and to some it matters a great deal. Since it turns out to be relatively simple to design a universal, high-quality, not-too-expensive healthcare system that allows patient choice, there is little reason not to permit it.

Markets are a very effective mechanism for improving quality and getting products and services to consumers at a low price, and most contemporary proposals for a socialist economy feature widespread use of markets. But markets don't work so well in healthcare. The problem is that medical care is very expensive, many consumers are unable to determine or predict exactly what they will need (medical diagnosis is complex and specialized), and sometimes consumers need treatment so quickly that even with knowledge and information they aren't able to make a sensible choice among alternatives.

For this reason, all rich democratic countries apart from the United States make very limited use of markets in healthcare. Prices aren't set by providers in response to supply and demand; they're determined by a government agency or by negotiated agreement between insurers and providers. Consumers contribute to the cost of healthcare by paying taxes or insurance premiums, but their access to healthcare isn't limited by their ability to pay. Providers and insurers aren't permitted to make profits. They can make more money by being good at what they do and thereby getting more customers, but they can't boost their bottom line by raising prices or by prioritizing some customers over others. And if they do generate more revenue, it doesn't go to shareholders.

There are two principal types of healthcare systems in the affluent democracies. These are sometimes referred to as the Beveridge model and the Bismarck model. I'll call them "single payer" and "insurance funds."[5] The single-payer healthcare model is more socialist than the insurance-funds model. Is the single-payer model better?

Single Payer Systems

In a single-payer system, the government pays providers (from tax revenues), decides prices, decides what procedures are covered, decides copayments, and more. It also runs some or most of the hospitals and employs some or most of the medical providers. The best-known example of this type of system is the United Kingdom's National Health Service (NHS).

Britons don't pay health insurance premiums; healthcare is paid for via taxes. There are no copayments for diagnosis and treatment, whether for a visit to the doctor or specialized surgery. There is a small copayment for medicines, but it is waived for the elderly, people with chronic conditions, and other needy groups.

Not everything is covered. A government agency decides, based on medical research, what treatments and medications are effective enough to justify coverage. And some basic things, like eyeglasses and some types of dental care, aren't covered. Patients must see their general practitioner first and get a referral in order to see a specialist, much like with health maintenance organizations (HMOs) in the United States. Patients can see any general practitioner of their choosing, and once they get a referral they can choose which specialist to see next.

The chief mechanism for controlling costs is that a single agency decides what tests, procedures, and medicines will be covered and how much providers will be paid. In addition, administrative costs are very low because there are no disputes about eligibility, there is a single set of rules, and there is a single price list.

General practitioners are paid based on the number of patients they have ("capitation"), not the number of patient visits or the number of tests and procedures they perform or the number of referrals they make to specialist doctors. General practitioners in the United Kingdom aren't government employees. Formally, they are self-employed doctors who contract with the government. But this is a distinction that makes little difference, as what they can do and how much they can charge are determined by the NHS. Doctors can provide private medical care on the side, charging what they like. But the private market is used by a small minority of Britons; 90 percent use only the NHS for their healthcare.

Britons pay for healthcare via their taxes and some small copayments. And if they want to avoid waiting to see a specialist or if they'd like to get a procedure that isn't covered by the NHS, they pay out of pocket.

Among the world's rich longstanding-democratic nations, Australia, Canada, Ireland, New Zealand, Italy, Portugal, Spain, Denmark, Finland, Norway, Sweden, and South Korea have healthcare systems that are broadly similar to the British one. The United States does too; nearly half of Americans get their healthcare via Medicare (elderly), Medicaid (low income), the Veterans Administration (former military), or the Military Health System (current military). So this is the type of system favored by the English-speaking nations, the southern European countries, the Nordic countries, and most recently South Korea.

There are differences among these countries: whether or not medical providers are formally government employees, what tests and procedures are covered (two out of three nonelderly Canadians have private insurance to supplement the government package), whether patients must see a primary-care physician first or can go straight to a specialist, the degree of choice patients have about doctors and hospitals, the existence and size of copayments, whether key decisions are made by a central government agency (UK) or by local governments (Canada, Denmark, Sweden), whether private health insurance can cover the same procedures as the public system (in Canada it can't), and more. But the basic structure is the same: government decides what tests, procedures, and medicines are covered, how much providers are paid, and where the money comes from.

In this type of system, these matters are political decisions. If citizens aren't satisfied with their access to medical care, with its quality, with waiting times, with the amount of taxes they're paying to fund it, or with something else, they can vote in a new government that will make changes.

A transition to this type of system in the United States wouldn't be too difficult. We could lower the age at which Americans are eligible for Medicare, raise the income limit below which they qualify for Medicaid, and add a Medicare-like program ("public option") that individuals and families can purchase on health insurance exchanges and that companies can purchase for their employees. Or we could simply allow any employer or individual to buy into Medicaid or Medicare, with subsidies for those who need them, and automatically assign stragglers into one or the other of these programs. Eventually, much of the population would be covered by Medicare and Medicaid. This would achieve universal coverage, and the government, as the dominant payer, would be in a strong position to control healthcare costs.[6]

Insurance Funds Systems

Austria, Belgium, France, Germany, Japan, Netherlands, and Switzerland—the continental European democracies plus Japan—organize healthcare differently. Health insurers, usually referred to as insurance funds, are the principal payers. Citizens pick an insurance fund and pay it a fee, often supplemented by a payment from their employer. The insurance fund determines what tests, procedures, and medications will be covered. Hospitals and doctors are mostly nonprofit or private; relatively few are owned, administered, or employed by the government.

In this respect, things work similarly to the way they do for a majority of working-age Americans who get health insurance through an employer-sponsored plan and get treated by nonprofit or private physicians and hospitals, with the insurer paying most or all of the cost. But there the similarity ends. First, unlike in the United States, everyone is covered. Individuals typically are required to purchase health insurance through an insurance fund, and those who don't or can't are either assigned to a fund or are covered by the government. The insurance funds must accept all applicants; they can't refuse coverage on grounds of age, risk, preexisting conditions, or for any other reason. Second, there is a basic plan that all insurers must offer at a fixed price. Typically they also can offer better plans, which cover more services or allow more choice among doctors or shorter waits, at a higher price. Third, prices are tightly controlled. Sometimes, as in France and Japan, government sets the prices in consultation with representatives of hospitals and doctors. In other countries, such as Germany and the Netherlands, prices are determined, for the nation as a whole, via bargaining between representatives of the insurance funds and representatives of medical providers. If those negotiations break down, government steps in to impose a resolution. Fourth, insurance funds can't be for-profit. They can compete via the type of premium plans they offer, or by reimbursing more quickly than others, or offering better customer service. But they can't do so by denying payment for covered services or by charging a lower premium for the basic package or by cutting employees' wages.

There are differences across these countries. The number of funds varies: France has about 15, Germany 150, Japan 3,500. In most, people can choose to join whatever insurance fund they like, but in France they must go with the one set up for their line or work or the region where they live, and they stay with that fund for life, even if they move across the country or lose their job. Japanese must go with their employer's fund. In some nations people can switch between funds on short notice (Germany, Switzerland), whereas in others switching can only be done once a year (Netherlands). In some countries patients can go to whatever doctor or hospital they like (France, Japan), while in others they must first see a primary-care physician. Some charge copayments; some don't. In some, lots of people purchase supplementary private insurance to cover things the insurance plan doesn't (90 percent of the working-aged in France). In Germany, but not in most other countries, people are allowed to opt out of this system and purchase private insurance on their own (about 7 percent do so).

Using employer payments as a major source of financing for healthcare might seem outdated. In a society where people switch jobs frequently, it makes little sense for insurance against a potentially major and very costly risk to be tied to one's employer. Moreover, providing health insurance is expensive for firms, putting them at a disadvantage relative to small firms and foreign competitors. And it likely acts as a brake on wage increases. Nevertheless, employer-funded health insurance seems to work reasonably well in these countries. An important reason why is that if people quit or lose their job, they are automatically kept with their existing insurance fund or switched into a government health insurance plan. And the cost of healthcare is contained, so it's less of a burden for employers.[7]

Would Democratic Socialism Be Better in Healthcare?

Does the single-payer healthcare model perform better than the insurance-funds model?[8]

Figure 9.1 shows average life expectancy since 1980 in the 12 countries that have a single-payer system and the seven countries that have an insurance-funds system. There is no meaningful difference between them.

Life expectancy is influenced not only by a nation's healthcare system but also by lifestyle, diet, education, affluence, violence, and more. A measure that can more directly gauge the impact of the healthcare system on longevity is "avoidable deaths," defined as deaths among persons aged 0 to 74 from diseases or conditions that are treatable or that could have been prevented through better public health interventions. Comparable data are available only for European nations and only for recent years. This includes nine countries with a single-payer system and six countries with an insurance-funds system. As we see in Figure 9.2, the avoidable death rate is virtually identical across the two system types.

Figure 9.3 shows health expenditures as a share of GDP. Here we see a slight advantage for single-payer countries. It may be that this is due to greater efficiency—for instance, lower administrative costs or less waste. Then again, it could be a result of political choices to cover fewer procedures or medications, which might result in longer wait times or less use of medical care. We lack data that would permit the sort of detailed comparison we need in order to reach

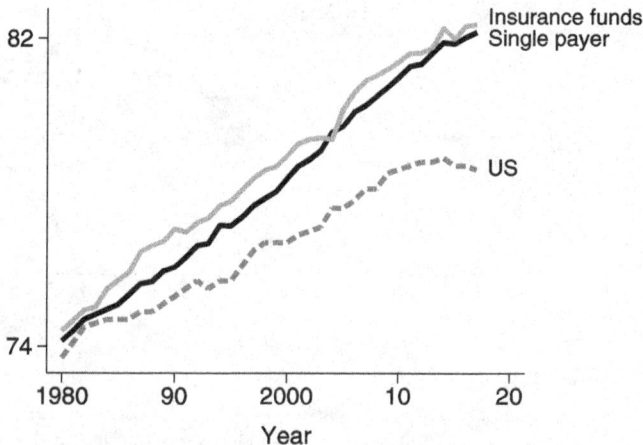

Figure 9.1 Life expectancy

Years of life expectancy at birth. The vertical axis doesn't begin at zero. The "single payer" countries are Australia, Canada, Denmark, Finland, Ireland, Italy, New Zealand, Norway, Portugal, Spain, Sweden, and the United Kingdom. The "insurance funds" countries are Austria, Belgium, France, Germany, Japan, Netherlands, and Switzerland. Data source: OECD.

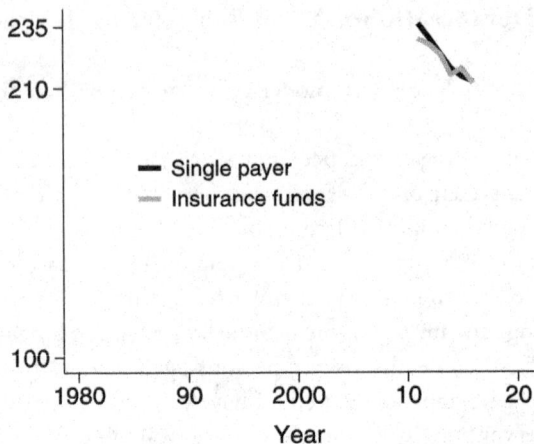

Figure 9.2 Avoidable death rate

Per 100,000 persons aged 0 to 74. Deaths from diseases or conditions that are treatable ("treatable" deaths) plus deaths that could have been prevented through better public health interventions ("preventable" deaths). The vertical axis doesn't begin at zero. The "single payer" countries are Denmark, Finland, Ireland, Italy, Norway, Portugal, Spain, Sweden, and the United Kingdom. The "insurance funds" countries are Austria, Belgium, France, Germany, Netherlands, and Switzerland. Data source: Eurostat, "Preventable and Treatable Mortality Statistics."

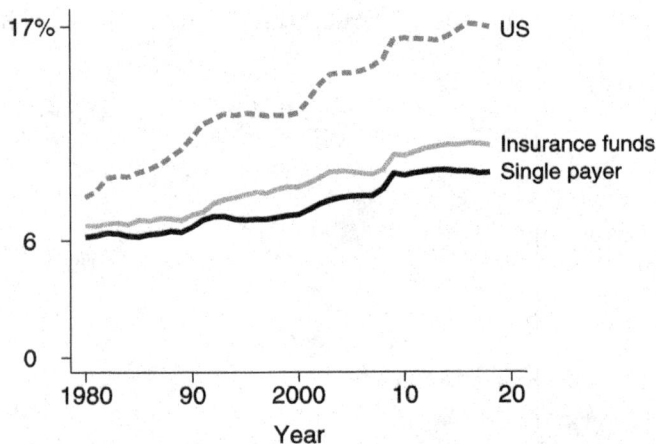

Figure 9.3 Health expenditures

Share of GDP. Total (public plus private) expenditures. The "single payer" countries are Australia, Canada, Denmark, Finland, Ireland, Italy, New Zealand, Norway, Portugal, Spain, Sweden, and the United Kingdom. The "insurance funds" countries are Austria, Belgium, France, Germany, Japan, Netherlands, and Switzerland. Data source: OECD.

a confident conclusion about the source and value of this difference in health expenditures.

In 2013 and 2016, the Commonwealth Fund conducted thorough assessments of the healthcare systems of 11 of these countries. They included six countries that have a single-payer system (Australia, Canada, New Zealand, Norway, Sweden, and the United Kingdom) and four with an insurance-funds system (France, Germany, the Netherlands, and Switzerland), along with the United States. They scored each nation in five areas—care process (preventive care, safe care, coordinated care, and engagement and patient preferences), access (affordability and timeliness), administrative efficiency, equity, and healthcare outcomes—and they used these scores to determine an overall ranking.

Figure 9.4 shows the countries' ranking in each year along with the averages for the two groups. In 2013 the average rank for countries with a single-payer system was exactly the same as the average for countries with an insurance-funds system. In 2016 the average rank was better for single-payer countries than for insurance-fund countries. But the difference was small—small enough that it easily could disappear if more nations from each group were included. It might also be a product of error; while these assessments are careful and thorough, that doesn't mean they are perfectly accurate.

Given what we observe in the data, I see no empirical grounds for expecting that socialist healthcare would be better. The type of healthcare system that is

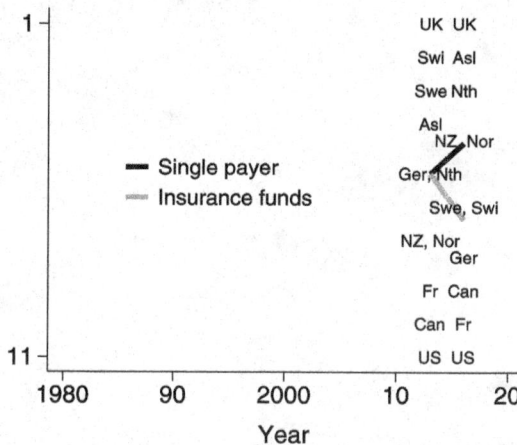

Figure 9.4 Healthcare system performance rank

The rankings are for 2013 and 2016. Data sources: Karen Davis, Kristof Stremikis, David Squires, and Cathy Schoen, "Mirror, Mirror on the Wall: How the Performance of the US Health Care System Compares Internationally," Commonwealth Fund, 2014, exhibit 2; Eric C. Schneider, Dana O. Sarnak, David Squires, Arnav Shah, and Michelle M. Doty, "Mirror, Mirror 2017: International Comparison Reflects Flaws and Opportunities for Better U.S. Health Care," Commonwealth Fund, 2017, exhibit 2.

closer to what we likely would have under socialism—a single-payer system— doesn't seem to do noticeably better when it comes to life expectancy, avoidable deaths, cost, or system quality.

Perhaps more important, the existence of single-payer healthcare in many of the world's rich democratic nations suggests that if we want socialist healthcare, we don't need a socialist economy in order to get it.

10

Helpful Finance

It is now clear that financial crises are not discrete events but are linked phenomena. . . . Capitalism as a system is structurally prone to generate financial crisis.

—Walden Bello[1]

When left-wing regimes have been democratically elected in the past, they have tended to get immediately battered and bruised by the economic fallout from those who control finance and investment. The attack from financiers and investors can be so strong that it forces the government to abandon their plans for reform—thus making a mockery of the people's sovereignty.

—Tom Malleson[2]

The process of financialization over the last four decades has channeled credit creation into several narrow tracks, so that a number of increasingly vital economic activities have been left without sufficient access to credit at reasonable interest rates.

—Fred Block[3]

Finance is vital to a good society. People need to be able to borrow money to fund expensive purchases such as education, homes, and cars. Entrepreneurs and firms need access to external funds in order to start up or expand a business, invest in research, and adjust to changing conditions.

What we want is a financial sector that will provide adequate funding for useful endeavors but won't cause economic crises and won't prevent government from doing good things. Is this impossible in a capitalist economy? Would democratic socialism do better?

Economic Stability

Two of the biggest economic crises of the past century were driven by financial bubbles that popped and spilled over to the broader economy, wreaking

Would Democratic Socialism Be Better?. Lane Kenworthy, Oxford University Press. © Lane Kenworthy 2022.
DOI: 10.1093/oso/9780197636800.003.0010

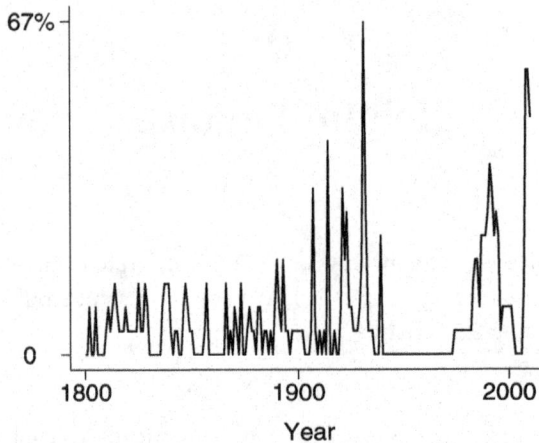

Figure 10.1 Share of rich democratic nations in banking crisis

The countries are Australia, Austria, Belgium, Canada, Denmark, Finland, France, Germany, Ireland, Italy, Japan, Korea (South), Netherlands, New Zealand, Norway, Portugal, Spain, Sweden, Switzerland, United Kingdom, United States. Data source: Carmen M. Reinhart and Kenneth Rogoff, "Dates for Banking Crises, Currency Crashes, Sovereign Domestic or External Default (or Restructuring), Inflation Crises, and Stock Market Crashes (Varieties)," carmenreinhart.com/data.

havoc on the lives of hundreds of millions of people and causing not just temporary agony but also long-term financial and psychological scarring.[4] Financial crises have occurred frequently in capitalist economies, as we see in Figure 10.1.[5]

It's possible that this is endemic to capitalism. It may be inevitable that a largely private financial sector will periodically overreach in search of new financial instruments and new customers, making too many risky investments and loans that eventually go bad, resulting in an economic downturn.

Then again, if we compare across the rich democratic nations, we see that over the past half century those with more of a social democratic capitalist orientation have tended to experience fewer banking crises. Figure 10.2 has a measure of social democratic capitalism on the horizontal axis and the number of years the country spent in a banking crisis since 1973 on the vertical axis.

Key to limiting financial crises is effective government regulation.[6] The aim is to allow flexibility and innovation while discouraging excess. One option is to break up financial firms that become "too big to fail." If a bank or investment firm knows that policy makers will be forced to bail it out in the event it becomes insolvent, it will have little incentive to refrain from overly aggressive lending or investing. Another element is a requirement that financial players maintain fairly large capital cushions—money on hand as a share of total loans—in case a large number of loans go bad in a short period of time, as in the 2008–09 crisis. It may

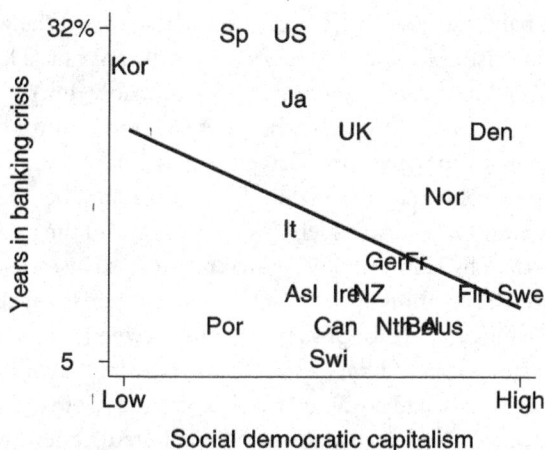

Figure 10.2 Social democratic capitalism and banking crises

Years in banking crisis: share of years, 1973–2010. Data source: Carmen M. Reinhart and Kenneth Rogoff, "Dates for Banking Crises, Currency Crashes, Sovereign Domestic or External Default (or Restructuring), Inflation Crises, and Stock Market Crashes (Varieties)," carmenreinhart.com/data. Social democratic capitalism: average standard deviation score on four indicators: public expenditures on social programs as a share of GDP, replacement rates for major public transfer programs, public expenditures on employment-oriented services, and modest regulation of product and labor markets. The data cover the period 1980–2015. Data source: Lane Kenworthy, *Social Democratic Capitalism*, Oxford University Press, 2020, pp. 39–40. "Asl" is Australia; "Aus" is Austria. The line is a linear regression line.

be helpful to require a sharp separation between commercial banks and investment banks, as America's Glass-Steagall law did from 1933 to 1999, though the jury is still out on this. A financial transactions tax can dampen speculation and volatility in markets for stocks and currencies. As with many areas of government policy, regulation of the financial industry should proceed in a trial-and-error fashion, using incremental learning to try to move steadily toward a "just right"—not too light, not too heavy—regulatory approach.

An increasingly prominent notion is that capitalism causes financial crises because it generates high levels of income inequality.[7] There are several potential pathways. One is that households with stagnant incomes increase borrowing in order to sustain consumption growth, and their debt levels eventually become unsustainable. Another is that as the rich get a larger and larger portion of the income, they end up with excess savings, which fuels speculative investment and financial bubbles. A third is that the rich use their money and consequent political influence to press policy makers to loosen regulations on finance, and this leads to bubbles.

Anthony Atkinson and Salvatore Morelli have done the most comprehensive study of financial crises across countries and over time. They conclude that "The history of systemic banking crises in different countries around the world does not suggest that either rising or high inequality is a significant causal factor."[8]

What about the 2008–09 crisis in particular? We probably don't yet have the final story on the Great Recession's causes, but there are grounds for skepticism about income inequality's contribution.[9] Growing demand for loans by middle- and low-income households may have been driven more by the rising cost of homes and college, along with relaxed lending standards and the availability of home equity loans, than by slow household income growth. Risky lending may have been spurred by the creation of new financial instruments that appeared to spread risk and by rising pressure for profits in publicly owned investment firms. Finally, the Federal Reserve could have quashed the housing bubble, the proximate precipitant of the crisis, had it wanted to. That it chose not to do so arguably owed more to Fed Chair Alan Greenspan's ideological predilections than to the political influence of America's rich.[10]

A Free Hand for Government

An influential Marxian adage holds that the government in a capitalist society is structurally dependent on capital.[11] Policy makers need the economy to perform well, in part because this is good for people and in part because it boosts politicians' likelihood of getting reelected. This dependence enables businesses to exert significant influence on policy choices by withholding investment or threatening to move to another country. Providers of finance are especially powerful, because money is more mobile than factories and offices and because finance feeds every sector of the economy. In modern economies, international finance also can influence policy makers by increasing a government's cost of borrowing in the bond market.[12] James Carville, an advisor to President Bill Clinton, once said "I used to think if there was reincarnation, I wanted to come back as the president or the pope or a .400 baseball hitter. But now I want to come back as the bond market. You can intimidate everybody."[13]

The fact of structural dependence is not in dispute. There are plenty of examples, from France's Mitterrand government feeling compelled to retreat from its nationalization and government spending plans in the early 1980s to pressure on governments in all rich democracies to reduce tax rates to particular policies that have been blocked or abandoned due to worry about capital flight or a negative reaction from the bond market.[14]

If a country's financial sector were mostly public, the threat of capital flight would be reduced. But existing capitalist democracies can decrease this threat by adopting capital controls, and most did so in the 1950s, 1960s, and 1970s.[15] Since then, their governments have tended to judge that the benefits of access to international financial markets outweigh the damage incurred from capital flight.

How big a problem is the threat of capital flight in the typical affluent democratic nation? Some analysts contend that it is much smaller than the conventional image holds. Domestic providers of finance can in principle move their funds wherever they like. But most of the time they don't leave, because they can make money by lending to firms and individuals in these nations, and most of those firms stay put because they, in turn, can make money by utilizing the employee skills, network ties, and high-quality infrastructure in these countries. Torben Iversen and David Soskice put the point as follows:

> Advanced capital is geographically embedded in the advanced nation-state rather than footloose. . . . The value added of advanced companies is geographically embedded in their skilled workforces, via skill clusters, social networks, the need for colocation of workforces, and skills cospecific across workers and the implicit nature of a large proportion of skills. The nature and pattern of industrial organization has changed substantially through the century but the insight of economic geographers that competences are geographically embedded has not. Thus, while advanced companies may be powerful in the marketplace, advanced capitalism has little structural power.[16]

Even if socialization of finance were to significantly reduce the threat of capital flight, it wouldn't remove what may be an equally if not more important obstacle to progressive policy choices—conservative political parties. The Republican Party in the United States, for instance, favors low taxes, limited regulation, and a weak welfare state not just because of pressure from the financial sector or other business interests but also because this has become a core element of its ideology and of its electoral strategy.[17]

Also, a socialized domestic financial sector wouldn't solve the problem of international finance. Indeed, a socialist country probably would face higher borrowing costs in the global bond market.

Effective and Fair Provision of Finance

In principle, an advantage of a private, market-driven financial system is that it will direct funds toward any borrower that has a good shot at succeeding. In practice, biases may cause lenders to underinvest in certain types of businesses, communities, and individuals—companies with little potential for good short-term returns, low-income communities, racial or ethnic minorities, entrepreneurs aiming to challenge large monopolistic firms, and worker cooperatives, among others. In addition, society might want to direct investment toward firms or sectors that are likely to achieve a particular social goal, such as climate stability, but may not yield much in the way of profits.

What is the best way to achieve effective and fair provision of finance? Tom Malleson offers a thoughtful proposal for a socialist financial system.[18] At the national level, "What is required . . . is public investment by a body that operates at a sufficiently large geographical scale, is publicly accountable, and technically expert. The options here range from a ministry of the central government (as is standard today) to a State Bank to a National Investment Fund."[19] At the local level, he proposes a system of "public community banks," under control of both the central government and a democratically elected local advisory board. This would allow them to respond both to overall national funding priorities and to local needs.

These two institutions could help to ensure that funding gets directed toward sectors and firms that will serve socially useful purposes and to ensure that businesses don't get underfunded because of lender biases. Where they may fall short is in providing funds to enterprises that might yield a product or service that improves living standards in a way elected boards or central funding directors can't foresee. Part of the genius of markets is that they facilitate unplanned but beneficial economic behavior. It's very difficult to anticipate where such firms or sectors will come from, so the best bet is to have multiple sources of financing.[20]

An ideal financial system might therefore look much like what exists in most contemporary rich democratic nations, but with a stronger role for a national funding agency and for local public community banks along with, in some, more effective regulation.[21]

Would Democratic Socialism Be More Likely to Produce Helpful Finance?

Capitalist financial systems tend to underfund disadvantaged individuals, businesses, and communities. They can potentially block valuable government policies. And they sometimes cause economic crises. But each of these can be remedied without abandoning capitalism. And while a socialist financial system might do better at avoiding these problems, it is likely to be less effective at funding startups that look unpromising but that end up contributing, in small ways or large, to improved living standards and quality of life.

11

Truly Democratic Politics

We must make our choice. We may have democracy, or we may have
wealth concentrated in the hands of a few, but we can't have both.

—Louis Brandeis[1]

The high concentrations of wealth and economic power generated
by capitalist dynamics subvert principles of democratic political
equality. Political equality means that there are no morally irrelevant attributes—such as race, gender, religious affiliation, wealth,
income, and so on—generating inequalities in the opportunity of
people to participate effectively in democratic politics and influence
political decisions. . . . Capitalism violates this condition. . . . The
wealthy and those who occupy powerful positions in the economy
invariably have a disproportionate influence on political outcomes
in all capitalist societies. There are many mechanisms in play here.
Wealthy people have a much greater ability to contribute to political
campaigns. Powerful people in corporations are embedded in social
networks which give them access to policy makers in government,
and are in a position to fund lobbyists to influence both politicians
and bureaucratic officials.

—Erik Olin Wright[2]

Can democracy survive in a capitalist economy? Eventually, according to skeptics,
capitalists' desire to escape from regulations, taxes, and other hindrances imposed
by a popularly elected government will turn them against democracy, resulting in a
shift to autocracy.

The historical record isn't consistent with this prediction. As capitalism has
emerged and spread, so too has democracy. In Figure 11.1, we see that two centuries ago the average country had a political system that was the near antithesis of
democratic. Since then, democracy has been on the rise, interrupted only briefly
in the 1930s and the 1960s. Moreover, in countries with a GDP per capita above
$10,000, democracy, once established, has hardly ever been overturned.[3]

In recent years pundits and journalists have issued a stream of warnings that
citizens in Europe and the United States are turning away from democracy

Would Democratic Socialism Be Better?. Lane Kenworthy, Oxford University Press. © Lane Kenworthy 2022.
DOI: 10.1093/oso/9780197636800.003.0011

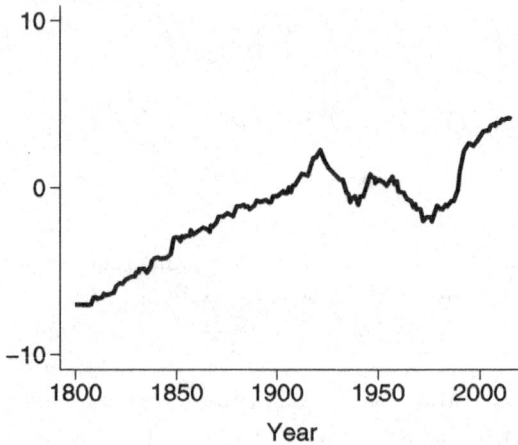

Figure 11.1 Democracy

Average for all nations with population greater than 500,000. -10 is a hereditary monarchy; +10 is a consolidated democracy. Data source: HumanProgress, "Democracy versus Autocracy over Time," using data from Polity IV Annual Time-Series.

and that authoritarian parties and politicians are on the verge of eviscerating democratic institutions. But careful assessment of the evidence suggests there is no crisis of democracy. Public support for democracy and for democratic institutions hasn't declined. And while far-right parties have increased their vote share, they haven't done so by swaying voters to embrace antidemocratic views but rather by tapping into already existing conservative sentiments. And these parties' vote shares remain relatively small.[4]

A different concern is that democracy is warped by the economic inequality capitalism generates. Democracy is a system of decision making in which participants have approximately equal opportunity to influence policy choices.[5] This entails, first, that each person has the same number of votes in electing policy makers (representative democracy) and in direct policy making (direct democracy). Second, each person has roughly the same opportunity to influence policy makers' views and actions via organization, lobbying, monetary donations, protest, and other activities. Third, individuals have access to adequate information in order to develop informed preferences. Fourth, decisions are made according to majority rule (though the majority can't abridge the other conditions).

The political system in a nation with a capitalist economy is unlikely to be perfectly democratic. Under capitalism the distribution of income and wealth will inevitably be unequal, and those with more money will be able to exert disproportionate influence over policy making. The question is: Can the political system be democratic *enough*?[6]

Economic Inequality and Plutocracy: The Hypothesis

Let's consider the United States, which is a good candidate for the worst-case scenario among the rich capitalist nations. Economic inequality between the rich and the nonrich is greater in America than in other countries, and it has increased sharply since the late 1970s.[7] As top-end economic inequality grows, a country like the United States may increasingly get government by the wealthy.

There are five main ways that the rich, along with companies they own or control, can deploy money to increase their influence over policy makers' decisions. First, they can donate to politicians and political parties. Election campaigns are expensive, and private donations account for most of the money that campaigns spend. Expenditures in the 2020 US election totaled nearly $14 billion, up from $5 billion in 2000.[8] The share of campaign contributions that come from the highest-income Americans has been rising steadily in recent decades; according to one estimate, around 40 percent of the total now comes from those in the top 0.01 percent of incomes.[9] It wouldn't be surprising to find that candidates and elected officials listen most attentively to the policy preferences of their most generous donors.

Second, rich Americans can run for office themselves. In 2020, more than half of the 535 members of the Senate and the House of Representatives had a net worth of more than $1 million.[10] A billionaire, Donald Trump, succeeded in getting elected president in 2016, and fellow billionaires Michael Bloomberg and Tom Steyer ran for the Democratic nomination in 2020, albeit unsuccessfully.

Third, the rich and their companies can spend money to lobby elected policy makers. Lobbying expenditures in the United States total about $3.5 billion each year, and they increased sharply in the 2000s before leveling off in the 2010s.[11]

Fourth, those with money can fund organizations and movements that pressure policy makers in other ways—calling their office, showing up at town hall meetings, generating online petitions, canvassing voters, marching in the streets.

Fifth, affluent Americans can use their money to influence ideas. They can finance research. They can establish and fund think tanks. They can create or buy media outlets. They can sponsor and promote like-minded opinion leaders.

The result of these efforts, according to a growing chorus of voices, has been an erosion of democracy in America due to rising inequality of income and wealth. According to Paul Krugman, "Extreme concentration of income is incompatible with real democracy. Can anyone seriously deny that our political system is being warped by the influence of big money, and that the warping is getting worse as the wealth of a few grows ever larger?" Jacob Hacker and Paul Pierson put it as follows: "Runaway inequality has remade American politics, reorienting power and policy toward corporations and the superrich. . . . The rise of plutocracy is the story of post-1980 American politics."[12]

Yet money in politics likely is subject to diminishing returns. There was considerable economic inequality in the United States in the late 1970s. In all likelihood, America's affluent had a good bit more political influence than the rest of the citizenry at that point in time, and it's conceivable that their advantage had already reached its maximum. If so, then even though the rich have gotten a rising share of the country's income and wealth during the ensuing four decades, this might not have widened their advantage in influencing policy outcomes.

Economic Inequality and Plutocracy: The Evidence

What kinds of things would we expect to observe if the inequality-plutocracy hypothesis is correct? Do we observe them?

Do the Rich Have Disproportionate Political Influence?

Scholars have been actively researching the political influence of economic elites since the middle of the twentieth century. Studies have tended to focus on individual policies, or sometimes a handful of related policies. This is helpful, but to really answer the question we need a more comprehensive analysis. Surprisingly, we have very little. There are a number of quantitative analyses of the determinants of social policy and some other types of programs, but these too give us an incomplete picture, and most of them don't consider the impact of America's rich.

In one of the few attempts at a comprehensive study, Larry Bartels uses public opinion survey data to identify the policy preferences of Americans in three income groups: low, middle, and high.[13] He then examines the degree to which these opinions correlate with votes by people's elected representatives in the House and the Senate in the early 1990s and early 2010s. Bartels concludes that policy makers' voting tends to correspond much more closely to the desires of people with high incomes. This kind of study is a big advance, in that it gives us evidence on the influence of different income groups across an array of policies and issues. But legislators' voting may or may not translate into actual policy outcomes.

In his book *Affluence and Influence*, Martin Gilens takes this next step.[14] He begins by measuring the policy preferences of high-income, middle-income, and low-income Americans in public opinion surveys from 1981 through 2002. Where the preferences of people at these various income levels differed, Gilens looks to see whether policy changed over the ensuing four years, and if so in what direction. The data include a total of 1,779 policy outcomes. Gilens finds that when policy did change, the change was more likely to conform to the expressed preferences of high-income Americans than of middle-income or low-income Americans.

So yes, Americans with more income do seem to have more political influence than those with less income, as the inequality-plutocracy hypothesis predicts.

However, there are limits to how confident we should be about this conclusion. For one thing, research has uncovered very little evidence that campaign contributions and lobbying influence policy outcomes.[15] There are, as I noted earlier, other pathways through which money can affect policy decisions, but it's surprising that researchers haven't identified a connection via the campaign donation and lobbying routes.

Perhaps more important, despite the heroic efforts of Gilens and some others, social scientists don't yet have the evidence we really would want for testing the inequality-plutocracy hypothesis. Most of the attention in discussions of plutocracy focuses on the top 1 percent of incomes, but the sample sizes in public opinion surveys are too small to get an accurate reading of the views of this group. Thus, "high income" in Gilens's analysis refers to roughly the 90th percentile of the income distribution rather than the top.

Also, the policy outcomes in Gilens's data are limited to those that public opinion surveys have asked about. This leaves out a lot of policy. An alternative strategy is to begin with the full array of potential policy changes and study a random sample of them. Paul Burstein uses this approach in a recent study.[16] He begins with all of the policy proposals considered by Congress during the 1989–90 legislative session, draws a sample of 60 (manifested in a total of 417 bills), and then tracks their fate. Unfortunately, he, like Gilens, is unable to identify the views of rich Americans, so his analysis doesn't speak to the inequality-plutocracy hypothesis. And his data cover only two years.

It probably doesn't make sense to weight all potential policy changes equally, since both affluent and ordinary Americans likely care much more about some than others. In a statistical analysis this can be handled by differentially weighting the cases.

An ideal database probably would be something like Burstein's. However, it would cover not just legislation but also executive branch actions such as implementation of laws and regulations and issuance of executive orders. And it would cover many more years. How to address the lack of hard data on the policy preferences of the rich? Here we would need researchers to make educated guesses, based the type of information that scholars studying individual policy changes typically have drawn upon, about when and to what degree the policy desires of the wealthy differed from those of ordinary citizens.

In the absence of this ideal database, I agree with Larry Bartels that "Gilens's work provides the best evidence we have regarding the responsiveness of the

American political system to the preferences of its citizens."[17] Gilens's findings suggest, consistent with the inequality-plutocracy hypothesis, that higher-income Americans very likely do have disproportionate influence on policy decisions.

Has the Gap in Political Influence between the Rich and the Rest Increased Over Time?

Income and wealth inequality in the United States have increased sharply since the late 1970s.[18] If the inequality-plutocracy hypothesis is correct, this rise in economic inequality should have led to a rise in inequality of political influence during these past four decades.

But in a study tracing policy wins by rich Americans and by business in recent decades, Jacob Hacker and Paul Pierson don't find a rise in the frequency of such wins.[19] Nor do Gilens's *Affluence and Influence* data suggest an increase in inequality of political influence. In addition to his core period of 1981 to 2002, Gilens examines the correlation between income and influence on policy for a selection of earlier and later years. He finds that the gap in influence between high-income Americans and those with middle or low incomes was small during the Johnson presidency in the 1960s, larger during the presidencies of Reagan and Clinton in the 1980s and 1990s, but then smaller during George W. Bush's presidency in the 2000s.[20] Christopher Wlezien and Stuart Soroka conduct an analysis similar to Gilens's and covering the years 1972 to 2008, though for a relatively small set of policies. They find no indication of a rise in policy makers' responsiveness to Americans with higher incomes.[21]

This isn't the final word. It's quite possible that when someone updates Gilens's analyses through the 2010s, or when researchers compile something like the ideal database I outlined in the previous section, the data will reveal that the rich-versus-the-rest gap in political influence has indeed increased in concert with economic inequality. But that isn't what's suggested by the best research we have at the moment.

Is the Gap in Political Influence between the Rich and the Rest Larger in the United States Than in Other Affluent Democratic Nations?

The income and wealth gaps between the rich and the nonrich are larger in the United States than in any other affluent democratic country.[22] If the inequality-plutocracy hypothesis is correct, we would therefore expect more inequality of political influence in America than abroad.

There are single-country studies of the link between preferences of people at different income levels and policy outcomes in Germany, the Netherlands, Sweden, and Switzerland.[23] These analyses conclude that, as in the United States, when the views of higher-income persons differ from the views of those with lower incomes, policy changes are more likely to reflect the desires of people with more income.

The best comparative analysis I'm aware of is a recent paper by Larry Bartels, which looks at the degree to which policy changes tend to correspond to the expressed preferences of people at different income levels in an array of affluent democratic nations.[24] Bartels focuses on just one type of government policy: social programs. Contrary to what the inequality-plutocracy hypothesis predicts, he finds no difference in the magnitude of the rich–poor disparity in policy responsiveness across countries that have very different levels of income inequality. Instead, it turns out that inequality in policy responsiveness is "rampant in contemporary affluent democracies, not limited to the United States."

Bartels's finding is consistent with the large research literature attempting to explain why the United States has one of the least expansive and generous welfare states among the rich democratic nations. That literature emphasizes culprits other than America's high level of economic inequality, such as our winner-take-all elections and consequent two-party political system, our large number of government veto points, our weak labor unions, our lack of corporatist concertation, our racial and ethnic diversity, and our absence of a feudal history.[25]

Have Top-End Tax Rates, Financial Regulation, and Unionization Decreased More in the United States Than in Other Rich Democratic Countries?

Top-end income and wealth inequality have increased more in the United States than elsewhere. So according to the inequality-plutocracy hypothesis, we should expect greater movement toward policy outcomes desired by the well-to-do in America than in other rich democratic nations.

Begin with taxes. The top statutory federal income tax rate was indeed reduced more sharply in the United States than in most other affluent democracies. Yet some other countries where income inequality barely increased at all, such as Japan and Norway, made similar changes to their top statutory tax rates.[26] Just as puzzling, nearly all of the change in the United States occurred at the beginning of the rise in income inequality, in the 1980s, rather than toward the end. Moreover, the top statutory rate is of limited relevance if there are numerous loopholes and deductions that allow the rich to shield a sizable portion of their income from taxation. What really matters to taxpayers is the "effective" tax rate—taxes paid divided by pretax income. Estimates of the top effective tax rate in the United States suggest that while it has fluctuated—decreasing under Reagan, increasing under the first Bush and Clinton, decreasing again under the second Bush, and increasing again under Obama—it was about the same in 2017 as when Reagan entered office.[27] The 2018 Trump tax cut will reduce it (we don't have the data yet), but the Biden administration and Democrats in the House and Senate have said they intend to raise it again.

What about financial regulation? The United States did reduce regulations on the financial sector, but here too the most significant change occurred at the beginning of the era of rising economic inequality, around 1980. And most of the other rich democratic countries for which data are available have made bigger deregulatory reforms in finance than America did.[28]

Unionization has dropped sharply in the United States. But that decline began in the 1950s, long before income and wealth inequality started to rise. And since the late 1970s, unionization rates have been falling in most affluent nations, at about the same pace as in America.[29]

None of these patterns is consistent with what the inequality-plutocracy hypothesis predicts.

Do Republicans Receive More Campaign Money Than Democrats and Consequently Win More Elections?

Let's return to the US story. Most of the money spent in political campaigns comes from private donations. Although we have limited direct information about the policy preferences of America's rich, a 2011 survey suggests that they have views on core economic policy issues, such as taxes and government spending, that are much closer to those favored by Republicans than to those of Democrats.[30] It's no surprise, therefore, that the affluent tend to give more money to Republicans and conservative groups than to Democrats and progressive groups.[31]

If the well-to-do favor Republicans, the inequality-plutocracy hypothesis would expect Republican candidates to have enjoyed a steadily rising advantage in campaign spending in recent decades. But they haven't. Since the late 1990s, when comprehensive and reliable data on campaign expenditures begin, Democrats and their supporters have kept pace with Republicans.[32] That's continued even after the Supreme Court's 2010 *Citizens United* ruling, which made it easier for donors to hide their contributions. And in the most recent election, in 2020, Democrats enjoyed a huge spending advantage.

Nor has money led to Republican electoral dominance. Democratic candidates have won the popular vote in seven of the last eight presidential elections. It's true that Republicans have fared better in House and Senate elections than they did in the middle of the twentieth century. But in that earlier era Democrats had a big advantage because of their perceived success in dealing with the Great Depression and World War II and because the legacy of the Civil War and Reconstruction gave them a virtual monopoly in the South. By the 1990s, both of those advantages had evaporated. And in recent decades Democrats have been hurt in House elections by the fact that their voters are highly concentrated in urban areas, in Senate elections by the fact that low-population conservative states such as Wyoming get the same number of seats as high-population liberal states such as California, and in presidential elections by the Electoral College.[33]

Maybe America's plutocrats haven't needed Republicans in order to get their desired policies enacted. If the rich have become much more politically powerful, presumably they're able to sway Democrats as well. The Clinton administration's embrace of financial deregulation seems to fit with this view. But the fact that center-left parties in other far-less-economically-unequal countries did the same thing suggests reason for skepticism. And trends in top income tax rates aren't consistent with the notion that America's rich have been effective at getting Democrats to do their bidding. As I noted earlier, the Clinton and Obama administrations increased top tax rates, offsetting the reductions under Reagan and George W. Bush.

Have Policy Trends over the Long Run of American History Corresponded to Trends in Economic Inequality?

In a recent book, *Democracy in America?*, Benjamin Page and Martin Gilens attempt a rough tracing of trends in economic inequality and inequality of political influence over the long arc of American history. They conclude that there is substantial correspondence: "Economic inequality—the concentration of wealth and income in a few hands, with a big gap between rich and poor—has risen and fallen at various times. And democracy—popular control of government—has tended to move in the opposite direction. When citizens are relatively equal, politics has tended to be fairly democratic. When a few individuals hold enormous amounts of wealth, democracy suffers."[34] Specifically, Page and Gilens say the federal government's responsiveness to the policy wishes of ordinary Americans was low in the 1790s, higher in the Jacksonian era, lower in the second half of the 1800s, and higher in the 1950s.

I think it's worth treating this conclusion with skepticism. Consider the period for which the story seems, on the surface, most clear-cut: the second half of the 1800s. This was the era of industrialization and the Gilded Age. Inequality of income and wealth increased significantly.[35] According to Page and Gilens, this led to a shift in government attentiveness away from commoners and in favor of the affluent. But did key policy choices during the second half of the 1800s really go against what ordinary Americans wanted, or at least what was good for most? Slavery was outlawed. Real living standards doubled each generation.[36] As government created and expanded a nationwide public education system, average years of schooling rose steadily from four in 1870 to six in 1900 to eight in 1930. With advances in medical knowledge and public health systems, life expectancy jumped from 39 in 1880 to 50 in 1900 to 60 in 1930.

Does Policy in States with Greater Economic Inequality Conform More to the Preferences of the Rich?

Social scientists have compiled data on top-end income inequality not only for countries but also for the US states.[37] As of the most recent year for which these data are available, 2015, the 12 states in which the top 1 percent's income share is largest include eight—New York, Connecticut, Massachusetts, California, Washington DC, Illinois, New Jersey, and Washington state—where Republican vote shares tend to be lowest, state tax systems are least regressive, and state public social programs are most expansive and generous.[38] That isn't what the inequality-plutocracy hypothesis would predict.

California is a particularly striking case. Between 1979 and 2015, the share of income going to the top 1 percent of households in California soared from 10 percent to 24 percent. If the United States is on the road to plutocracy, California ought to be leading the charge. Yet California currently has the least regressive tax system of any state in the country, in part due to new taxes on high incomes added in recent years. Since 1999 California has enacted paid sick leave, paid parental leave, an automatic-enrollment pension system for people whose employer doesn't offer a plan, a large Medicaid expansion (it now covers one in three Californians), an expansion of Temporary Assistance for Needy Families (TANF) eligibility, a phased-in $15 per hour minimum wage indexed to inflation, a state Earned Income Tax Credit, increased money for K-12 schooling funded by two tax increases on high-income households, an array of services for residents with severe mental illnesses, low-cost public auto insurance for persons with low income, new funds for roads and high-speed rail, a significant reduction in incarceration, and more. In 2018 California passed a law requiring an end to the use of fossil-fuel-based electricity by 2045, and

the governor issued an executive order committing the state to full carbon neutrality by that same year.

What Should We Conclude?

The available evidence suggests two conclusions. First, economic inequality has
an impact on inequality of political influence. America's rich very likely have
more influence on policy decisions than the nonrich do. Second, because there
is a tipping point beyond which this effect diminishes, wealthy Americans may
have roughly the same degree of political advantage nowadays that they did in
the late 1970s or early 1980s.

Would Democratic Socialism Be Better at Achieving Truly Democratic Politics?

The case for socialism as better for democracy in the political realm rests mainly
on its promise to reduce inequality of income and wealth and thereby equalize
opportunity for political influence. But when we compare across countries, or
when we compare over time within the United States, the level of economic inequality doesn't seem to correlate very strongly with the degree of inequality of
political influence.

It's possible, then, that the real gains in enhancing democracy will come from
improving education, expanding economic opportunity, revitalizing civic organizations, increasing access to voting, expanding public campaign financing,
making use of deliberative citizen assemblies, and other reforms that don't necessarily require a reduction in income or wealth inequality.[39] All of these are
achievable within capitalism.

12

Economic Democracy

People have every right to democratize any institution that they're part of.

—Noam Chomsky[1]

If democracy is justified in governing the state, then it must *also* be justified in governing economic enterprises.

—Robert Dahl[2]

Ownership is not an acceptable source of governmental authority in cities and towns. If we consider deeply why this is so, we will have to conclude, I think, that it should not be acceptable in companies or factories either.

—Michael Walzer[3]

The social democratic model . . . does not empower workers and citizens as much as one could hope for this century. . . . Most of the key decisions are made over their heads.

—Marc Fleurbaey[4]

The idea that "what touches all should be decided by all" underpins the widely shared view that, in politics, democracy is the fairest system. This encourages us to ask: Why shouldn't democracy also apply in the economic sphere?[5] Economic democracy, in the firm and/or in the broader economy, is at the heart of many contemporary visions of democratic socialism.

Economic Democracy in the Firm

In existing capitalist economies, there are five main ways through which employees can exercise voice within their company: worker participation, labor unions, works councils, board-level employee representation, and worker control.

Would Democratic Socialism Be Better?. Lane Kenworthy, Oxford University Press. © Lane Kenworthy 2022.
DOI: 10.1093/oso/9780197636800.003.0012

Worker Participation

Employees, either individually or in groups, may have partial or full decision-making authority over aspects of the work process—what the goal should be, how to pursue it, how to allocate time, and more. This can take a variety of forms, from individual jobs with extensive autonomy to suggestion boxes to quality circles to joint safety committees to self-managed work teams. In the United States, a little more than half of employed persons report having "a lot of freedom to decide how to do my own work." One-third say they often "take part with others in making decisions that affect" them. And one-quarter say they're involved in a "group, team, committee, or task force that addresses issues such as product quality, cost cutting, productivity, health and safety, or other workplace issues."[6] Studies find that such participation tends to boost worker productivity, commitment, and satisfaction.[7]

This kind of participation is, however, a long way from economic democracy. It's akin to having a benevolent dictator who allows his subjects some control over their affairs.

Labor Unions

Historically, the chief way in which employees have had a voice in their company is via labor unions. In the rich democratic nations, unions arose with the industrial revolution beginning in the mid-to-late 1800s. Their principal aim usually is to increase wages, and they frequently achieve this goal. Unionized workers tend to have higher wages, and faster rising wages, than similarly skilled nonunionized workers. If we compare across states or countries, wages tend to be higher in those with greater unionization.[8]

Unions tend to want not only higher pay but also less inequality of pay.[9] Among the rich capitalist democracies, a sizable portion of the cross-country variation in earnings inequality can be explained by the degree of wage bargaining coverage and the degree of wage bargaining centralization.[10]

Much of the rise in income inequality in recent decades consists of separation between the top 1 percent and everyone else.[11] Where unions are sufficiently strong, they can pressure firms to distribute more of the profits to ordinary workers and less to top executives. Unions also can affect top-end income inequality via a political channel, by lobbying policy makers and influencing election outcomes. Several recent quantitative studies that examine developments over the past generation, in the United States alone or in the United States along with other affluent democracies, have found unionization to be one of the better predictors of variation in top-end income inequality.[12]

Since the inception of labor unions, a host of analysts have worried that they will harm the economy.[13] But if we compare across the affluent democratic countries over the past generation, there is no association between unionization levels and economic growth. The same is true for over-time patterns in the United States.[14]

What are the prospects for a revitalization of labor unions? In the United States, where the decline began earliest, hope springs eternal. There are various reasons for this: When asked, many workers say they would like to have a union or union-like organization represent them.[15] Changes to several aspects of US labor policy—the 1949 Taft-Hartley Act's permission for states to implement anti-union "right to work" laws, the lack of a Canadian-style card check procedure for forming a union, weak enforcement of labor laws under Republican administrations, and more—might potentially facilitate an increase in union membership. And we have myriad proposals for how the American labor movement could organize more effectively.[16]

Yet optimism about unions' future must come to terms with the comparative experience in recent decades. In a handful of the rich longstanding-democratic countries, procedures established nearly a century ago require that workers be a member of a labor union in order to have access to unemployment insurance, and unionization rates there have remained fairly high. But as we saw in chapter 7, in virtually every other affluent democratic nation, despite policies and governments far less hostile to unions than in the United States, union membership has fallen just as sharply as it has in America.[17]

Works Councils

Works councils are employee-elected bodies that negotiate with management over work conditions such as tasks, safety, scheduling, and hiring and firing procedures. They are similar to unions except that they seldom negotiate pay and are confined to individual firms. In many western European nations, works councils were set up after World War II to promote cooperation between labor and management and forestall communist sympathy among workers. By the 1960s, many had disappeared or fallen into disuse because of opposition by employers or unions. In the 1970s and 1980s, however, works councils revived, sometimes due to legal mandate and in some instances voluntarily.[18]

Works councils' prominence and rights vary a good bit across the rich democratic countries, as Figure 12.1 suggests.[19] A score of 3 on this measure indicates that works councils have economic and social rights, including joint decision-making authority on some issues (such as mergers and restructuring). A score of 2 means works councils have economic and social rights via consultation; they

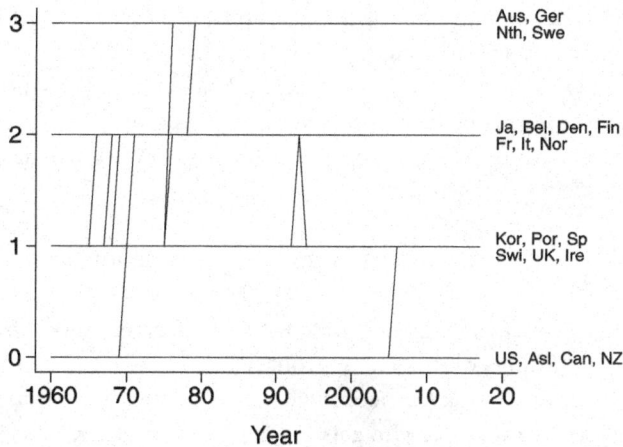

Figure 12.1 Works councils

Rights of works councils. 3 = economic and social rights, including codetermination on some issues (e.g., mergers, takeovers, restructuring); 2 = economic and social rights, consultation (advice, with possibility of judicial redress); 1 = information and consultation rights (without judicial redress); 0 = works council or similar (union or nonunion) institutions of employee representation confronting management do not exist or are exceptional. Data source: Jelle Visser, "ICTWSS: Database on Institutional Characteristics of Trade Unions, Wage Setting, State Intervention, and Social Pacts," version 6.0, 2019, Amsterdam Institute for Advanced Labour Studies, series wc_rights. "Asl" is Australia; "Aus" is Austria.

are able to give advice to management and can, if needed, request enforcement of rights through the legal system. A score of 1 indicates that works councils have information and consultation rights but little or no ability to use the legal system to ensure enforcement. Countries with a score of zero, such as the United States, have few or no works councils.[20]

Here's an example of what this means in practice: In the Netherlands, a works council is mandatory in any establishment with 50 or more employees, though in practice they exist in only three-quarters of such establishments. Works councils have extensive information and consultation rights: "They monitor the firm's implementation of legislation on equal opportunities, health and safety, and other work-related areas. They enjoy consultation rights on economic and financial matters, and must be informed and consulted in a timely manner. Further, they have codetermination rights over pension insurance, the arrangement of working hours and holidays, health and safety, and rules concerning hiring, firing, promotion, training, and grievance handling. In disagreements over plans for restructuring or redundancies, the employer must postpone their implementation while an amicable solution is sought."[21]

Because works councils give employees greater ability to block automation, new forms of work organization, and large-scale layoffs, some fear they will reduce productivity. On the other hand, by providing an ongoing forum in which management and workers must consult and negotiate with one another, works councils may boost information sharing and yield more frequent agreement on strategies for improving firm performance.[22] Studies have found little or no systematic tendency for works councils to either help or hurt firm productivity.[23]

Board-Level Employee Representation

Unions and works councils negotiate with management about matters such as wages and working conditions. A stronger form of employee voice would give workers a say in electing the people who make far-reaching decisions about the firm's direction and about who gets to be the management. The most common way this is done is via board-level employee representation (sometimes called codetermination), whereby employees elect a portion of their company's board of directors.

In Germany, workers have been able to elect 50 percent of the directors in firms with 2,000 or more employees since the early 1950s and 33 percent of the directors in firms with 500 to 2,000 employees since the mid-1970s. As of the mid-2010s, similar rules existed in Austria, Denmark, Finland, France, Ireland, the Netherlands, Norway, and Sweden. Board-level employee representation is rare or nonexistent in Australia, Belgium, Canada, Italy, Japan, Korea, New Zealand, Portugal, Spain, Switzerland, the United Kingdom, and the United States.[24]

Board-level representation tends to have limited reach. About one-quarter of German workers are employed in firms that have it.[25] In 2018, Democratic lawmakers in the United States proposed the Accountable Capitalism Act, which would require employee election of 40 percent of the board of directors in large US corporations—those with annual revenues of $1 billion or more. The roughly 1,300 firms that meet this criterion employ approximately 45 million Americans, or about one-third of all workers.[26]

Are there benefits of board-level employee representation apart from its greater fairness for workers? Where employees elect some of the directors, companies might be able to pursue more of a long-term orientation. But there is little research on this question.[27] Some advocates believe board-level employee representation will boost wages.[28] But the available evidence doesn't support this hope.[29]

Critics of board-level employee representation often suggest that it will weaken firms' performance. However, it appears to have had no such adverse effect in the European countries where large firms operate under codetermination requirements.[30]

Worker Control

In some companies, employees have full control over decision making, or at least in deciding who gets to be the decision makers. In a capitalist economy, this happens when employees are the owners.

A common form of employee ownership is an "employee share ownership plan" (ESOP). In the United States, as of the mid-2010s about 6,500 companies had such a plan. Approximately 10 million people work in these firms, or about 8 percent of the American work force.[31] However, in most of these companies the ESOP owns less than half of the stock shares, so the workers have far less than full control. According to one estimate, the number of American workers in a firm where the ESOP has 50 percent or more ownership is approximately 1 million, and the number in a company with 100 percent ESOP ownership is about 500,000.[32] This is fewer than 1 percent of employees.

Firms in which workers have full decision-making authority because they are majority or sole owners, and which operate on a one-person-one-vote (rather than one-stock-share-one-vote) basis, are typically called "worker cooperatives." There are about 400 such firms in the United States, with roughly 7,000 workers. That's 0.005 percent of the US labor force.[33] In the United Kingdom the share is 0.3 percent.[34]

Although hard data are scarce, it appears that employee share ownership is more prominent in the United States and the United Kingdom than in other rich democratic nations.[35] Cooperatives are uncommon in all of these countries.[36]

In principle, employees could own a large number of firms collectively. One version of this would gradually transfer stock shares in large companies to a fund controlled by unions or some other worker-elected representative body. Sweden's government adopted such a scheme—called "wage-earner funds," or the "Meidner Plan"—in the early 1980s but then abandoned it within a decade, and it hasn't been tried anywhere else.[37]

People seem to like the idea of employee ownership and control. As we see in Figure 12.2, a survey question asked in 1975 and again in 2018 found that a healthy majority of Americans would prefer to work for a firm "owned by the employees who appoint the management to run the company's operations" rather than one in which outside investors or the government owns the firm and appoints the management.

These companies also tend to perform well economically. Research on employee share ownership and worker cooperatives tends to find that, on average, they match other firms on productivity, profitability, and other performance indicators.[38]

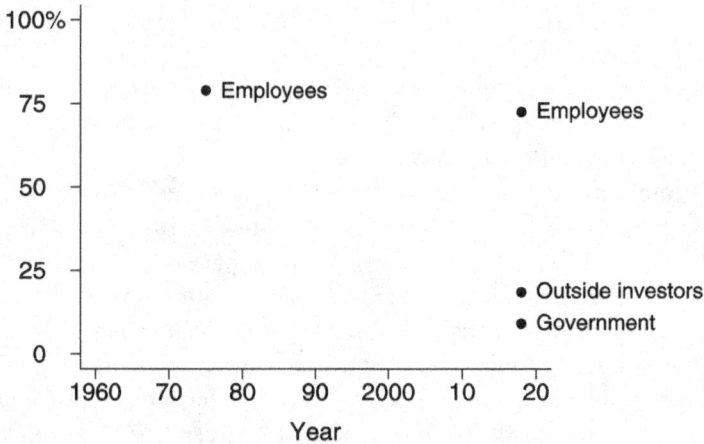

Figure 12.2 Who should control the company you work for?

Share of US adults. 1975 question: "I'm going to describe three different kinds of companies to you, and, regardless of the job you now have, I'd like you to tell me which one of these three kinds of companies you think you would like to work for if you had the choice. 1: A company in which the stock is owned by outside investors who appoint their own management to run the company's operations. 2: A company in which the stock is owned by the employees who appoint their own management to run the company's operations. 3: A company in which the government owns the stock and appoints the management to run the company's operations." Data source: John F. Zipp, Paul Luebke, and Richard Landerman, "The Social Bases of Support for Workplace Democracy," *Sociological Perspectives*, 1984, table 3, using data from a poll by Peter Hart Inc. 2018 question: "Which company would you prefer to work for? 1: A company in which the government owns the stock and appoints the management to run the company's operations. 2: A company whose stock is owned by the employees who appoint the management to run the company's operations. 3: A company whose stock is owned by outside investors who appoint the management to run the company's operations." Data source: General Social Survey (GSS), sda. berkeley.edu, series company.

If people like employee-owned firms and cooperatives and they perform relatively well, why are there so few of them? Part of the problem may be limited access to financing.[39] If so, it shouldn't be too difficult for government to improve matters by creating a fund dedicated to providing affordable financing for employee-owned and worker-controlled companies.[40]

Yet the idea and the practice of worker ownership and control have existed since the late 1800s, and in the United States ESOPs have had tax-advantaged status since 1974.[41] Given this, the fact that majority ESOPs and worker cooperatives are so rare suggests that democracy in the workplace may not be a key concern for many people. While a large share of people apparently think it's better if companies are controlled by employees than by outside investors or by government, workplace democracy perhaps isn't something they care about very strongly.[42]

Would Democratic Socialism Be Better at Achieving Democracy in the Firm?

Under socialism, the people might vote to require democracy in the workplace—one-person-one-vote within each firm. However, voters already have the ability to do that under capitalism, so we should ask why they don't.

It could be that people would prefer democracy in the workplace if it were mandated, but they don't currently have this preference because they have no experience with workplace democracy. This is plausible. It very likely was true of democracy in the political realm in predemocratic times. Once people experience economic democracy, according to this view, they will like it and see no reason to go back to control by outside owners.

Here, though, it's worth returning to the normative case for democracy in the workplace. The principle is that "what touches all should be decided by all." Proponents of workplace democracy acknowledge that this need not apply to every aspect of our lives, but they say it should apply to ones that we find it necessary to be part of or where we spend a good bit of our time, which certainly includes the workplace.

But what about others? Suppose a couple owns their house, and their three children, aged 25, 23, and 21, still live with them. Should we require that all decisions in such a household be made on a one-person-one-vote basis? What about rental housing? Should tenants each get a vote on all decisions regarding the building, maintenance, rent, and other matters? Should congregants each get a vote on decisions made by their church or religious organization? I suspect many would say no.[43]

It's conceivable that when, at some point in the future, a polity takes seriously the question of whether to require democracy within companies, they will decide that democracy should be actively promoted but not mandated. Tom Malleson offers a sensible approach:

> Just as justice requires that women should not be compelled to be subservient in their marriages, justice requires that workers should not be compelled to be subservient at work. This does not mean that people should be forced to adopt workplace democracy; people should be allowed to sign up for subservience at work if they so choose (. . .). The point is only that the choice needs to be genuine; people must have a real choice about whether to work in a hierarchy or a democracy. And for that to happen there need to be real alternatives. The bottom line is that justice requires the state to foster the background conditions so that just as women are free (but not forced) to choose egalitarian relationships, workers become likewise free (but not

forced) to choose democratic workplaces. Concretely this requires that the state foster the expansion of workplace democracy so that this choice becomes readily accessible.[44]

Right now, voters in democratic capitalist nations could choose to promote workplace democracy—for example, by passing a law that allows any firm's workers, if a majority of them vote in favor, to buy out the owner(s) and turn the company into a cooperative.[45] Why don't voters do this? One possibility is that they believe any such attempt would be blocked by corporations and rich individuals who oppose firm-level democracy. If so, socialism would, arguably, provide a more favorable context.

Another possibility is that, as I just suggested, democracy at work isn't very important to people. A healthy majority of Americans say they would prefer to work in a company where employees appoint the management, as we saw in Figure 12.2. But even if they prefer democracy in their firm, they may not care strongly about it. In the 1970s there was nontrivial interest among labor unions in democratizing the firm, but since then there have been no noteworthy efforts or movements in that direction.[46] When people are asked what issues matter most to them or to their country, workplace democracy is seldom mentioned.[47] This too could be a product of capitalism. Under socialism more people would see workplace democracy as a realistic possibility, and maybe that would cause them to desire it deeply rather than superficially. But this is merely a hypothesis. We don't, to my knowledge, have any evidence to support it.

Democracy in the Broader Economy

To achieve economic democracy, is it enough for people to have equal voice within the firm for which they work? Shouldn't the overall economy be subject to democratic decision making? There are two main ways to do this.

A Democratic Polity

In principle, the government in a democratic nation can do most anything it wants by way of guiding the economy. It can steer investment toward selected industries or firms. It can limit or discourage imports. It can regulate much of what businesses do—who they sell to, what price they charge, safety requirements they must meet, and much more. It can subsidize or in other ways assist particular types of firms, such as worker cooperatives. It can create government-run providers of goods and services. All governments in existing capitalist democracies have done these sorts of things to one degree or another, and they could do more if policy makers were in favor.

Don't affluent individuals and corporations block more active government intervention? Yes, to some extent. But they aren't all-powerful. Over the past 150 years governments in the rich capitalist democracies have massively expanded their role in economic affairs, from welfare states to regulation to heavy taxation to provision of schooling and medical care and more, and they've frequently done so despite opposition from moneyed interests. So there is reason to expect they could and perhaps would do more, if they were pressured by citizens to do so.

Concertation

In a democratic polity, workers have the same input as any other individuals. It may make sense to give workers a direct, regularized voice in decision making, and a number of rich democratic nations have done this. Typically this involves labor union representatives sitting together with employer representatives and government officials to discuss or negotiate over issues of economic and social policy—sometimes a single issue, sometimes the full range of government economic interventions. This institution is called concertation (or corporatist concertation).[48]

Figure 12.3 shows one measure of the prominence of concertation in these countries. A score of 2 on this measure indicates regular and frequent involvement by unions and employers in government decisions on social and economic policy. A score of 1 indicates irregular and infrequent involvement. A score of zero means involvement is rare or nonexistent. Austria, Belgium, Denmark, the Netherlands, Norway, Sweden, and Switzerland have had extensive and regularized concertation throughout the past half century, while Canada, France, Japan, the United Kingdom, and United States have made little or no use of it. Other countries have been in between. Some have increased or decreased over time.

Concertation improves policy makers' access to information. It may encourage workers and employers to act in the collective interest rather than selfishly. And it might enable quicker and more adaptive responses to economic changes than would come from parliaments. For these reasons, many researchers have hypothesized that concertation will improve national economic performance.[49] A generation ago there was some support in the data for this hypothesis, but that no longer seems to be true.[50]

Even so, concertation offers a supplementary mechanism, beyond ordinary democratic channels, for workers to ensure their voice is heard in the making of key economic policy decisions.

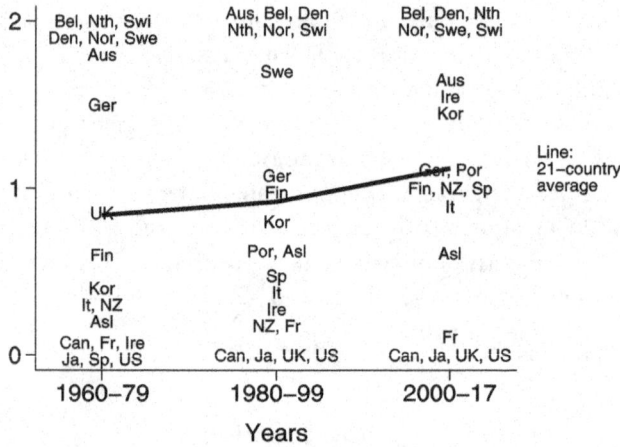

Figure 12.3 Concertation
Routine involvement of unions and employers in government decisions on social and economic policy. 2 = full concertation, regular and frequent involvement; 1 = partial concertation, irregular and infrequent involvement; 0 = no concertation, involvement is rare or absent. Countries' position indicates their average score during the time period. Data source: Jelle Visser, "ICTWSS: Database on Institutional Characteristics of Trade Unions, Wage Setting, State Intervention, and Social Pacts," version 6.0, 2019, Amsterdam Institute for Advanced Labour Studies, series ri.

Would Democratic Socialism Be Better at Achieving Democracy in the Broader Economy?

Modern capitalist democracies already have economic democracy in the form of democratic oversight of the overall economy. In most such countries the government chooses to intervene heavily in some respects and to use a light touch in others.

One of the areas in which a light touch has come to dominate is steering of investment toward particular sectors, projects, or firms. All such nations have done this at times, and some—particularly Japan, South Korea, and France—have done so extensively. Some observers believe the reason governments have reduced such steering is pressure from businesses or the influence of neoliberal ideology. But apart from directing investment away from fossil fuels and toward clean energy sources, which all governments should now be doing, it isn't clear that there are significant benefits from this type of picking and choosing, though debate on this question continues.[51] Some socialist proposals feature such steering as integral.[52] Yet if the goal is economic democracy, and a democratically elected government decides to give markets a large say in how investment is allocated, heavy government steering may be inconsistent with the goal.

Would Socialism Be Better at Advancing Economic Democracy?

There likely would be less resistance under democratic socialism to a requirement of democracy within firms. But while a large share of people say they would rather their firm be controlled by employees than by outside investors or by the government, we have no evidence on whether people want to mandate workplace democracy for all or most companies. It seems more likely that people would prefer a policy that facilitates but doesn't require worker cooperatives, and it would seem quite possible—not easy, but possible—to enact such a policy under capitalism.

Rich democratic capitalist nations already have democratic control over the economy as a whole, at least in principle. And regularized discussion and negotiation between representatives of business, labor, and government ("concertation") provides, in the countries that use it, an additional avenue for worker influence. Advocates of democratic socialism contend that ordinary persons would have more political influence under socialism—companies and wealthy individuals would be less able to dominate policy making. But as we saw in chapters 10 and 11, the available evidence suggests reason to doubt that.

13

Less Economic Inequality

Something is wrong with capitalism. There must be a better distribution of wealth, and maybe America must move toward a democratic socialism.

—Martin Luther King Jr.[1]

In a period marked by internationalization of trade and rapid expansion of higher education, social-democratic parties failed to adapt quickly enough, and the left-right cleavage that had made possible the mid-twentieth-century reduction of inequality gradually fell apart. The conservative revolution of the 1980s, the collapse of Soviet communism, and the development of neo-proprietarian ideology vastly increased the concentration of income and wealth in the first two decades of the twenty-first century. . . . The study of history has convinced me that it is possible to transcend today's capitalist system and to outline the contours of a new participatory socialism for the twenty-first century—a new universalist egalitarian perspective based on social ownership, education, and shared knowledge and power.

—Thomas Piketty[2]

Income inequality is inevitable. There is no practical way to ensure that everyone's income is the same. It's also helpful. We need financial incentives in order to encourage work, investment, entrepreneurship, and innovation.

Yet too much inequality is unfair. Much of what determines a person's earnings and income—intelligence, creativity, physical and social skills, motivation, persistence, confidence, connections, inherited wealth, discrimination—is a product of genetics, parents' assets and traits, and the quality of one's childhood neighborhood and schools. These aren't chosen; they are a matter of luck. A nontrivial portion of income inequality is therefore, arguably, undeserved.

Income inequality might also have harmful consequences for other outcomes we value, from education to health to democracy and more.

Would democratic socialism reduce economic inequality? How helpful would that be?

Would Democratic Socialism Be Better?. Lane Kenworthy, Oxford University Press. © Lane Kenworthy 2022.
DOI: 10.1093/oso/9780197636800.003.0013

Income Inequality between the Top 1 Percent and
the Bottom 99 Percent

Since the late 1970s, income inequality has been rising in most of the rich democratic capitalist nations. This is particularly true for inequality between those
at the top and everyone else. Figure 13.1 shows that top-end income inequality,
measured as the share of income that goes to those in the top 1 percent of the distribution, decreased steadily in many of these nations from the early twentieth
century through the late 1970s. But since then it has increased.

In the United States, the rise has been quite large, to the point that top-end income inequality has returned all the way back to the very high level of the early
1900s. But it isn't just the United States. There's been a rise in nearly all of these
countries, even the Nordics.

What has caused this increase in top-end income inequality? Explanations
often begin with education, but patterns of educational attainment can't tell
us much about why the top 1 percent's incomes have separated from everyone
else, because people in the top 1 percent don't tend to be better educated than
those just below them in the income distribution. That also holds for some other
factors commonly invoked in explanations of rising income inequality. High
earners more commonly couple with other high earners today than in former
generations, but this doesn't distinguish the top 1 percent from the rest of the
top 10 or 20 percent of households. Manufacturing employment has declined,
the statutory minimum wage has been flat, and unskilled immigration has risen

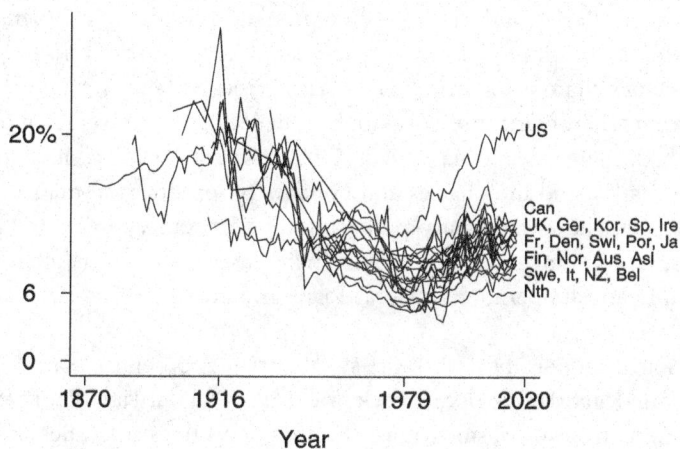

Figure 13.1 Income inequality between the top 1 percent and the bottom 99 percent
Top 1 percent's income share. Pretax income. Excludes capital gains. Data source: World Inequality
Database. "Asl" is Australia; "Aus" is Austria.

sharply, but these are more likely to have increased the income gap between the middle and the bottom than between the top and everyone else.

There appear to have been seven key causes of the rise in top-end income inequality.[3]

One is increases in product market size. By expanding the size of product markets, technological advance and globalization have produced large increases in firm revenues, and this translates into big payoffs for superstar athletes, entertainers, and CEOs. A related logic applies to the financial sector. Computerization and modern communications technology have enabled a big expansion in the volume of trades, as well as creation of new financial tools and instruments (leveraged buyouts, junk bonds, home equity loans, subprime mortgages, derivatives, collateralized debt obligations, credit default swaps). These in turn have increased the volume of fees earned by large financial firms, which has made it possible for these companies to handsomely reward their top creators, analysts, deal makers, and traders.

A second contributor to rising top-end income inequality, particularly in the United States and the United Kingdom, is changes in corporate governance and executive pay-setting. During the "golden age" of post–World War II capitalism, boards of directors of large publicly owned corporations saw the firm's mission as increasing market share, revenues, and profits. Profits were invested in research or equipment, passed on to employees in the form of wage increases and new hires, or distributed to shareholders as dividends. Beginning in the late 1970s, this orientation was replaced by the notion that the principal aim should be to maximize "shareholder value" by increasing the firm's stock price. Around the same time, firms switched to hiring CEOs from outside the company, paying them large salaries, and adding stock options as part of their compensation.

A third contributor is financialization. Over the past century, the financial sector's share of America's GDP has correlated fairly strongly with the top 1 percent's share of income; it was high in the 1920s, then lower for about 50 years, then high again since the late 1970s. Financial firms' revenues have grown in recent decades, and the salaries and bonuses of top financial managers, traders, and analysts have risen sharply. The amounts for some, particularly hedge fund managers, are staggering. Moreover, many large nonfinancial companies have added financial operations such as loans and credit cards on top of their core business.

A fourth important part of the story of rising top-end income inequality in the United States is the rise in stock prices. The Standard and Poor's (S&P) 500 is a common measure of stock-market values. Over the six decades since the mid-1950s, the correlation between the inflation-adjusted value of the S&P 500 and the top 1 percent's income share is + 0.92. Both were flat through the late 1970s and then shot up.

Fifth, labor unions have weakened. Where unions exist and are sufficiently strong, they can force firms to distribute more of the profits to ordinary workers and less to top executives. Computers, robots, the ability to move to another state or country, immigration, high unemployment rates, and other developments have increased employers' leverage vis-à-vis workers, and in this context union strength is likely to be especially critical. Unions also can affect income inequality via a political channel, by pressuring policy makers and influencing election outcomes. As we saw in chapter 7, unionization has declined in recent decades in all but five of the affluent democratic countries.

A sixth contributor to rising top-end income inequality has been reductions in top tax rates. While the Reagan, Bush, and Trump tax cuts in the United States get a lot of attention, all of the affluent democracies have reduced their top income tax rate. Lower tax rates allow the rich to keep more of their earnings, but they also can affect the pretax distribution of income. When top income tax rates are lower, people and households at the top have greater incentive to try to maximize their income.

A seventh contributor is increases in the power of large firms in some industries. Firms with a dominant position in their product market can deter potential entrants, weaken existing competitors, and extract more revenue from customers. They then pass on the resulting above-market profits, or "rents," to their top executives.

Will the rise in income inequality between the top 1 percent and the bottom 99 percent continue? There is no way to know. Perhaps a new development—a deep economic downturn, a shift in political priorities, or something else—will produce another reversal like the one in the middle of the twentieth century. All we can say with confidence is that this hasn't happened yet.

Income Inequality within the Bottom 99 Percent

In many of the rich democracies, inequality also has increased within the bottom 99 percent, as we see in Figure 13.2. (Here the comparable data only go back to the 1960s.) Once again, the rise in inequality has occurred not only in the United States but also in most of the affluent democratic nations, including the Nordics.

In most of these countries, much of the rise in bottom-99-percent income inequality has happened above the median. The spread between households at the 90th percentile and those at the median (50th percentile) has increased steadily and to a greater extent than the spread between households at the median and those at the bottom.[4]

There are two principal sources of rising inequality within the bottom 99 percent.[5] The first is increased wage inequality. Since the late 1970s, wages above

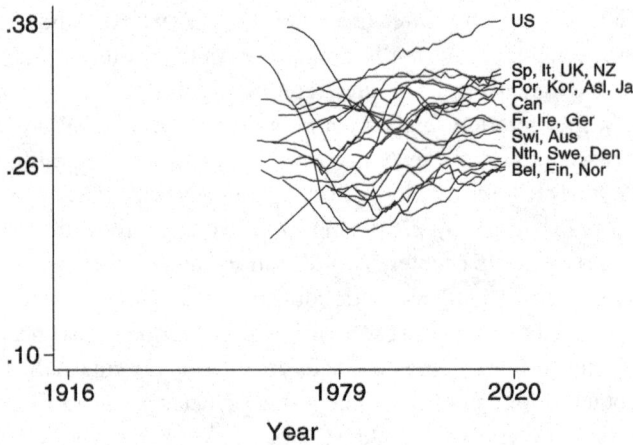

Figure 13.2 Income inequality within the bottom 99 percent

Gini coefficient (equal to 0 if everyone's income is the same and 1 if a single household gets all the income). Posttransfer-posttax income, adjusted for household size. The vertical axis doesn't begin at zero. Data source: Frederick Solt, Standardized World Income Inequality Database, using data from the Luxembourg Income Study, the OECD, and other sources. "Asl" is Australia; "Aus" is Austria.

the middle have risen faster than for those in the middle. This development has multiple causes, including shifts in educational attainment, globalization, technological change, and union decline.

The second source is changes in household structure and employment. Initially, the rise in women's employment tended to reduce income inequality by reducing the share of households with zero earners or a single earner. More recently, however, the employment rate has been growing faster among women who have an employed partner, and this tends to boost income inequality. The share of households with just one adult has been rising, which increases household income inequality by increasing the share of households with only one earner or no earners. Rising marital homogamy is another contributor to rising inequality; more people are coupling with a person whose employment and wages are similar, so high earners are becoming more likely to be paired with other high earners, moderate earners with moderates, and low earners with other lows.

Shifts in taxation or government transfers could have contributed to the rise in income inequality between upper-middle-income and middle-income households, but there is little evidence to suggest that they did.

Why didn't income inequality increase between households in the middle versus those at the bottom? Increased movement of women into paid work helped household incomes grow a bit for those in the middle, while increases in government transfers did the same for those at the bottom.[6]

Is Income Inequality Harmful?

In recent decades a growing number of observers have concluded that income inequality has adverse effects on an array of outcomes we value, including education, health, economic growth, happiness, and more.[7]

Is income inequality harmful? In şeparate research, I've examined the experiences of the world's affluent democratic countries during the period of rising inequality.[8] Many of the most prominent predictions of harmful effects are supported only weakly or not at all. The evidence suggests that income inequality hasn't slowed the growth of college completion. It either hasn't reduced the increase in life expectancy or the decrease in infant mortality or, if it has, the impact has been small. It looks unlikely to have contributed to the rise in obesity. It hasn't slowed the fall in teen births or homicides since the early 1990s. It hasn't reduced economic growth. It hasn't hindered employment. It isn't systematically linked to the occurrence of economic crises. It hasn't reduced income growth for poor households. It doesn't appear to have affected average happiness. In the United States it has had little or no impact on trust in political institutions, on voter turnout, or on party polarization.

For some outcomes—interpersonal trust, the Great Recession, and household debt—the evidence is ambiguous or it is too soon to make an informed judgment.

On the other hand, in the country with the highest level of inequality, the United States, the evidence pretty strongly suggests that income inequality has reduced middle-class household income growth. It also has increased disparities in education, health, family formation, family stability, and happiness, and it has reduced residential mixing.

Wealth Inequality

Wealth typically is distributed more unequally than income. In the United States, for instance, the top 1 percent of households get about 15 percent of the income in any given year, while the top 1 percent of wealth holders have about 35 percent of the wealth.

Figure 13.3 shows the top 1 percent's share of the wealth since the early 1900s in four countries for which long-run data are available—France, Sweden, the United Kingdom, and the United States. In each of the four, wealth inequality decreased in the first half of the twentieth century, then was flat until around 1970 or 1980, and since then has increased a bit.

What accounts for the significant reduction in wealth inequality during the first half or two-thirds of the twentieth century? Four developments appear to have been crucial.[9]

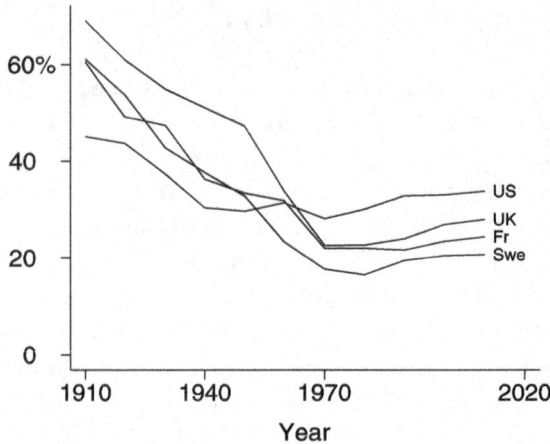

Figure 13.3   Wealth inequality between the top 1 percent and the bottom 99 percent
Top 1 percent's wealth share. Wealth = assets minus liabilities. Data source: Thomas Piketty, *Capital in the Twenty-First Century*, Harvard University Press, 2014, ch. 10.

A key part of the story was declines in the value of private assets, which are disproportionately owned by those at the top. Businesses and property were destroyed during the two world wars. Land values fell as economies transitioned from agriculture to manufacturing. The value of businesses and stocks plummeted during the Great Depression. Persistent lack of confidence in the stock market along with new financial regulations and new taxes on dividends and profits kept corporate and stock values relatively low through the 1950s and 1960s. In western European nations, there also was some post–World War II nationalization of formerly private firms.

Second, homeownership rates increased significantly, particularly after the invention of government-backed 30-year fixed-interest-rate mortgage loans in the 1930s. This facilitated wealth accumulation among the middle class.

A third contributing factor was historically rapid rates of economic growth in the 1940s, 1950s, and 1960s, coupled with institutions—strong labor unions, in particular—that ensured a significant amount of this growth trickled down to the middle and lower parts of the distribution via rising wages and employment. This reduced the income share of the top 1 percent, which in turn reduced its grip on wealth.

Fourth, during these decades all affluent countries enacted and expanded new taxes on income, and in some instances on wealth.

The OECD has current wealth inequality data for more countries. According to those data, shown on the vertical axis in Figure 13.4, the United States has the most top-end wealth inequality of any rich nation.[10]

As I just noted, homeownership and home values have been a key determinant of over-time trends in wealth inequality. When comparing across countries,

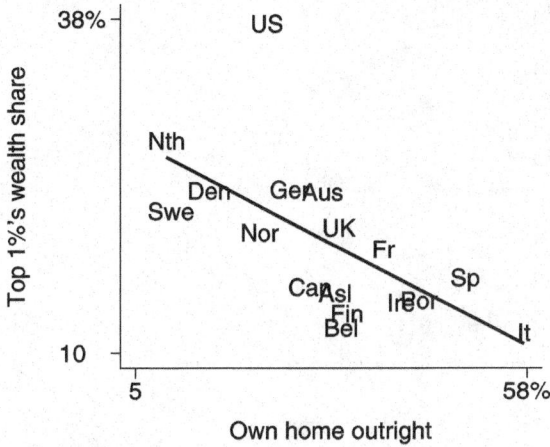

Figure 13.4 Wealth inequality by homeownership

Wealth inequality: top 1 percent's wealth share. Wealth = assets minus liabilities. The estimate for Sweden is imputed using top 5 percent wealth share data. Data source: OECD Wealth Distribution Database. Homeownership: share of the population that owns a home outright (without a mortgage loan). Data source: OECD Affordable Housing Database. 2014 or nearest available year. "Asl" is Australia; "Aus" is Austria. The line is linear regression line, calculated with the United States excluded. The correlation is -.62.

a helpful measure is the share of the population that owns a home outright—that is, without a mortgage loan. This is strongly correlated with the top 1 percent's wealth share, as we see in Figure 13.4. Wealth inequality tends to be higher where fewer people are homeowners who have fully paid off their home loan.[11]

Does wealth inequality correspond to income inequality when we look across the rich capitalist democratic nations? Perhaps surprisingly, the answer is no, as Figure 13.5 reveals. The top 1 percent's income share is on the horizontal axis, and the top 1 percent's wealth share is on the vertical. The position of the United States is consistent with what we might expect; it has the most income inequality and the most wealth inequality. But across the other nations there is no correlation at all.[12] Especially notable is the position of the Netherlands, Denmark, Sweden, and Norway. These countries have among the lowest levels of top-end income inequality but some of the highest levels of top-end wealth inequality.

Would Democratic Socialism Be Better at Reducing Economic Inequality?

Democratic socialism is very likely to reduce top-end income inequality, even compared to the relatively low levels achieved in the Nordic countries. In John Roemer's "coupon socialism" version, for example, there would be no private owners of large quantities of stock shares, nor of stock options. Firms might still

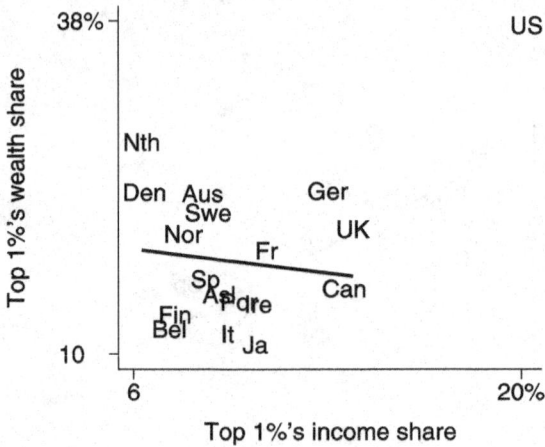

Figure 13.5 Wealth inequality by income inequality

Wealth inequality: top 1 percent's wealth share. Wealth = assets minus liabilities. The estimate for Sweden is imputed using top 5 percent wealth share data. Data source: OECD Wealth Distribution Database. Income inequality: top 1 percent's income share. Pretax income. Excludes capital gains. Data source: World Inequality Database. 2014 or nearest available year. "Asl" is Australia. The line is a linear regression line, calculated with the United States excluded.

choose to pay very large salaries and bonuses to their CEO and their top performing employees. But in the absence of privately owned stock shares, top-end income inequality almost certainly would be reduced.

It seems likely that democratic socialism also would reduce income inequality within the bottom 99 percent of the population. Particularly if many firms are worker cooperatives, there is less likelihood of very large differences in pay. But this outcome is less certain. Many of the affluent capitalist democracies, especially the ones with strong labor unions, have been able to achieve significant wage compression. When combined with government tax-and-transfer programs that redistribute income, the result has been modest levels of income inequality within the bottom 99 percent. Roemer himself has said "The Nordic countries have achieved admirable economic equality using taxation but maintaining . . . private ownership of most firms. If that could be a model for the United States, I'd be all for it."[13]

Even if democratic socialism reduces income inequality, there is no guarantee it will also reduce wealth inequality. We can see this from the lack of an association between the two in Figure 13.5. A socialism with extensive public ownership surely would yield less wealth inequality, because it would make it difficult for individuals to compile large quantities of financial assets. It's less certain whether a socialism centered on economic democracy would do so.

One of the best ways to reduce wealth inequality is to boost home equity among the middle class. But is that a good policy goal? There are benefits to homeownership, but it also has drawbacks. It may reduce geographic mobility by tying people to a particular home.[14] And it renders their wealth vulnerable to swings in housing market prices. This debate is far from settled.

How Much Should We Care about Reducing Economic Inequality?

Let's stipulate that democratic socialism very likely would reduce income inequality and that there is a good chance it also would reduce wealth inequality. How much should this matter to us?

To some, the answer is obvious: economic inequality is the defining challenge of our time. That's because economic inequality may worsen other things we value—health, education, safety, economic growth, democracy, happiness, and more.[15] If it does so, then it probably should matter quite a bit.

However, as I've noted, there is little evidence that it has such effects. In the United States, it does appear to have reduced middle-class income growth and to have increased disparities in education, health, family formation, family stability, and happiness.[16] But those effects may be unique to this nation that has such exceptionally high inequality.

So the case for caring deeply about less inequality comes down mainly, in my view, to normative considerations. The amount of income and wealth inequality that exists in the United States, and probably in some other affluent democracies, is unfair, because much of what determines where people end up on the economic ladder is beyond their control. This suggests that less economic inequality would be fairer.

But while less income and wealth inequality might be better in terms of fairness, how critical is it? How high should it be on our list of priorities?

In a society where many of life's needs and wants—safety, housing, childcare, schooling, medical care, work, time for family and leisure, retirement income, eldercare, and much more—are assured by government programs, it isn't clear that a moderately high level of income or wealth inequality is especially problematic.[17] Denmark, Norway, and Sweden have some of the highest levels of wealth inequality among the rich capitalist democracies, and while Bernie Sanders has argued that there should be no billionaires, Sweden and Norway have more billionaires per capita than the United States.[18] Despite this, in the contemporary Nordic countries there is plenty of economic security, little material hardship, abundant freedom, and most people (including immigrants) say they are quite satisfied with their lives.[19] On the whole, life there is very good.[20] In this kind of context, people may not be especially bothered by the fact that some persons have a lot of income or wealth, just as they aren't too upset that some persons are exceptionally intelligent or good looking or socially adept.

14

Gender and Racial Equality

To understand why the United States seems so resistant to racial equality, we have to look beyond the actions of elected officials or even those who prosper from racial discrimination in the private sector. We have to look at the way American society is organized under capitalism. Capitalism is an economic system based on the exploitation of the many by the few. Because of the gross inequality it produces, capitalism relies on various political, social, and ideological tools to rationalize that inequality while simultaneously dividing the majority, who have every interest in uniting to resist it. How does the 1 percent maintain its disproportionate control of the wealth and resources in American society? By a process of divide and rule.

—Keeanga-Yamahtta Taylor[1]

Capital feeds on existing norms of sexism, compounding the exploitative nature of wage work. When women's ambitions and desires are silenced or under-valued, they are easier to take advantage of. Sexism is part of the company toolkit, enabling firms to pay women less . . . and otherwise discriminate against them.

—Nicole Aschoff[2]

Income inequality is inevitable, as I noted in the previous chapter. However, it isn't inevitable that there be inequality between groups that differ on some ascriptive characteristic, such as sex or race. Across groups we could have levels of living standards, well-being, and representation that are equal or nearly equal.

On one view, capitalism is a force for progress in this realm. Market competition encourages firms to care about how well a person works or how much they can buy, rather than the color of their skin or how many X chromosomes they have.

An opposing perspective contends that bosses benefit from keeping workers divided. Doing so enables firms to pay less and gives them greater discretion over hiring and firing procedures, work conditions, and working time. Sexism and racism are helpful in sowing division, so companies will tend to foster these

Would Democratic Socialism Be Better?. Lane Kenworthy, Oxford University Press. © Lane Kenworthy 2022.
DOI: 10.1093/oso/9780197636800.003.0014

views. And firms will discriminate against members of less-advantaged groups in order to help perpetuate the notion that they are inferior and therefore deserving of prejudice and hostility.

Is capitalism compatible with between-group equality? Would democratic socialism do better?

Gender Equality

In the United States, women couldn't own and control property until 1849. They weren't allowed to vote until 1920. Prior to 1965, employers were free to discriminate against women in hiring, pay, and promotion. The country has never elected a female president.

Yet in the United States and in other democratic capitalist nations, there has been significant progress toward equality. Figure 14.1 shows the gap between men and women in college completion. Comparable data for most nations don't go back very far in time, but in the United States they show a decline in men's advantage beginning around 1980 and steady progress toward and beyond equality since then. In all of the 16 countries for which data are available, college completion has been rising for both groups, but at a faster rate among women. Women

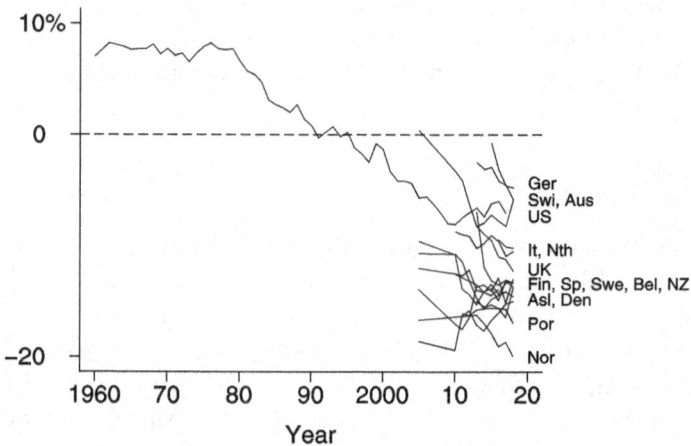

Figure 14.1 Male–female gap in college education

College completion among men minus college completion among women. A negative gap means the college completion rate is higher for women than for men. All countries other than the United States: share of persons reaching age 30 with a bachelor's degree. Data source: OECD, "Tertiary Graduation Rate," data.oecd.org. United States: share of 25- to 34-year-olds with 4 or more years of college. Data source: Census Bureau, "CPS Historical Time Series Tables," table A-1. The line that begins in 1960 is the United States. "Asl" is Australia; "Aus" is Austria.

now are more likely than men—in some countries *much* more likely—to get a bachelor's degree.[3]

Figure 14.2 shows the gap in employment rates between men and women. Half a century ago this gap was enormous in some countries. In Italy in the early 1970s, about 88 percent of working-age men were employed, compared to just 27 percent of working-age women, so the gap was more than 60 percentage points. Today the largest employment gap is a little more than 20 percentage points, and in some of these nations it has shrunk to five percentage points or less.

The trend toward equality in employment rates owes partly to a decline among men, but it is due mainly to rising employment among women, as we saw in chapter 4. Norms have shifted, so more women want a paying job. Women have more education, so they are better qualified for good jobs. Discrimination has declined, enabling women to access better jobs. And many of these countries now have public programs that make it easier for women to combine employment with family—in particular, a year or so of paid parental leave, public childcare and preschool, and eldercare.[4]

Women can get employed, but do firms in a capitalist economy exclude them from the top positions? Historically that has been the pattern, but things have been changing rapidly in recent decades, as we see in Figure 14.3. The figure shows the share of board of directors seats in large companies that are held by women. In the leading countries, that share is now around 40 to 45 percent. A key contributor to the rapid rise in some nations is quotas—the tool of choice

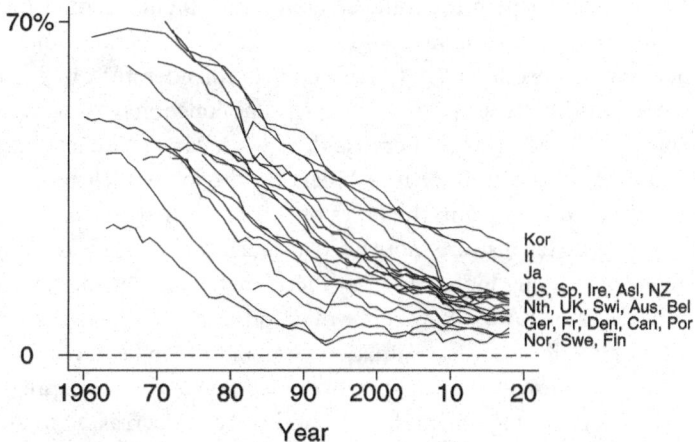

Figure 14.2 Male–female gap in employment
Employment rate among men minus employment rate among women. The employment rate is calculated as employed persons age 25–64 as a share of all persons age 25–64. Data source: OECD, "Employment Rate," data.oecd.org. "Asl" is Australia; "Aus" is Austria.

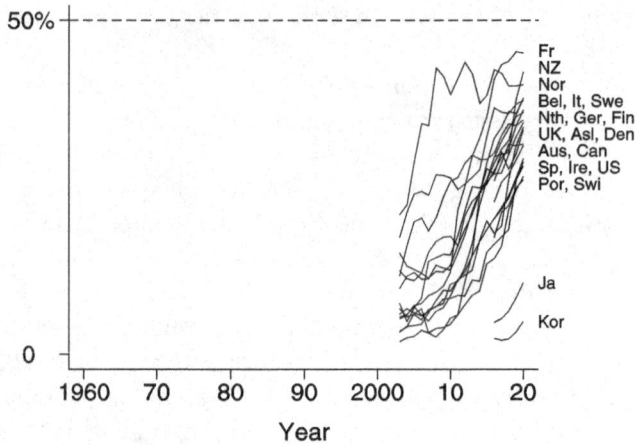

Figure 14.3 Women's share of corporate board positions

Women's share of board positions in large firms. Data source: OECD, "Female Share of Seats on Boards of the Largest Publicly Listed Companies," stats.oecd.org. "Asl" is Australia; "Aus" is Austria.

if one wishes to ensure equal outcomes.[5] Norway was the first nation to adopt one, requiring large firms to have at least 40 percent of their board members as women by 2008. In 2018, the state of California joined this list; it passed a law requiring all companies based in California to have at least one female board member by the end of 2019 and two or three (depending on the total number of directors) by the end of 2021.[6]

Can women get paid the same as men in a capitalist economy? They often don't, for several reasons. Men tend to work more hours than women. Men and women differ in productivity, though there is considerable disagreement about how much this matters. As we've seen, men no longer have an advantage in education. On the other hand, because their work careers are less likely to be interrupted, they tend to have more years on the job, which may contribute to productivity. Differences in the types of jobs women and men work contribute to the pay gap. Men also are more likely to work in core or monopoly industries, where profit rates are higher and pay therefore tends to be higher. And men are more likely to be union members, which on average boosts their pay. Finally, there likely is still some discrimination by employers in favor of men.

Figure 14.4 shows the pay gap between women and men, expressed as a percentage of median pay for men. The gap has been decreasing in all of the rich democratic nations. In some, such as South Korea and Japan, it remains quite high. In the United States it is about 20 percent. In the leading countries, it is down to just five percent or less.

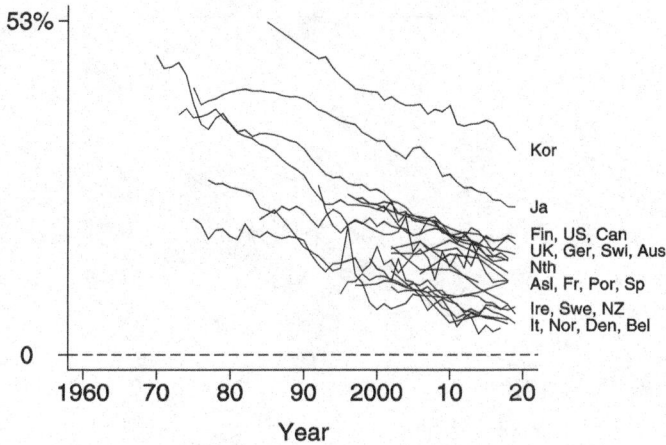

Figure 14.4 Male–female gap in pay
Difference between median full-time male pay and median full-time female pay as a share of median full-time male pay. Data source: OECD, "Gender Wage Gap," data.oecd.org. "Asl" is Australia; "Aus" is Austria.

What about other components of well-being? Figure 14.5 shows the gap in life expectancy between men and women. Here, as with education, women have an advantage; they tend to live longer than men in all of the affluent capitalist democracies. The magnitude of the difference has ebbed and flowed over the past sixty years, but it remains substantial, averaging four to five years across these countries.

Figure 14.6 shows the gap in subjective well-being between men and women. The measure is from a question the World Values Survey has asked regularly since the early 1980s: "All things considered, how satisfied are you with your life as a whole?" Respondents answer by choosing a value between 1 and 10, with larger numbers indicating greater life satisfaction. In most countries there is little difference between men and women, but if anything women tend to be happier than men, and that has been true throughout the past four decades.

If rich capitalist democracies have achieved or surpassed gender equality in education, health, and happiness and are moving rapidly in that direction in jobs and pay, what about in politics? Is equality in political representation possible under capitalism? The trends in women's share of parliamentary seats, shown in Figure 14.7, suggest grounds for optimism. Women remain under-represented in every rich capitalist democracy, but they have been gaining ground everywhere. In the leading countries they now hold 40 percent or more of the seats.

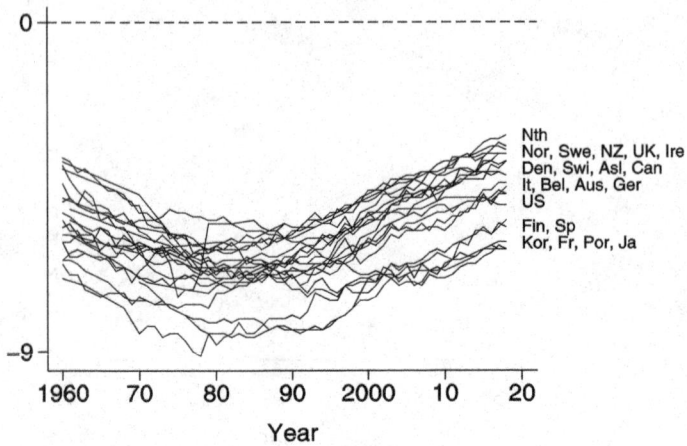

Figure 14.5 Male–female gap in life expectancy

Difference between life expectancy at birth for men and life expectancy at birth for women.
A negative gap means life expectancy is higher for women than for men. Data source: OECD, "Life
Expectancy at Birth," data.oecd.org. "Asl" is Australia; "Aus" is Austria.

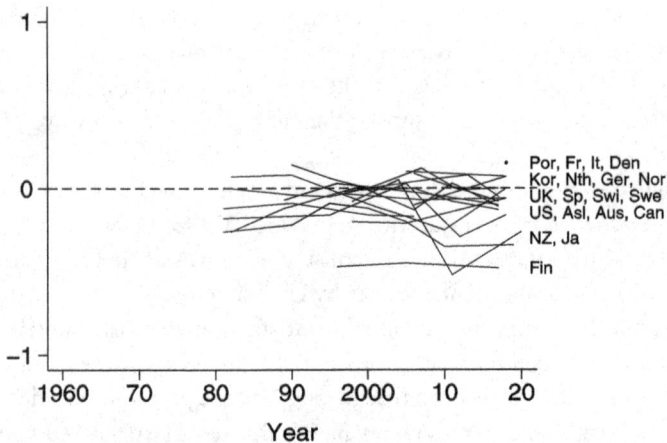

Figure 14.6 Male–female gap in life satisfaction

Difference between average life satisfaction among men and average life satisfaction among women.
A negative gap means life satisfaction is higher among women than among men. Question: "All
things considered, how satisfied are you with your life as a whole these days?" Scale from 1 to 10,
with larger numbers indicating higher life satisfaction. Data source: World Values Survey. "Asl" is
Australia; "Aus" is Austria.

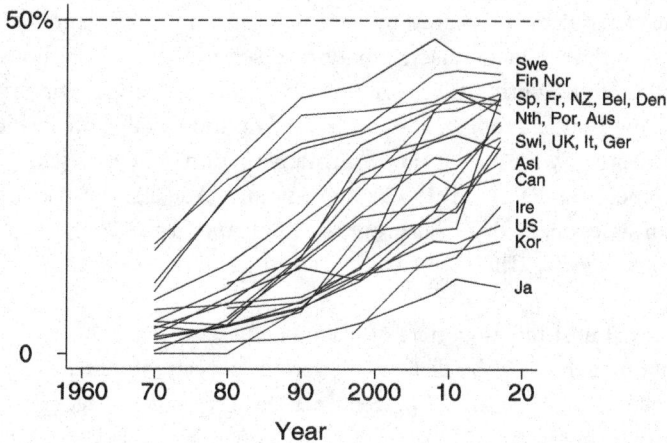

Figure 14.7 Women's share of legislative seats

Women's share of seats in the lower (main) parliamentary body. Data source: Inter-Parliamentary Union, ipu.org. "Asl" is Australia; "Aus" is Austria.

Racial Equality

The story for gender equality in the rich capitalist democracies is encouraging. Let's turn now to what may be the most challenging between-group inequality in these countries: white versus Black Americans.

Allowing the enslavement of Black persons in the 17th, 18th, and 19th centuries is one of the worst things the United States has done, and progress in rectifying our policies and institutions came slowly. Slavery was outlawed in 1865, following the union victory in the Civil War. Yet physical violence, sharecropping arrangements, segregation laws, and poll taxes and literacy tests were used to subjugate Blacks for another century in much of the South, and residential segregation and employer discrimination hindered opportunity in the rest of the country.[7]

In *An American Dilemma*, published in 1944, Gunnar Myrdal concluded that race relations in the United States were locked in a vicious cycle in which whites oppressed Blacks and then used the consequent poor outcomes for Blacks as justification for the oppression.[8] In 1968, the Kerner Commission, appointed by President Johnson in the wake of urban disorders and violent protests, concluded that "Our nation is moving toward two societies, one black, one white— separate and unequal."[9]

Yet in some respects the tide had begun to turn. In 1954 the Supreme Court ruled racial segregation in public schools to be unconstitutional. Following a decade of activism and protest by the civil rights movement, the Civil Rights Act of 1964 outlawed racial discrimination in school admissions, housing, hiring, and pay and the Voting Rights Act of 1965 outlawed discriminatory barriers to voting and political representation. In the late 1960s state laws forbidding inter-racial marriage were banned and affirmative action policies began.

A generation later, in 1997, Stephen and Abigail Thernstrom published a major assessment of racial progress titled *America in Black and White: One Nation, Indivisible.* Their conclusion was positive and optimistic:

> Today, almost three-quarters of black families are above the poverty line. In 1940, 87 percent of black families were in poverty; the figure was down to 47 percent in 1960 and 26 percent in 1995. The black college population has grown from 45,000 in 1940 to over 1.4 million today, a thirtyfold increase. Sixty percent of employed black women were domestic servants in 1940; today very few are. A majority, in fact, hold white-collar jobs. The number of black men in professional occupations has also risen impressively. Power and influence were exclusively white prerogatives in 1940; there was no Vernon Jordan and no Michael Jordan.[10]

Nor, we can now add, was there a Barack Obama—America's first Black president, elected in 2008 and again in 2012.

Has there in fact been real progress? If so, how much? And how far are we from equal outcomes?

Rates of college completion have been rising for all racial groups since the middle of the twentieth century. There hasn't been much change in the gap between whites and Blacks, as we see in Figure 14.8. However, focusing on the inequality distracts us from the significant improvement for African Americans, whose rate of college completion today is higher than it was for whites as recently as the mid-2000s. And it's worth noting that in high school completion there has been significant equalization.[11]

The employment rate, shown in Figure 14.9, moves up and down with the business cycle. While it has been lower among African Americans than among whites throughout the past half century, there was significant progress in the 2010s. By 2019, before the Covid-19 pandemic hit, the employment rate gap was down to three percentage points.

As is true for women, Black Americans' share of corporate board positions has been rising, though we lack reliable data until very recently. By the end of 2020, African Americans held 9 percent of those positions, as we see in Figure 14.10. That's less than their 13.5 percent share of the population, but it's not far away.

The typical employed Black American earns about $12,000 per year less than her or his white counterpart. That hasn't changed much in recent decades, as we

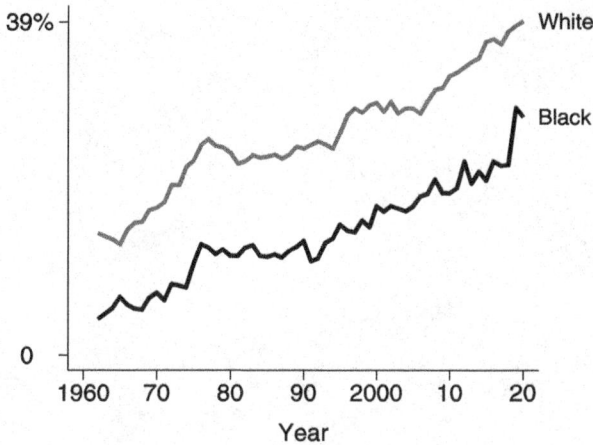

Figure 14.8 College education: Black and white Americans

Four-year college degree. Share of persons age 25–29. Data source: Census Bureau, "Educational Attainment," CPS Historical Time Series Tables, table 2.

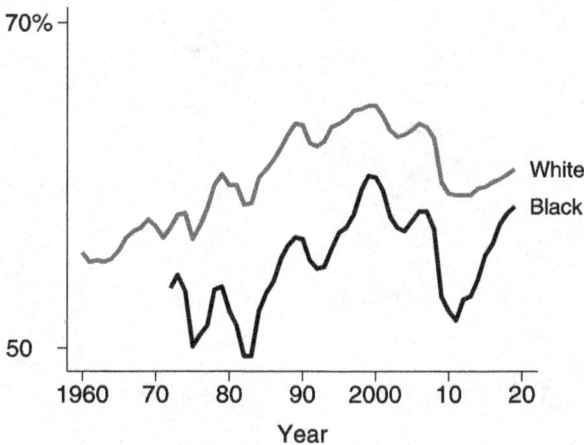

Figure 14.9 Employment: Black and white Americans

Employed persons as a share of the population. Data source: Federal Reserve Bank of St. Louis (FRED), series LNS12300006 and LNS12300003, using Current Population Survey data.

see in figure 14.11. Since the late 1970s earnings have risen slowly for many ordinary Americans.[12]

Median wealth among Blacks is far lower than among whites, and that has been true at least since the 1980s, when systematic data collection began. This is mainly a function of homeownership patterns. For most middle-class

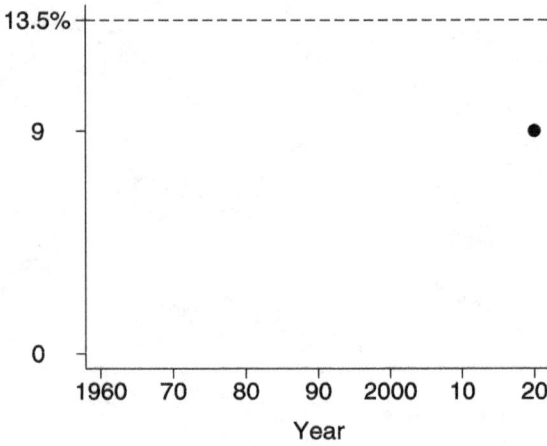

Figure 14.10 Blacks' share of corporate board positions

African Americans' share of board positions in S&P 500 firms. Data source: Equilar, via Ross Kerber and Jessica DiNapoli, "What Happened When a U.S. State Required Details on Corporate Diversity?," Reuters, May 11, 2021.

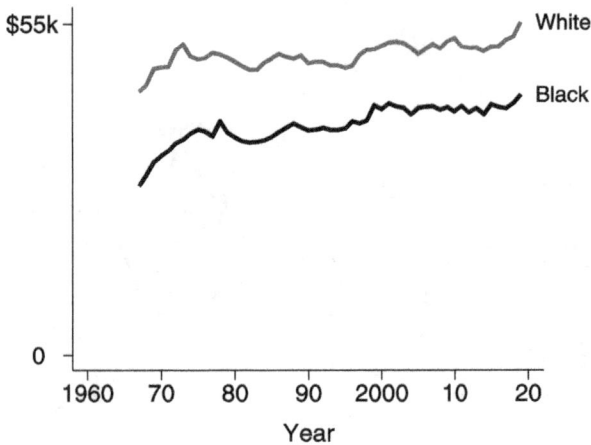

Figure 14.11 Pay: Black and white Americans

Median annual earnings for persons employed full-time year-round. "k" = thousand. Data source: Census Bureau, "Historical Income Tables," table P-38, using Current Population Survey data.

Americans, owning a home facilitates wealth accumulation, which otherwise tends to remain close to zero. About 65 percent of white households are homeowners, so the median white household owns a home. Among Blacks, the homeownership rate has never reached 50 percent, so the median household has tended to have very little wealth.[13]

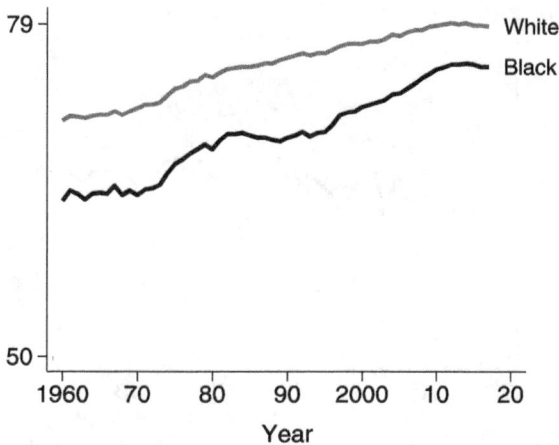

Figure 14.12 Life expectancy: Black and white Americans
Years at birth. The vertical axis doesn't begin at zero. Data source: National Center for Health Statistics, *Health, United States*, 2019, table 4.

How big a problem is the wealth gap? It matters, but mainly because America's underdeveloped public safety net renders people with little wealth economically vulnerable. Once public social programs in the United States catch up to their counterparts in the Nordic countries, lack of wealth likely will have limited impact on people's well-being and life chances, as I suggested in chapter 13.

Whites in the United States live longer than Blacks, but as we see in Figure 14.12, the gap in life expectancy has been shrinking. In the 1970s it was seven years. By the late 2010s, it was down to 3.5 years. That's about the same as the gap between Japan and Denmark.[14]

White Americans have tended to be happier than Blacks, as Figure 14.13 shows. But here too the gap has been decreasing. In the 1970s it averaged about 1.2 points on a scale of 0 to 10. By the second half of the 2010s it had declined by half.

Finally, what of equality in political representation? Here too there is persistent but decreasing inequality, as we see in Figure 14.14. The country has achieved relatively little progress toward fair representation of Blacks in the Senate. But in the House of Representatives there has been steady progress for more than half a century, and equality is nearly at hand.

Would Democratic Socialism Be Better at Achieving Gender and Racial Equality?

It's reasonable to suspect that, if implemented 150 or 100 or perhaps even 50 years ago, democratic socialism might have achieved faster progress toward gender

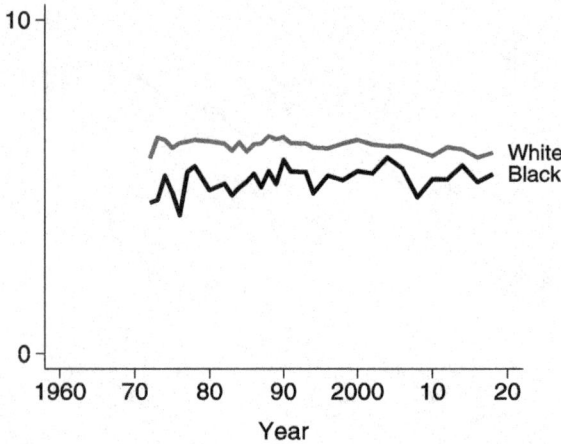

Figure 14.13 Happiness: Black and white Americans

Average happiness. Calculated with not too happy scored as 0, pretty happy scored as 5, and very happy scored as 10. Question: "Taken all together, how would you say things are these days—would you say that you are very happy, pretty happy, or not too happy?" Data source: General Social Survey, series happy.

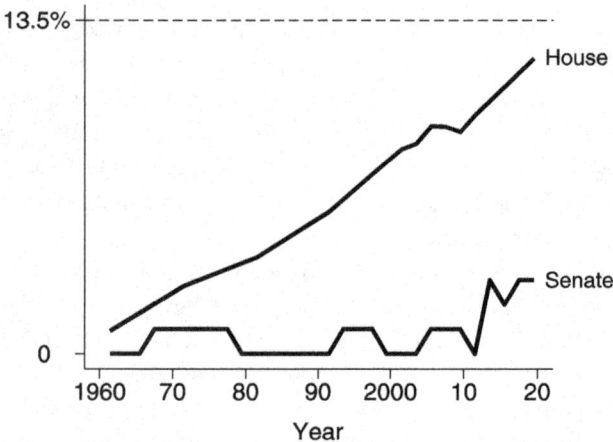

Figure 14.14 Blacks' share of legislative seats

African Americans' share of seats in the House of Representatives and the Senate. Data source: Congressional Research Service.

and racial equality than the rich capitalist nations actually have. But given how close to equality those countries are now, there is reason for skepticism that democratic socialism would do better.

In all of these nations, women have surpassed men in education. They tend to live longer than men and to be at least as happy if not happier. They still lag when it comes to employment and earnings, but the gap has been closing rapidly. The same is true in political representation.

In historical terms, the inequality between white and Black Americans is perhaps the worst case of between-group disparities in the affluent democracies. Yet while significant Black–white inequality persists, particularly in pay and wealth, there has been considerable progress—in education, in employment, in high-end corporate positions, in life expectancy, in happiness, and in political representation.

The hypothesis that capitalism needs inequality between ascriptive groups is a plausible one. The evidence, however, suggests it is almost certainly wrong. This isn't to say that capitalism is good for between-group equality; on that question, I think the jury is still out. What it means is that gender and racial equality are achievable under capitalism.

15

More Community

All human beings . . . feel insecure, lonely, and deprived of the naive, simple, and unsophisticated enjoyment of life. Man can find meaning in life, short and perilous as it is, only through devoting himself to society. The economic anarchy of capitalist society as it exists today is, in my opinion, the real source of the evil. We see before us a huge community of producers the members of which are unceasingly striving to deprive each other of the fruits of their collective labor—not by force, but on the whole in faithful compliance with legally established rules.

—Albert Einstein[1]

Capitalism undermines a sense of solidarity among people. . . . The forms of competition and conflict built into capitalism drive economic activities primarily on the basis of greed and fear. Instead of social interaction in economic life being normatively organized around the principle of helping others, it is organized primarily around taking advantage of the weakness of others for one's own gain. This underwrites a culture of selfish individualism and atomism.

—Erik Olin Wright[2]

An economic system first and foremost affects our living standards and our experience of work and leisure. But it also can influence the way we think about other people and interact with them. Is capitalism bad for tolerance, inclusion, trust, social connections, social support, unselfishness, and cooperation? Would democratic socialism do better?

Tolerance and Inclusion

On one view, capitalism fosters tolerance and inclusion. As an economic system in which actors engage in voluntary transactions in pursuit of financial gain, capitalism encourages people to hire, work for, sell to, and buy from whoever will

Would Democratic Socialism Be Better?. Lane Kenworthy, Oxford University Press. © Lane Kenworthy 2022.
DOI: 10.1093/oso/9780197636800.003.0015

improve their well-being. In the long run, this should tend to discourage discriminatory behavior and prejudiced beliefs.[3]

As I noted in chapter 14, another perspective holds that capitalism encourages employers to look for ways to divide workers. Easily observable differences such as sex, race, and language are obvious targets, so capitalism, according to this view, will tend to promote and perpetuate sexism, racism, and nativism.[4]

There are plenty of historical instances of firms in rich democratic nations attempting to sow divisions among workers by pitting a mainly male, white, native-born workforce against women, racial and ethnic minority groups, and immigrants. And no nation has fully succeeded in stamping out intolerance and prejudice.

Yet developments over the past half century are encouraging. As we saw in chapters 4 and 14, employment rates among prime-working-age women have been rising steadily in recent decades, while those for men have been falling. We are not yet at parity, and perhaps, given differing female and male preferences for spending time with young children, we'll never get there. But the gap has been shrinking, and that's also true for the gap in pay. Partly as a consequence of these changes and partly as a cause of them, attitudes toward gender roles have been shifting. Figure 15.1 shows the large increase over the past century in the share of Americans who approve of a married woman earning money in business or industry if she has a husband capable of supporting her.[5]

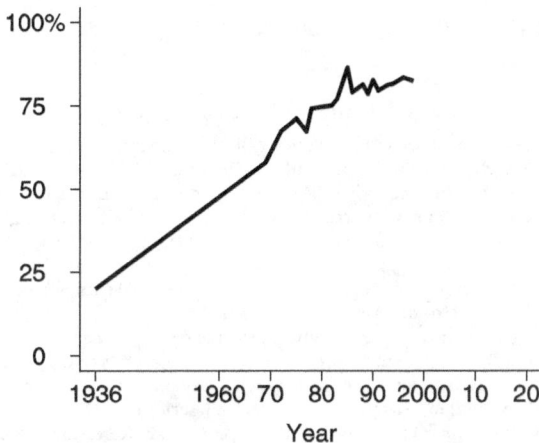

Figure 15.1 Approve of a married woman earning money in business or industry if she has a husband capable of supporting her

Other response options: disapprove, don't know. Don't know responses are excluded. Data source for 1936 and 1969: Gallup. Data source for 1972ff: General Social Survey (GSS), sda.berkeley.edu, series fework. The GSS stopped asking this question after 1998.

While the United States is the rich democratic nation with the deepest and most longstanding racial divisiveness, we observe considerable progress on some indicators of education and economic well-being, as chapter 14 documented. Attitudes, too, have shifted in recent decades, as suggested by the trend lines in Figure 15.2.

Hostility toward immigrants has contributed to the rise in vote share for anti-immigrant "populist" candidates and political parties in the affluent democratic countries.[6] Yet the share of Americans who favor a reduction in immigration has been decreasing in recent decades, not increasing.[7] And as we see in Figure 15.3, a rising share of Americans say they believe immigrants strengthen the country because of their hard work and talent.

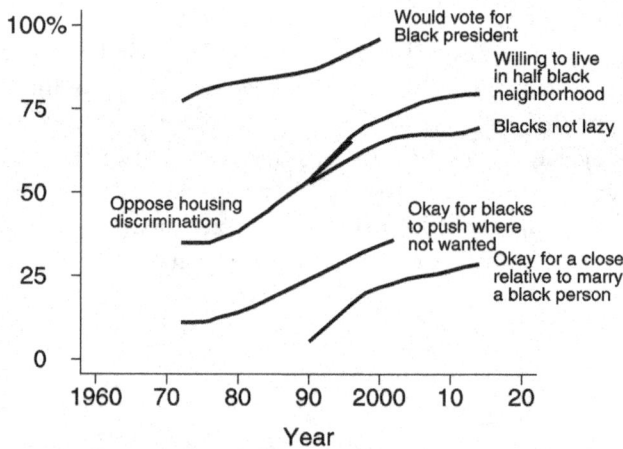

Figure 15.2 Whites' tolerance and embrace of African Americans

Share of white adults. The lines are loess curves. Vote for Black president. Question: "If your party nominated an African-American for President, would you vote for him if he were qualified for the job?" Response options: yes, no. The line shows the share responding yes. Data source: General Social Survey (GSS), sda.berkeley.edu, series racpres. Willing to live in half Black neighborhood. Question: "Would you be favorable or opposed to . . . living in a neighborhood where half of your neighbors were black?" Data source: GSS, series liveblks. Oppose housing discrimination. Question: "Do you agree or disagree: White people have a right to keep African-Americans out of their neighborhoods if they want to, and African-Americans should respect that right." Response options: agree strongly, agree slightly, disagree slightly, disagree strongly. The line shows the share responding disagree strongly. Data source: GSS, series racseg. Blacks not lazy. Question: "Do people in the group tend to be hard-working or lazy? Blacks." The line shows the share choosing 1–4 on a scale of 1 (hardworking) to 7 (lazy). Data source: GSS, series workblks. Okay for Blacks to push where not wanted. Question: "Do you agree or disagree: African-Americans shouldn't push themselves where they're not wanted." Response options: agree strongly, agree slightly, disagree slightly, disagree strongly. The line shows the share responding disagree strongly. Data source: GSS, series racpush. Okay close relative marry Black person. Question: "What about having a close relative marry a black person? Would you be very in favor of it happening, somewhat in favor, neither in favor nor opposed to it happening, somewhat opposed, or very opposed to it happening?" The line shows the share responding very in favor. Data source: GSS, series marblk.

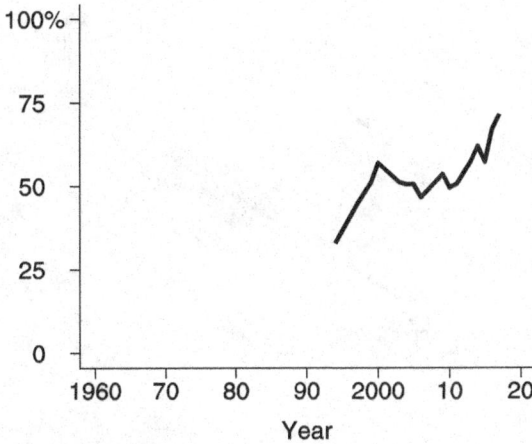

Figure 15.3 Immigrants today strengthen our country
Estimated share of US adults. Question: "I'm going to read you some pairs of statements that will help us understand how you feel about a number of things. As I read each pair, tell me whether the first statement or the second statement comes closer to your own views, even if neither is exactly right. 'Immigrants today strengthen our country because of their hard work and talents' or 'Immigrants today are a burden on our country because they take our jobs, housing, and health care.' " The line shows the share responding "strengthen," with "don't know" responses excluded. Data source: Pew Research Center.

The same story holds for sexual orientation. Until relatively recently, many Americans viewed homosexuality as wrong. Public opinion has shifted dramatically since around 1990, as Figure 15.4 shows. A steadily rising share of Americans say they think that homosexuality should be accepted by society, homosexuals should have equal job opportunity rights, gay and lesbian sex should be legal, same-sex marriage should be legal, and gay and lesbian couples should be allowed to adopt children.

The driving force behind this rise in attitudes of tolerance and inclusion is material prosperity.[8] As people get richer, they tend to want more fairness in their society. Drawing on several decades of public opinion survey data from multiple countries, Ronald Inglehart and Christian Welzel have found that once people can be confident of survival and a decent standard of living, they tend to shift away from a worldview that emphasizes traditional sources of authority and traditional social roles. This is replaced by a "postmaterialist" or "emancipative" orientation, a key element of which is universalistic humanism, which deems all persons, including members of "outgroups," as equally worthy of rights, opportunities, and respect.

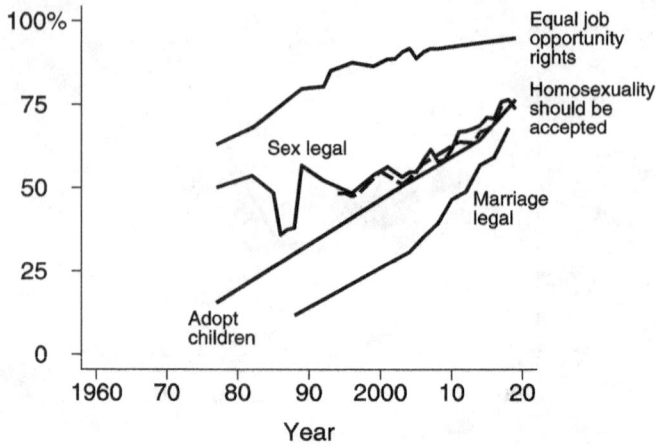

Figure 15.4 Tolerance and inclusion of homosexuals and homosexuality

Equal job opportunity rights question: "As you may know, there has been considerable discussion in the news regarding the rights of homosexual men and women. In general, do you think homosexuals should or should not have equal rights in terms of job opportunities?" Response options: yes should, no should not, depends, no opinion. "Depends" and "no opinion" responses are excluded here. Data source: Gallup, "Gay and Lesbian Rights," Gallup Historical Trends. Homosexuality should be accepted question: "I'm going to read you some pairs of statements that will help us understand how you feel about a number of things. As I read each pair, tell me whether the first statement or the second statement comes closer to your own views—even if neither is exactly right. 'Homosexuality should be accepted by society' or 'Homosexuality should be discouraged by society.'" Don't know responses are excluded. Data source: Pew Research Center. Sex legal question: "Do you think gay or lesbian relations between consenting adults should or should not be legal?" Response options: should be legal, should not be legal. Data source: Gallup, "Gay and Lesbian Rights," Gallup Historical Trends. Marriage legal question: "Do you agree or disagree: homosexual couples should have the right to marry one another?" Response options: strongly agree, agree, neither agree nor disagree, disagree, strongly disagree. The line shows the share who strongly agree or agree. Data source: General Social Survey, sda.berkeley.edu, series marhomo. Adopt children question: "Do you think gays and lesbians should or should not be allowed to adopt children?" No opinion responses are excluded. Data source: Gallup, "Gay and Lesbian Rights," Gallup Historical Trends.

Trust

Public opinion surveys often ask respondents whether "most people can be trusted" or "you need to be very careful in dealing with people." The share who choose the first option is treated by social scientists as a measure of the degree of generalized interpersonal trust in a society. In the United States, the level of interpersonal trust is comparatively low, and it has decreased sharply since the middle of the twentieth century. Figure 15.5 shows a sharp drop in trust between the mid-1960s and the early 1980s, with a continued but smaller decline since then.

As we see in the figure, the degree of interpersonal trust in the United States tracks very closely with the degree of trust in government. There is good reason to suspect this correlation is causal. Government is one of our most important institutions,

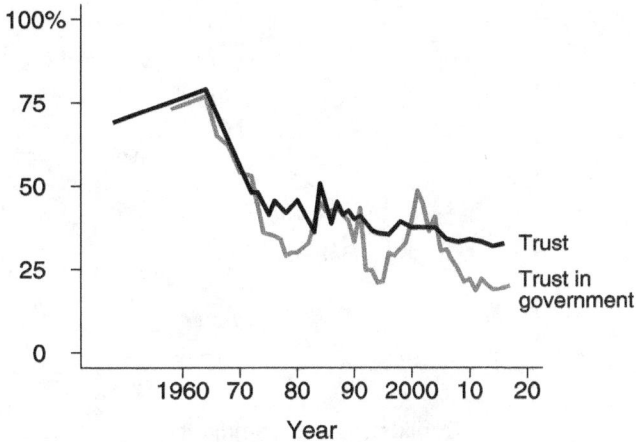

Figure 15.5 Interpersonal trust and trust in government

Share of adults. Trust in government question: "Do you trust the government in Washington to do what is right always, most of the time, some of the time, or never?" The line shows the share responding always or most of the time. Data source: Pew Research Center, "Public Trust in Government, 1958–2017," using data from assorted public opinion surveys. Trust question: "Generally speaking, would you say that most people can be trusted or that you can't be too careful in life?" Response options: can trust, cannot trust, depends. The line shows the share responding can trust, with depends responses omitted. Data sources: General Social Survey, sda.berkeley.edu, series trust; National Opinion Research Corp, cited in Robert E. Lane, "The Politics of Consensus in an Age of Affluence," *American Political Science Review*, 1965, p. 879. The correlation is +.85.

and over time it has played a growing, and increasingly visible, role in the lives of citizens. The degree to which people have trust or confidence in their government may therefore influence the degree to which they trust other individuals.

Americans' trust in their government was high through the 1950s. But it dropped sharply in the 1960s and 1970s due to the Vietnam War and the Watergate scandal, and since then it has decreased a bit more. The over-time pattern for generalized interpersonal trust is very similar.

The association across countries also is quite strong. As Figure 15.6 reveals, nations where confidence in government is greater tend to have higher levels of interpersonal trust.

In Figure 15.7 we see that the relatively low level of trust in the United States isn't representative. In a number of the rich democratic countries, more than 50 percent of the population think most people can be trusted, and in some it is closer to 75 percent.

Figure 15.7 also shows that in most of these countries there has been relatively little change in the degree of interpersonal trust over the past four decades. In this era of neoliberal, "greed is good" capitalism, people in some of the rich longstanding-democratic countries have become a little less trusting, but in most the level of trust has remained constant or even risen.

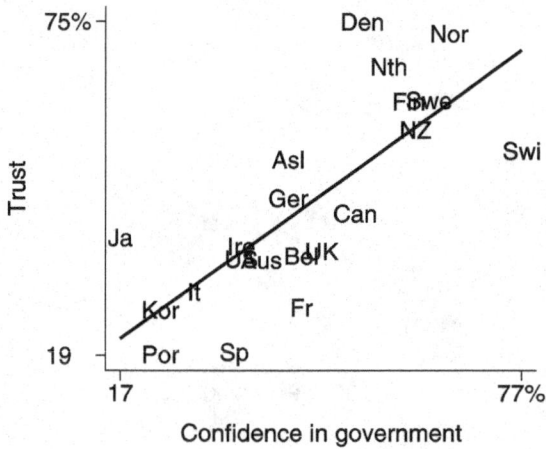

Figure 15.6 Confidence in government and interpersonal trust

Trust: Share of adults saying "most people can be trusted." The other response option is "You can never be too careful when dealing with others." Data source: World Values Survey. Confidence in government question: "Do you have confidence in the national government: yes or no?" Data source: Gallup World Poll, via the OECD. "Asl" is Australia; "Aus" is Austria. The line is a linear regression line. The correlation is +.76.

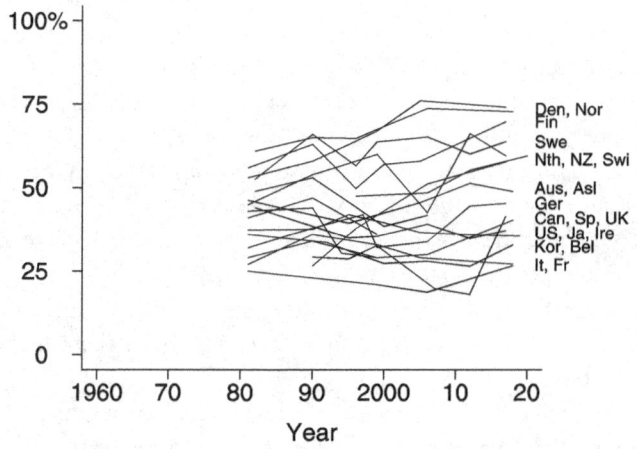

Figure 15.7 Interpersonal trust

Share of adults saying most people can be trusted. Question: "Generally speaking, would you say that most people can be trusted or that you need to be very careful in dealing with people?" Data source: World Values Survey. "Asl" is Australia;"Aus" is Austria.

Social Connections

Isolation and loneliness can be harmful. For evolutionary reasons, they may produce a subconscious search for threat, which can increase anxiety and depression, worsen physical health, and shorten lives.[9]

For at least 150 years, analysts and pundits have worried that modernity—or specifically *capitalist* modernity—would reduce social connections and ties. Better transportation, greater access to college, and the concentration of jobs in cities increases the incentive for people to move away from family and childhood friends. Cities are crowded, which can make it more difficult to develop lasting bonds. Technological advance provides more sources of distraction and access to individualized entertainment, reducing the time available for friends or family. As more women move into paid work, they have less time to socialize. And as government public insurance programs cushion more of the risks and hardships we face, voluntary organizations, a key source of interaction and community, may diminish in prevalence.

In the late 1800s and early 1900s, Fernand Tonnies, Max Weber, and Emile Durkheim described the shift from the "gemeinschaft" society of small villages, which emphasizes personal relationships and family, to the individualistic, atomistic "gesellschaft" society common in large cities. Since the middle of the twentieth century, a steady stream of analysts and commentators has concluded that the United States is in the midst of a loneliness epidemic. David Riesman's *The Lonely Crowd* in 1950, Vance Packard's *A Nation of Strangers* in the 1970s, Robert Putnam's *Bowling Alone* in 2000, and David Brooks's *New York Times* op-eds in the 2000s and 2010s are among the many contributions suggesting that personal connections and social supports have weakened.[10]

The United States may be a useful test case. We know that Americans' participation in civic organizations has declined since the mid-1960s. In addition, attendance at religious services, and religiosity more generally, have fallen during this period (they decreased earlier in most other affluent democratic nations). America's version of capitalism has tended to be a relatively individualistic one, especially in the period since 1980.[11] If there were a country and era in which we might expect to observe a rise in isolation and loneliness, this is it.

However, the best available data suggest that the conventional picture is wrong. In his 2011 book *Still Connected*, the most comprehensive and detailed examination of evidence on social connections and ties, Claude Fischer concluded as follows:

> The question that this book has posed is whether and how Americans' relationships with family and friends changed between 1970 and 2010. The short answer, based on a canvass of published research and available survey

data, is: not much. Some of the ways in which Americans engaged with people in their immediate circles changed, but the intimacy and support of close family and friendship ties stayed about the same. Few Americans were socially isolated, and the percentage of those who were did not increase. The number of family and friends with whom people reported being close stayed about the same. Americans got together with one another in set-aside home activities like dinner parties less often, but they communicated with one another electronically more often. Americans expected to get about as much help from family and friends as they had earlier. And American feelings about their social relationships stayed about the same or became more upbeat.[12]

A look at the available evidence since 2010 suggests no reason to revise Fischer's conclusion.[13]

Social Support

Since the mid-2000s the Gallup World Poll has regularly asked, "If you were in trouble, do you have relatives or friends you can count on to help you whenever you need them, or not?" As Figure 15.8 indicates, in about half of the rich democratic nations the share responding yes has decreased since the mid-2000s. However, this appears to owe mainly to the 2008–09 economic downturn.

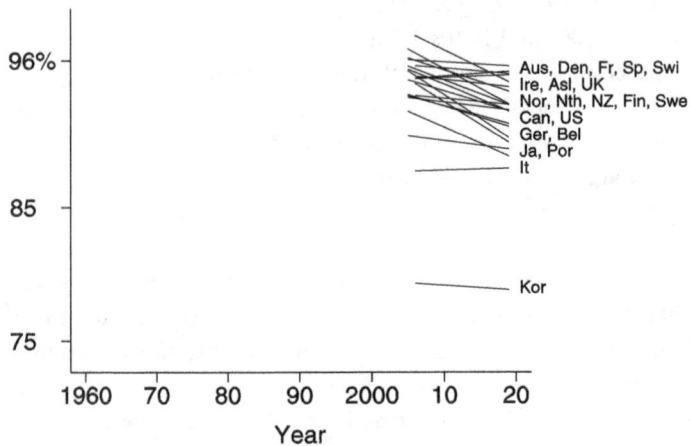

Figure 15.8 Social support
Share of adults responding yes to the question: "If you were in trouble, do you have relatives or friends you can count on to help you whenever you need them, or not?" The vertical axis doesn't begin at zero. Data source: Gallup World Poll, via the *World Happiness Report 2020*, online appendix. The lines are linear regression lines. "Asl" is Australia; "Aus" is Austria.

In any case, the levels remain quite high, with more than 85 percent of respondents in every rich democratic nation apart from South Korea saying they do have relatives or friends they can count on for help.

Unselfishness

Part of the genius of capitalism is that it takes selfish behavior and channels it into activities that end up benefiting everyone.[14] But in doing so capitalism doesn't just allow for selfishness; it encourages it. In the view of some proponents of democratic socialism, we can do better.

Generalized Altruism

Altruism consists of individuals putting the well-being of the larger group, or society, ahead of their self-interest. People do this, but typically in specific and limited instances rather than as a general behavior. A person may donate to a charity, let someone cut ahead of them in a checkout line at a store, and even fight in a war at considerable risk of getting killed. But most of us aren't guided by altruistic motives in our regular, ongoing actions.

In one conception of community, we would be. Andrew Levine suggests that "When the whole people rule, they are not motivated . . . by self-interest. Their votes do not register preferences for alternative outcomes in contention, but opinions as to what is best for the collective entity they freely constitute. In other words . . . individuals view themselves as indivisible parts of collective entities, and they make the interests of these collectivities their own."[15]

This seems unlikely to be a realistic goal for the not-too-distant future. And it might not be a good thing even if it were feasible. One finding from research on subjective well-being is that people tend to be happier in societies with "individualist" rather than "collectivist" value orientations. That is, they are happier in a context of cultural norms that encourage people to think of themselves as autonomous individuals as opposed to norms that encourage conformity.[16]

Communal Reciprocity

G.A. Cohen has suggested that socialism, by minimizing inequality of opportunity and limiting inequality of income and wealth, will facilitate a better way of interacting with our fellow humans: cooperation for its own sake. Cohen calls this "communal reciprocity."

Communal reciprocity is the antimarket principle according to which I serve you not because of what I can get in return by doing so but because you need or want my service, and you, for the same reason, serve me. Communal reciprocity is not the same thing as market reciprocity, since the market motivates productive contribution not on the basis of commitment to one's fellow human beings and a desire to serve them while being served by them, but on the basis of cash reward. The immediate motive to productive activity in a market society is (not always but) typically some mixture of greed and fear, in proportions that vary with the details of a person's market position and personal character. It is true that people can engage in market activity under other inspirations, but the motives of greed and fear are what the market brings to prominence, and that includes greed on behalf of, and fear for the safety of, one's family. Even when one's concerns are thus wider than those of one's mere self, the market posture is greedy and fearful in that one's opposite-number marketeers are predominantly seen as possible sources of enrichment, and as threats to one's success. These are horrible ways of seeing other people. . . . Within communal reciprocity, I produce in a spirit of commitment to my fellow human beings: I desire to serve them while being served by them, and I get satisfaction from each side of that equation.[17]

Cohen notes that communal reciprocity is the way people typically interact when on a camping trip. Equipment is shared. Tasks—setting up tents, preparing food, cleaning—are shared. No one gets too much more than anyone else. We tend to like this way of interacting.

The question is whether this mode of interaction and the pleasure it evokes is generalizable. I am skeptical. We have no particular reason to think that cooperation for its own sake would work well for most types of economic interaction, nor to presume that, if it did, this would make us happy.[18] The spirit of the camping trip is probably best considered a special case, much like parenting. Parenting is heavily infused with altruism but also extremely hierarchical. We wouldn't want to extend this to most other realms of life.

Would Democratic Socialism Be Better at Promoting Community?

Capitalism might discourage tolerance, inclusion, trust, personal interconnections, and social support. But the available evidence for the rich longstanding-democratic capitalist nations suggests that some of these elements of community have been getting better, and in some countries they are quite strong.

Some advocates of socialism want more. They would like most of our behavior to be unselfish, not just some of it. I suspect this isn't feasible, and I have doubts about whether it is even desirable.

16

A Livable Planet

Our economic system and our planetary system are now at war. What the climate needs to avoid collapse is a contraction in humanity's use of resources; what our economic model demands to avoid collapse is unfettered expansion. Only one of these sets of rules can be changed, and it's not the laws of nature.

—Naomi Klein[1]

Capitalism is overwhelmingly the main driver of planetary ecological collapse and it can't be reformed enough to save humans.

—Richard Smith[2]

We are causing the planet to warm, with potentially devastating consequences. Do we need democratic socialism in order to avert climate catastrophe?

We Are Warming the Planet

In various ways, but especially by burning fossil fuels, we've dramatically increased greenhouse gas emissions. If the amount of greenhouse gases emitted from earth is larger than natural processes can remove, it traps more infrared radiation (sunlight that bounces off the earth) in the atmosphere, leading to a rise in temperature. Also, warm air holds more water vapor than cold air, and water vapor causes additional trapping of heat.

As Figure 16.1 shows, carbon dioxide (CO_2) emissions have increased steadily since 1750, when the industrial revolution began, and the rise has been especially pronounced since 1950. As carbon dioxide emissions have increased, the amount of carbon dioxide in the atmosphere has increased. We have direct measurement of CO_2 atmospheric concentration only since 1959, but data from ice core drilling in Antarctica suggest that in the 800,000 years prior to 1750, it never exceeded 300 ppm (parts per million). Between 1750 and 1959 it rose from 280 to 316. As we see in Figure 16.2, between 1959 and 2018 it increased from 316 to 409.[3]

Carbon dioxide isn't the only problematic greenhouse gas. Methane and nitrous oxide play a role too. Here a major contributor is the raising of animals for

Would Democratic Socialism Be Better?. Lane Kenworthy, Oxford University Press. © Lane Kenworthy 2022.
DOI: 10.1093/oso/9780197636800.003.0016

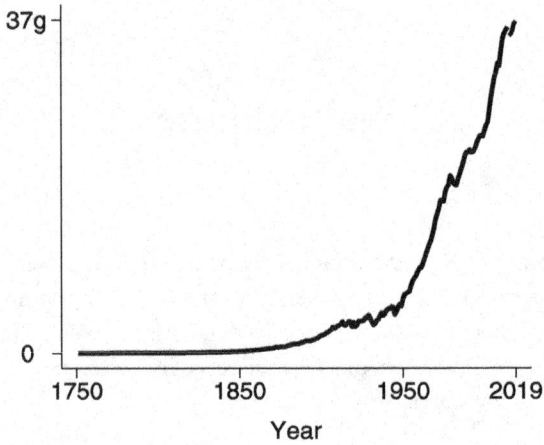

Figure 16.1 Carbon dioxide emissions

"g" = gigatonnes. Data source: Carbon Dioxide Information Analysis Center, cdiac.ess-dive.lbl.gov; Global Carbon Project.

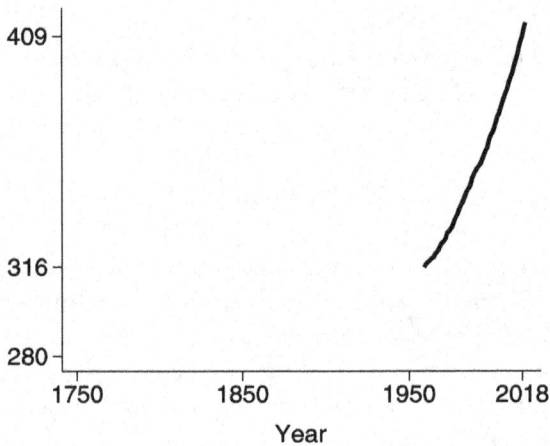

Figure 16.2 Carbon dioxide concentration in the atmosphere

Parts per million. 280 is the estimated level in 1750. Data source: Earth System Research Laboratory, National Oceanic and Atmospheric Administration, US Department of Commerce, esrl.noaa.gov/gmd/ccgg/trends.

food, which accounts for approximately 15 percent of all greenhouse gas emissions.[4] That's roughly the same as all cars, trucks, airplanes, and ships combined.[5] Methane concentration in the atmosphere has increased sharply since scientists began measuring it in the mid-1980s. The concentration of methane is much

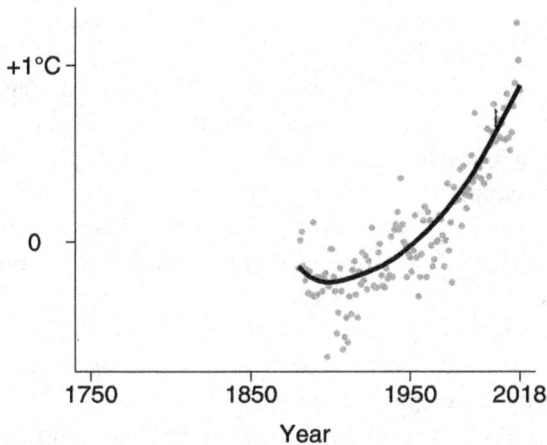

Figure 16.3 Earth's average temperature

Difference from the 1901–2000 average. Degrees Celsius. Land and ocean. The line is a loess curve. Data source: National Centers for Environmental Information, National Oceanic and Atmospheric Administration, ncdc.noaa.gov/cag/time-series/global.

lower than of carbon dioxide, but methane's potency as a greenhouse gas is about 30 times greater.[6]

The result of rising greenhouse gas concentration in the atmosphere has been an increase in the planet's temperature. Figure 16.3 shows direct measurements of temperature, which began in 1880. Average temperature has risen sharply, particularly since 1950. Indirect measures going back much farther in time suggest the same conclusion.[7]

Could the observed temperature rise be a result of something else? That's unlikely. Computer simulations that project temperature patterns in scenarios with little or no human emission of greenhouse gases don't come close to matching the earth's actual temperature patterns. When the simulations add human-generated greenhouse gases, they closely match the observed temperature patterns.[8]

The most thorough survey of the evidence is by the Intergovernmental Panel on Climate Change (IPCC). Its conclusion is that "It is extremely likely that human influence has been the dominant cause of the observed warming since the mid-20th century."[9]

The Consequences Are Potentially Dire

Climate change is likely to have an array of effects. Many are difficult to project, both because the climate is a complex system and because it isn't clear how much progress we will make in slowing or reversing the carbonization of the atmosphere.

In the absence of quick and effective action to reduce greenhouse gas emissions, warming is likely to have damaging effects on health via, among other things, heat waves, urban smog, lack of access to water, and displacement.[10] In the United States, for example, the number of 100-degree-or-more days is projected to increase significantly almost everywhere, and by the end of this century a good bit of the country will have summer weather similar to today's Texas and Arizona.[11] In some parts of the world, things will be worse. The World Health Organization projects that, in the absence of action to slow climate change, by 2050 an additional 250,000 people (0.002 percent of the world's population) will die each year directly due to greater heat.[12]

Climate change also will increase the frequency and intensity of weather events and weather-related events—storms (hurricanes, typhoons, tornadoes), floods, droughts, fires.

The most significant impact of warming could come via melting of the Greenland and West Antarctic ice sheets, each of which has enough ice to raise sea levels by 15 to 20 feet. A significant rise in sea level could threaten hundreds of millions of people who live in coastal areas. The United Nations estimates that by 2050 as many as 1 billion people, or 10 percent of the world's population, may be climate migrants.[13] Predicting how much the two ice sheets will melt and what impact that will have is extremely difficult. In a 2013 report, the IPCC concluded that melting from the two ice sheets may cause a sea level rise of 1 to 3 feet by the year 2100. Since then, scientists have discovered that ice loss in the Greenland and West Antarctic ice sheets has been faster in recent years than previously thought and that a large glacier in the East Antarctic ice sheet is now vulnerable to melting. According to one knowledgeable observer, these recent findings "have led top climatologists to conclude that we are likely headed toward what used to be the high-end of projected global sea-level rise this century (i.e., 4 to 5 feet) and that the worst-case scenarios where humanity fails to take aggressive action to cut greenhouse gas emissions are considerably higher than that."[14]

Most ominously, Gernot Wagner and Martin Weitzman estimate that in the absence of significant policy change there is perhaps a one in ten chance that the globe's average temperature will rise by 6°C or more.[15] The consequences could be quite grim, as David Wallace-Wells explains:

The earth has experienced five mass extinctions . . . , each so complete a wiping of the fossil record that it functioned as an evolutionary reset, the planet's phylogenetic tree first expanding, then collapsing, at intervals, like a lung: 86 percent of all species dead, 450 million years ago; 70 million years later, 75 percent; 125 million years later, 96 percent; 50 million years later, 80 percent; 135 million years after that, 75 percent again. Unless you are a teenager, you probably read in your high school textbooks that these extinctions were the result of asteroids. In fact, all but the one that killed the dinosaurs involved climate change produced by greenhouse gas. The most notorious was 250 million years ago; it began when carbon dioxide warmed the planet by five degrees Celsius, accelerated when that warming triggered the release of methane, another greenhouse gas, and ended with all but a sliver of life on Earth dead.[16]

What Do We Need to Do?

Many climate scientists believe we should aim for an increase in average temperature of no more than 1.5°C or at most 2°C (it's already risen about 1°C). Not too long ago, knowledgeable observers calculated that this would require reducing greenhouse gas emissions by more than half by 2050 and to zero by 2100.[17] More recent calculations suggest we need to move faster, cutting emissions in half by 2030 and to zero by 2050.[18]

How can we do it? Advocates frequently emphasize personal behaviors and lifestyles, but the key will be to change large-scale actors, institutions, and systems.[19]

1. Shift from fossil fuel energy to clean energy. Government could simply mandate the phase-out of fossil fuel energy sources by a particular date, but the most common policy tools here are carbon taxes and cap-and-trade programs. If necessary, government could purchase a majority stake in fossil fuel companies and rapidly reduce coal, oil, and gas production.[20]

National and local governments can act alone, but better would be an international agreement that reduces emissions in most or all countries. Efforts over the past several decades haven't been very successful, though the 2015 Paris Climate Accord offers some grounds for optimism. An alternative to voluntary agreements, which are vulnerable to free riding, is the idea of a "climate club." According to William Nordhaus, "Under the club rules, participating countries would undertake harmonized but costly emissions reductions.... Countries who are outside the club—and do not share in the burden of emissions reductions—are penalized."[21]

Humans currently use about 160,000 terawatt hours of energy per year. There is more than enough energy available from solar and wind, the two leading nongreenhouse gas ("clean") energy resources, to provide this amount and more.[22] The challenge is getting it to everyone throughout the year and throughout the day. For that, we need further improvement in storage and batteries. An important advantage, however, particularly for solar energy, is that it can be generated close to where it is needed—on the roofs of buildings, houses, and parking lots. And because it is much more efficient than fossil fuel energy sources, one estimate concludes that "without changing the size of our homes, or our cars, or fundamentally changing the fabric of our lives, a fully electrified energy economy using non-carbon fuel sources would require less than half of the total amount of energy we use today."[23]

The remainder of the needed clean energy can be provided by a mix of biofuels, geothermal, and nuclear.

2. Geoengineering. We can try to alter the earth or its biosphere. One approach aims to limit the warming of the planet. The main idea here is to deflect more sunlight, for example by injecting large quantities of aerosols into the stratosphere. This is at best a partial approach, as it wouldn't stop or even slow carbonization, but it might buy us some time. A second approach is to actually remove carbon from the atmosphere. In a pair of reports issued in 2015, the US National Academy of Sciences concluded that while geoengineering efforts are worth further exploration, "There is no substitute for dramatic reductions in the emissions of carbon dioxide and other greenhouse gases to mitigate the negative consequences of climate change."[24]

3. Research. A rapid shift to clean energy sources is feasible with existing technology. But this problem is so big, and political obstacles to rapid decarbonization are so formidable, that it makes sense to invest heavily in research and development of new energy sources, new methods of storage and delivery, and more.[25]

Grounds for Optimism

There are some encouraging technological developments.[26] In the 2010s, the cost of solar panels fell by nearly 90 percent and the cost of wind turbines by 60 percent. Clean energy is now cheaper than 40 percent of coal plants worldwide and most natural gas plants. Partly as a result, more than 80 percent of all new electricity around the world in 2019 and 2020 came from clean sources, and that figure is projected to reach 95 percent in the early 2020s.

The cost of batteries for electric cars is expected to reach parity with internal combustion engines by the early 2020s. And Toyota has developed a new solid-state (rather than lithium-ion) battery for electric vehicles that will allow a car to travel 300-plus miles on a charge that takes 10 minutes. Sales of internal-combustion vehicles have been declining since 2017. Fiat, Ford (in Europe), and Mercedes have pledged to sell only zero-emission vehicles by 2030, General Motors by 2035, and Honda by 2040.

Climate Trace, a coalition of nonprofits and businesses, uses artificial intelligence, machine learning, and satellite image processing to measure worldwide greenhouse gas emissions in real time, with updates every 6 hours. This kind of accurate, up-to-date information should help voters, activists, and other actors to monitor governments and corporations and apply pressure where appropriate.

There also are some hopeful signs on the political front.[27] Signatories to the 2015 Paris Climate Accord, including 197 nations, pledged to take action to hold "the increase in the global average temperature to well below 2°C above preindustrial levels and to pursue efforts to limit the temperature increase to 1.5°C above preindustrial levels." The Accord didn't commit any country to particular actions. Nor did it specify rewards or punishments.

A small but growing number of countries have passed laws requiring zero net greenhouse gas emissions ("carbon neutrality") by 2050: Norway in 2016; Sweden in 2017; France, New Zealand, and the United Kingdom in 2019; Canada, Japan, and South Korea in 2020. In 2020 China's government pledged to reach carbon neutrality by 2060. In 2021, the US president issued an executive order instructing the country to reach zero net emissions by 2050. In all, 125 nations, which together account for more than two-thirds of global emissions, either have adopted or are debating a goal of net zero emissions by the middle of the century.

A small but growing number of US states have passed laws requiring large reductions in greenhouse gas emissions by 2050. In 2019, California, which has the world's fifth-largest economy, passed a law mandating zero net carbon emissions in the state's electricity sector by 2045, and its governor issued an executive order requiring zero net emissions across the entire economy by the same year. In 2019, New York state passed a law mandating 85 percent reduction in greenhouse gas emissions (from 1990 levels) by 2050.

In 2019, the Netherlands' Supreme Court ruled that the European Convention on Human Rights requires the Dutch government to significantly reduce the country's greenhouse gas emissions. This was the first time a court has required a nation to take action against climate change. In 2021, Germany's Federal Constitutional Court required the German government to make its climate law more aggressive in order to comply with commitments made in the 2015 Paris Climate Accord.

As I just noted, governments in countries that currently account for about two-thirds of global emissions have agreed to or are discussing pledges to reach net zero emissions by mid-century. Climate Action Tracker estimates that if all of these nations actually meet the targets, warming will reach 2.1 degrees. The organization also estimates that under current policies warming will reach 2.9 degrees. That's higher than we want, but it's an improvement compared to the estimate as of 2015, which was 3.7 degrees.[28]

Would Democratic Socialism Be Better at Achieving Climate Stability?

Proponents of democratic socialism offer two arguments for why it would help us to save the planet and our species. The first, expressed in the quote from

Naomi Klein at the beginning of this chapter, is that reducing greenhouse gas emissions requires reducing economic activity and output, whereas capitalism fosters, and perhaps requires, continuous growth.[29] This seems wrongheaded, because reducing greenhouse gas emissions is compatible with continued expansion of output. As I noted earlier, we already have the capability to generate the amount of energy we currently use and more from clean sources. What we need isn't a significant reduction in energy use but rather a shift to clean energy. Indeed, there is a case that continued economic growth will be helpful in achieving reduced greenhouse gas emissions, because people are more likely to support altruistic rather than selfish policies when the economy is advancing.[30]

The second argument for socialism is a political one. It says government's dependence on a healthy economy encourages it to perpetuate the existing fossil-fuel-based economic structure. In Paul Adler's words: "Government could tax the polluters to deter them, or it could regulate their activity to reduce the pollution. Unfortunately, however, government's subservience makes it incapable of assuming this responsibility. In a capitalist society, government is reluctant to impose the necessary taxes or regulations on business."[31] Or fossil fuel companies will inevitably have a great deal of political sway in a capitalist democracy, and they will use that influence to block policies that hasten a transition to clean sources of energy.[32]

There is no question that this has already happened.[33] But we also have compelling evidence that this problem isn't intractable. Cigarette producers had similar interests and incentives, and they succeeded for a while in blocking passage of policies that would reduce cigarette smoking, but in the end their efforts were overcome. As noted above, already a small but growing number of the rich capitalist democratic nations have enacted a carbon tax, a cap-and-trade program, or a mandate for the economy to get to zero net greenhouse gas emissions by the middle of this century.[34]

The central problem with advocating for socialism as a solution to climate change, however, is one of timing. Climate experts now tend to believe we need to cut greenhouse gas emissions in half by 2030 and to zero by 2050. The probability that any of the rich democratic nations will shift to socialism that quickly is very low. Whether socialism would help or not is therefore irrelevant. As Bhaskar Sunkara has rightly put it: "Fighting climate change can't wait until 'after the revolution,' and we'll have to find a way to shape capitalist investment priorities and win sweeping reforms in the here and now."[35]

17

Would Democratic Socialism Be Better Than Social Democratic Capitalism?

What can we conclude about whether, and if so in what ways, a modern democratic humane socialism would be superior to capitalism, and in particular to social democratic capitalism?

Democratic Socialism Might Turn Out to Be Better, but There Is Good Reason for Skepticism

Would democratic socialism be better at reducing or ending poverty in rich nations? The case that it would is weak. Social democratic capitalism has done well at boosting living standards for the least well off, even in the challenging post-1970s era. Moreover, the rich longstanding-democratic countries could eliminate poverty by increasing the generosity of their public social programs or by enacting a universal basic income or a negative income tax. Given the history of welfare state expansion over the past one hundred years, this seems doable within capitalism.

Would democratic socialism be better at reducing or ending poverty in the rest of the world? Here too the case that it would is weak. First, extreme poverty has decreased sharply in the era of global capitalism that began in the 1970s. Second, we don't know enough about how to achieve sustained economic growth in poor countries to be confident that socialism would help. Third, increased migration—ideally via fully open borders—clearly would help, and it might be more difficult to enact under socialism due to working-class opposition to immigration.

Would democratic socialism be better at achieving a plentiful supply of decent jobs? I see little reason to think so. Capitalism has proved capable of producing high employment rates. It doesn't look as though this requires a lot of government employment. And workers' control (worker cooperatives), a key feature of socialism in some proposals, might well reduce employment. The available data suggest that work conditions, job security, working time, and job satisfaction in capitalist economies have been getting better, not worse.

Would Democratic Socialism Be Better?. Lane Kenworthy, Oxford University Press. © Lane Kenworthy 2022.
DOI: 10.1093/oso/9780197636800.003.0017

Would democratic socialism be better at achieving rapid economic growth? I see no grounds for confidence that it would. We have very little understanding of what causes faster or slower growth in rich democratic nations. And the mechanisms through which socialism's advocates posit that it will boost economic growth—more government steering of investment, less income inequality, reduced frequency and depth of financial crises—have no compelling evidentiary support.

Would democratic socialism be better at achieving inclusive growth? Pay growth under socialism is unlikely to be faster than what we see in the contemporary Nordic countries with their strong labor unions. Would pay growth under socialism be better than under a capitalism with weak unions but with periodic tight labor markets, steadily rising sector-specific and occupation-specific minimum wages, widespread profit sharing, and an employment-conditional earnings subsidy that is indexed to GDP per capita? Perhaps, but it's reasonable to be skeptical.

Do we need democratic socialism in order to get an expansive supply of public goods and services? The record of existing affluent capitalist democracies, particularly the Nordic countries, suggests not.

Would democratic socialism be better at achieving effective, affordable healthcare for all? I see no reason to think so. Among the rich democratic capitalist nations, those with an "insurance funds" healthcare system have achieved similar results in life expectancy, healthy life expectancy, and cost growth as countries with a "single payer" system. Moreover, a country can have socialist healthcare—single payer, with government also employing most medical providers—in an otherwise capitalist economy. The Nordic countries and some others already do.

Would democratic socialism do a better job at ensuring helpful finance? I think that's doubtful. Capitalist financial systems tend to underfund disadvantaged individuals, businesses, and communities; they can potentially block valuable government policies; and they sometimes cause economic crises. But each of these problems can be remedied without abandoning capitalism, and nations with a social democratic capitalist orientation have made significant progress in doing so. And a socialist financial system is unlikely to be as effective at funding startups that unexpectedly yield improvements in living standards and quality of life.

Would democratic socialism be better at ensuring truly democratic politics? The hypothesis that it would stems from the notion that in capitalism those with more money use that money to buy disproportionate influence on policy making. Evidence from the United States and from other affluent nations suggests that those with higher incomes do indeed tend to get what they want from government more often than those with lower incomes. However, neither the over-time pattern in America nor the pattern across rich democratic nations suggests that reducing inequality of income or wealth is the key to reducing inequality of political influence. The real gains in enhancing democracy may come from reforms such as improving education, expanding economic opportunity, revitalizing civic organizations, increasing access to voting, expanding public campaign financing, making use of deliberative citizen assemblies, and others that can be done within capitalism.

Would democratic socialism be better at achieving workplace democracy? Certainly yes, if it makes workplace democracy mandatory. But I'm not sure the normative case for worker cooperatives, with workers having full control over decision making, is more compelling than the case for what currently exists in the Nordic countries—employees electing half the board of directors, labor unions negotiating wages and benefits, works councils negotiating work conditions, and some direct employee participation in firm decision making. We probably don't want to mandate that all firms be worker cooperatives, just as we wouldn't want to mandate one-person-one-vote decision making within families. We could facilitate workplace democracy, without requiring it, via a law that allows any firm's workers, if a majority of them vote in favor, to buy out the owner(s) and turn the company into a cooperative.

Would democratic socialism be better at achieving democratic control over the economy as a whole? Possibly. But most rich democratic capitalist nations already have this in principle. And regularized discussion and negotiation between representatives of labor, business, and government—"concertation"—provides an additional dimension in countries that use it.

Would democratic socialism be better at reducing income inequality? Very likely yes. That's particularly true for income inequality between the top (e.g., the top 1 percent) and everyone else. While many progressives believe income inequality has harmful effects on health, economic growth, democracy, happiness, and other outcomes we value, there is little empirical basis for this conclusion. Still, the normative case for modest levels of income and wealth inequality is strong, so it would be better if there were less inequality than there is in the contemporary United States.

However, I'm not convinced that reducing economic inequality should be high on our list of priorities. In a society where many of life's core needs—housing, childcare, schooling, healthcare, a job, retirement income, eldercare, and much more—are assured by government programs, inequality of income and wealth isn't likely to cause much consternation. We can see this in today's Nordic countries, which have comparatively high levels of wealth inequality but also enviable quality of life and high levels of subjective well-being.

Would democratic socialism be better at achieving gender and racial equality? It surely isn't needed for gender equality. In most of the affluent capitalist nations, women have surpassed men in educational attainment and life expectancy, and they are at least equally happy. In employment, pay, and top-level positions in business and politics there is still a gap in men's favor, but in the leading countries, including the social democratic capitalist ones, that gap is now quite small.

The toughest case for between-group equality is probably Blacks and whites in the United States. Here we see persistent inequality on many outcomes yet also significant reductions in inequality on nearly all of them, including education, employment, pay, health, happiness, and top-level corporate and political positions. Could democratic socialism help? Maybe, but the evidence suggests no reason to think it is necessary.

Would democratic socialism be better at fostering community? While critics posit that capitalism discourages tolerance, inclusion, trust, personal interconnections, and social support, the available indicators for the rich longstanding-democratic capitalist nations suggest that in certain respects things have been getting better, and in some countries they are quite good. Some advocates of socialism want more. They would like most of our behavior, not just some of it, to be unselfish. I'm not sure this is feasible, and I have doubts about whether it is desirable.

Would democratic socialism be better at minimizing climate change? A common version of this hypothesis says that only with socialism can we achieve a sizable reduction in economic output. But we don't need to reduce economic output in order to reduce greenhouse gas emissions. In fact, doing so might be counterproductive, because people are more likely to support altruistic policies when the economy is advancing. A second version of the hypothesis says that in a capitalist democracy fossil fuel companies will block any attempt to move aggressively toward clean sources of energy. However, this has already begun to change—most notably in the Nordic countries and California, but in other nations as well. In any case, a transition to socialism wouldn't come soon enough to help us address the climate problem, which must be more or less solved within the next 30 years.

To sum up: Democratic socialism would boost firm-level economic democracy, but perhaps only by requiring it, and I doubt we want to require it. Socialism very likely would reduce income and wealth inequality, but in a society with expansive public goods and services I'm not certain this would be important to many people. For other outcomes, I don't see a compelling reason to conclude that democratic socialism would be better than social democratic capitalism.

Should You Favor Democratic Socialism?

If you believe strongly in workplace democracy and are willing to mandate it, or if you attach a high priority to low levels of income and wealth inequality, then possibly yes.[1] Otherwise, you might reasonably prefer to opt for social democratic capitalism, with which we have extensive experience, rather than take a chance on a system that is, to this point in history, untested.[2]

For some of the outcomes where I conclude that democratic socialism is unlikely to do better than capitalism, that's because I've assumed capitalism can be improved. For instance, in some of the rich democratic nations—perhaps most of them—labor unions have been weakening and may never regain their former strength, making it difficult to secure steadily rising wages for ordinary workers. I've pointed out that there are ways to compensate for this, including tight labor markets, statutory occupation-specific minimum wages, profit sharing, and an earnings subsidy indexed to GDP per capita, but there is no guarantee that countries such as the United States will in fact adopt the needed policies. Wouldn't democratic socialism be better at delivering growth that's inclusive in such a case? Yes, it might. The problem is that if advocates of inclusive growth can't get a majority of the population and policy makers to support these relatively modest reforms, how can they convince a majority to switch to socialism?

We Might End Up with Democratic Socialism Even if It Isn't Better

Even if democratic socialism isn't likely to be better than social democratic capitalism, we might go there anyway.

One possible path is that capitalism implodes. The prediction of capitalist collapse has a lengthy history, dating back at least to Marx and Engels.[3] A good recent expression is by Wolfgang Streeck in his book *How Will Capitalism End?*[4] Streeck sees a number of signs that suggest capitalism is in trouble: Economic growth has slowed. Government debt has been rising. Income and wealth inequality have increased. There's been a shift from Keynesian capitalism to Hayekian capitalism. We see unchecked fraud and corruption in the financial sector. Globalization increasingly renders national governments impotent, and it forces governments to reduce tax rates and to make tax systems less progressive, generating frustration among the middle class. Rising government debt (coupled with demographic change) encourages cuts in public services and public insurance. Unions are on the decline. In some countries, wages have been stagnant and incomes have grown slowly. Government decisions increasingly are turned over to nonelected agencies (e.g., independent central banks). There is growing political dissatisfaction, manifested in declining voter turnout and the rise of "populist" parties. With the United States no longer able to serve as a stable financial anchor, the global economic system is increasingly anarchic.

Capitalism has always had the potential to self-destruct, particularly by exploiting people and places too ruthlessly in search of financial gain.[5] For a few decades after World War II, a peculiar set of institutions and norms and strong economic growth dampened this tendency. But the tide began to turn in the 1970s, and, in Streeck's view, "capitalist progress has by now more or less destroyed any agency that could stabilize it by limiting it."[6]

Streeck isn't alone. The International Panel on Social Progress concluded recently that "contemporary capitalism is facing a profound multidimensional crisis (financial, economic, social, ecological crises) that undermines the main sources of wealth creation—labor and nature—to the point that it can be characterized as a civilizational crisis with a potentially catastrophic outcome."[7] Some other distinguished social scientists have come to a similar conclusion.[8]

How does Streeck envision capitalism ending? "What is most likely to happen," he says, "is a continuous accumulation of small and not-so-small dysfunctions. . . . In the process, the parts of the whole will fit together less and less; frictions of all kinds will multiply; unanticipated consequences will spread, along ever more obscure lines of causation. Uncertainty will proliferate; crises of every sort—of legitimacy, productivity or both—will follow each other in quick succession while predictability and governability will decline further (as they have for decades now). Eventually, the myriad provisional fixes devised for short-term crisis management will collapse."[9]

My own take is that this diagnosis identifies some genuinely dysfunctional elements of certain versions of contemporary capitalism. Yet if we look at how well the system works in the Nordic countries and some others in western Europe, at how much living standards have improved in recent decades for people in poorer parts of the world, at how much life expectancy has risen, at the degree to which tolerance and inclusion have increased, and at the sustained high levels of life satisfaction, I find it difficult to share this pessimism.[10]

Moreover, even if this "slow collapse" scenario were to come to pass, we shouldn't necessarily expect capitalism to be replaced by democratic socialism. At least as likely to emerge from the ashes, perhaps more so, is a nondemocratic version of capitalism, such as China's.[11]

Another potential path to democratic socialism is a slow, gradual transition to greater public ownership. In a number of contemporary affluent democratic nations, most people who work in education and healthcare are public employees. At the moment, these two sectors account for about 20 percent of GDP. It's conceivable that this share will rise significantly over time. If these sectors continue to be mainly government-run, these economies might thereby evolve, unintentionally, into ones in which most economic activity is in the public sector.

A more intentional evolutionary route also is conceivable.[12] In the early 1980s, a Social Democratic government in Sweden enacted a plan to gradually transfer stock shares in large companies to a "wage-earner fund" controlled by labor unions. Over a period of several decades, this would have shifted a considerable degree of ownership to this fund.[13] The program was abandoned by the subsequent government, but it's not hard to imagine something like this getting enacted in one of the affluent democratic nations in the not-too-distant future. Because the transition in ownership occurs slowly, it would be barely noticeable, especially to ordinary citizens. It might, therefore, have a decent shot at persisting despite shifts in partisan control of the government.

The likelihood of left and center-left parties wanting to pursue something like this is heightened by the fact that these parties have struggled electorally in recent decades. One reason for their struggles is that they've been forced to position themselves as defenders of the status quo. In the Nordic countries, in particular, the success achieved by the social democratic capitalist model has left these parties with little to propose by way of changes.

In this context, something like a wage-earner fund proposal, or perhaps a law that makes it easier for employees to buy the company they work for, may have considerable appeal to such parties. It would give them a mission for advancing to a next stage of humanistic capitalism. We see glimpses of this possibility even in the United States. In his 2020 campaign for the Democratic Party's presidential nomination, Bernie Sanders proposed a version of a wage-earner fund plan.[14]

A Social Democratic Capitalist Future Probably Would Be a Very Good One

I have no special insight into what our societies or even our species will look like far into the future. But over the coming half century, my best guess is that the dominant socioeconomic model among the world's rich democratic nations will be social democratic capitalism. It has proven effective at reducing poverty, economic insecurity, and inequality of opportunity. And it gets these desirable outcomes without sacrificing any of the multiple other things we want in a good society, from freedom to economic growth to health, happiness, and more.[15]

In recent decades the Nordic countries have enhanced, adjusted, and refined the social democratic capitalist model, and other rich democratic nations have been moving toward it. Even the United States has advanced slowly but fairly steadily toward social democratic capitalism, and likely will continue to do so.[16] As nations that currently are poor or middle-income get richer, some of them—perhaps many—also will embrace social democratic capitalism.

The social democratic capitalism of the not-too-distant future might evolve to include more economic democracy and more public ownership of firms. This would bring it closer to what contemporary democratic socialists would like. But even if there is no such evolution, that might be okay. Social democratic capitalism isn't perfect, but it is quite good.

Acknowledgments

For helpful comments on earlier drafts, I thank John Campbell, Alex Hicks, Jeff Manza, John Myles, Jelle Visser, and the Oxford University Press reviewers.

This book, like nearly all of my work, builds on a large body of research on the world's rich longstanding-democratic capitalist nations. I thanked a lengthy (though surely incomplete) list of scholars and organizations in a book published two years ago, *Social Democratic Capitalism*, so I won't repeat the names here. But my gratitude continues.

I also owe a debt to an array of scholars—particularly Noam Chomsky, G.A. Cohen, Jon Elster, Janos Kornai, Alec Nove, John Roemer, David Stark, and Erik Olin Wright—who have inspired me, at various points over the past four decades, to think seriously about alternatives to capitalism.

I'm grateful to David McBride at Oxford University Press for his continued interest and support.

I've been fortunate throughout my life to have a wonderfully large, interesting, fun, supportive family—immediate and extended. Thank you Kim, Mia, Hannah, Noah, Josh, Tom, Suzan, Randy, Owen, Lauren, Lee, Amy, Asa, Carroll, Mary, Wilmer, Fran, Leonard, Dorothy, Ralph, Carroll, George, Eloise, Ellie, Marti, Jonathan, Will, Matthew, Trey, Connor, Katherine, Lizzie, Henry, George, Mariel, Bryce, Jenna, Jasper, Adeline, Adele, Mark, Michelle, Jen, Greg, Carol, Tammy, Mike, Maureen, Josh, Hector, Aaron, Gina, Adam, Mikaela, Katie, Megan, Max, Emma, and Ella.

Notes

Chapter 1

1. Newport 2018; Hartig 2019; Younis 2019; Meyerson 2020.
2. *Jacobin* magazine; *Catalyst* magazine; *Current Affairs* magazine; People's Policy Project.
3. Elizabeth Bruenig. See Bruenig 2018.
4. Aronoff, Dreier, and Kazin 2020, p. 5; *Wikipedia*, "Democratic Socialists of America."
5. Kornai 1983; Nove 1983.
6. Milanovic 2019.
7. Przeworski 1985; McCarthy 2020.
8. For recent examples, see Sunkara 2016; Chibber 2019; Robinson 2019; Wright 2019; Bridge 2021; Thier 2021.
9. Kenworthy 2020.
10. Kenworthy 2020, ch. 2.
11. Kenworthy 2020, pp. 39–40.
12. See also Garritzmann, Häusermann, and Palier 2021; Kautto and Kuitto 2021.
13. A household at the tenth percentile isn't quite the least well-off, but below that point in the income distribution we worry about data quality.
14. Chapter 8 ("More Public Goods and Services").
15. Kenworthy 2020, ch. 2.
16. Berlin 1958; Sen 1999, 2009; Nussbaum 2011; Hick and Burchardt 2016; Robeyns 2018.
17. Renwick 2017.
18. Partanen 2016. See also Schall 2016, ch. 3.
19. Another measure of opportunity is intergenerational mobility, and social democratic capitalism correlates positively with this too. See Kenworthy 2020, ch. 2.
20. Bentham 1843; Layard 2005; Murray 2012.
21. Panitch 2014, 2020; Sunkara 2019; Wright 2019, ch. 3; Piketty 2020, ch. 11; Kuttner 2021b, 2021c.
22. Chapter 13 ("Less Economic Inequality").
23. Low-end income trends in the Nordic countries also matched or bettered those of other rich democratic nations. See chapter 2 ("An End to Poverty in Rich Countries").
24. Employment trends in the Nordic countries also matched or bettered those of other rich democratic nations. See chapter 4 ("More Jobs").
25. Life satisfaction trends in the Nordic countries also matched or bettered those of other rich democratic nations. See Kenworthy 2022b, "Happiness" chapter.
26. Kenworthy 2020, ch. 3.
27. Palier 2010; Hemerijck 2013, 2017; Andersen et al. 2015; Birnbaum et al. 2017.

28. Kenworthy 2020, ch. 8.
29. For an earlier debate on this question, see Korpi 1982; Esping-Andersen 1985; Przeworski 1985; Pontusson 1987; Steinmo 1988.
30. Here, for instance, is Nathan Robinson in a book titled *Why You Should Be a Socialist*: "The socialist is a utopian. They might believe that small reforms over a period of centuries are the best way of getting to the utopia, but they're fundamentally unsatisfied by the idea that the highest human ambition is simply to turn the United States into circa 2019 Scandinavia. It might be that we should borrow Scandinavian social policies, such as generous paid parental leave and universal healthcare. But this is not the dream. The dream is transformative. The dream is to see a total elimination of exploitation and hierarchy and a change in the structure of who owns capital. The dream is a decommodified life, where people have ownership over their work and cooperate for the common good." Robinson 2019, ch. 5.
31. For exceptions, see Devine et al. 2012; Hahnel 2012, 2021; Adler 2019.
32. Harrington 1978, 1989; Walzer 1978; Kenworthy 1990; Miliband 1994; Roemer 1994; Roemer et al. 1996; Burczak 2006; Wright 2010, 2019; Schweickart 2011; Cumbers 2012, 2020; O'Neill and Williamson 2012; Wolff 2012; Malleson 2014; Auerbach 2016; Day 2018; Gindin 2018; Panitch and Gindin 2018; Adler 2019; Bastani 2019; Blakeley 2019; Chomsky 2019; Gowan and Lawrence 2019; Robinson 2019; Sunkara 2019; Calnitsky 2020; Piketty 2020, 2021; Democratic Socialists of America 2021; Jackson 2021; Speth and Courrier 2021.
33. Settle 2015; Pickard and Shrimsley 2019.
34. US Bureau of Labor Statistics, "Employment by Major Industry Sector," bls.gov.
35. US Bureau of Labor Statistics, "Table F. Distribution of Private Sector Employment by Firm Size Class," bls.gov.
36. Pontusson and Kuruvilla 1992.
37. Roemer 1994; Roemer et al. 1996.
38. Malleson 2014, pp. 200–201.
39. Przeworski 1985, Calnitsky 2017, and Robin 2018 emphasize freedom from wage labor. Cohen 2009 and Roemer 2017b emphasize equality of opportunity and solidarity. Some identify socialism with a particular set of views. Kate Aronoff, Peter Dreier, and Michael Kazin, for example, write that "Democratic socialists set their sights on moving beyond capitalism as society's operating system, not simply to make it more tolerable. . . . Existing social democracies offer many lessons, but they are by no means a blueprint for building a sustainable and multiracial democracy in today's United States. Norway's generous social democracy has been furnished largely by oil wealth, and xenophobic politicians have gained clout across Europe on promises to defend their countries' generous welfare states from mostly nonwhite foreigners. Amid rising anti-immigrant sentiment, Denmark, for instance, sorts predominantly Muslim new arrivals into official 'ghettos' to be surveilled and assimilated; in hardening these laws, the country's Social Democrats have found common cause with its far right" (2020, pp. 10–11).
40. Esping-Andersen 1985; Berman 2006. For an example in the United States, see Walzer 1990, 2010.
41. See virtually any dictionary definition of "socialism."

Chapter 2

1. Marx 1867, ch. 25.
2. Chibber 2019, p. 9.
3. Quoted in Wagner 2018.
4. Olsen 2021, p. xiv.
5. Maddison 2007.
6. Acemoglu and Robinson 2012.
7. Kenworthy 2022b, "Progress" chapter; Deaton 2013; Dollar, Kleineberg, and Kraay 2016; Jetter, Laudage, and Stadelmann 2019; DeLong 2020; Pritchett 2020.
8. Wright and Rogers 2015, ch. 10.
9. Lampman 1971.
10. Kenworthy 2011a.
11. See also Figure 1.6 in chapter 1.
12. See also Figure 1.6 in chapter 1.
13. One is the share of households experiencing one or more of the following: arrears in mortgage or rent payment, arrears in utility bill payment, inability to adequately heat home, constrained food choices, overcrowding, poor environmental conditions (e.g., noise, pollution), difficulty in making ends meet (OECD 2008, pp. 186–188). These data are available for only 17 of the 21 countries and only for the mid-2000s. A second alternative hardship indicator is the share of the population living in households who say they cannot afford at least four of the following nine items: mortgage or rent payments, utility bills, hire purchase installments, or other loan payments; one week's holiday away from home; a meal with meat, chicken, fish, or vegetarian equivalent every second day; unexpected financial expenses; a telephone (including mobile telephone); a color television; a washing machine; a car; heating to keep the home adequately warm (Eurostat 2017). These data are available for years since 2012 but only for 15 European countries. In the United States, the US Department of Agriculture estimates food insecurity. See Keith-Jennings 2018.
14. Kenworthy 2022b, "Longevity" chapter.
15. Lee et al. 2015, Figure 3.2.
16. Truesdale and Jencks 2016. See also US Congressional Budget Office 2008; Jencks 2009; Olshansky et al. 2012; Lowrey 2014; Kenworthy 2022b, "Longevity" chapter.
17. Mackenbach 2016.
18. Marmor, Mashaw, and Pakutka 2014, ch. 9.
19. Kenworthy 2011b, ch. 2. See also Bruenig 2017.
20. Hayek 1979; Galbraith 1998; Van Parijs 2001; Murray 2006, 2008; Wright 2010; Matthews 2014; Atkinson 2015; Reich 2015; Tanner 2015; Zwolinski 2015; Stern 2016; Calnitsky 2017; Standing 2017; Van Parijs and Vanderborght 2017; Lowrey 2018.
21. Kenworthy 2020.

Chapter 3

1. Sunkara 2019, p. 240.
2. Chapter 2 ("An End to Poverty in Rich Countries").
3. See also Deaton 2013; Dollar, Kleineberg, and Kraay 2016; Jetter, Laudage, and Stadelmann 2019; Pritchett 2020.
4. Tversky and Kahneman 1992; *Wikipedia*, "Loss Aversion."
5. Friedman 2005; Welzel 2013; Inglehart 2018.
6. Welzel 2013; Inglehart 2018.
7. Welzel 2013, ch. 3; Inglehart 2018.
8. Welzel 2013; Inglehart 2018.
9. Welzel 2013; Inglehart 2018.
10. Kenworthy 2022b, "Progress" chapter.
11. Krugman 2021b.
12. Rodney 1972; Wallerstein 1974; Cardoso and Faletto 1979; Robinson 2014; Hickel 2018a.
13. Stiglitz 2006; Rodrik 2013.
14. Autor, Dorn, and Hanson 2015, using World Development Indicators data; Kochnar 2015. The global middle class is defined here as an income of $10 to $20 per day.
15. *Dollar Street*, gapminder.org/dollar-street.
16. Matthews 2019a.
17. Milanovic 2016.
18. Yang 2020.
19. Krugman 2021a.
20. Karma 2019.
21. Sachs 2005.
22. Hickel 2018b.
23. *Wikipedia*, " List of Development Aid Country Donors."
24. Clemens 2007. See also Collier 2007; Easterly 2009.
25. Pritchett 2006, 2018; Tabarrok 2015; Caplan and Weinersmith 2019.
26. Clemens, Montenegro, and Pritchett 2008.
27. Caplan and Naik 2014.
28. Gardner 2017; Knight and Gunatilaka 2018 (especially p. 71).
29. Massey 2008.
30. Caplan and Naik 2014, pp. 10–11.
31. The General Social Survey asks, "Do you think the number of immigrants to America nowadays should be increased a lot, increased a little, remain the same as it is, reduced a little, or reduced a lot?" (series letin1). As of 2014, the most recent year the question was asked, the share responding increased a lot or increased a little was 11 percent among those who self-identify as lower class or working class, 17 percent among those who self-identify as middle class, and 30 percent among those who self-identify as upper class.

Chapter 4

1. Robinson and Wilkinson 1977, p. 5.
2. Streeck 2016, ch. 10.
3. Wright 2019, pp. 106–107.
4. Kalecki 1943; Baker and Bernstein 2013.
5. Kenworthy 2008.
6. Jahoda 1982; Esping-Andersen et al. 2002; Layard 2005; Huo, Nelson, and Stephens 2008; Kenworthy 2008; Morel, Palier, and Palme 2012; Kleven 2014; Krueger 2016; Hemerijck 2017.
7. Kenworthy 2022b, "Trade" chapter.
8. Autor, Mindell, and Reynolds 2021.
9. Lucas 2003.
10. Krugman 2009.
11. Krugman 2009, 2012; Blyth 2013.
12. Bernard and Lieber 2020; Reuters 2020; Matthews 2021.
13. Kenworthy 2022b, "Good Government" appendix. See also Boix 1998; Pontusson 2011. "The boom, not the slump, is the right time for austerity at the Treasury," wrote Keynes in 1937. See Krugman 2018.
14. Chapter 12 ("Economic Democracy").
15. Pencavel 2012.
16. Kenworthy 2022b, "Employee Voice" chapter.

Chapter 5

1. Wright 2019, p. 2.
2. Standing 2011, p. 37.
3. Robinson 2019, ch. 5.
4. Schor 1991, p. 7.
5. See for example Engels 1845; Sinclair 1906; Terkel 1974; Garson 1994; Ehrenreich 2001; Guendelsberger 2019.
6. See also Kalleberg 2018, ch. 4; Oesch and Piccito 2019; Kenworthy 2022b, "Job Quality" chapter.
7. Hochschild 1997.
8. Damaske, Smyth, and Zawadzki 2014, 2016.
9. Kenworthy 2022b, "Job Quality" chapter.
10. General Social Survey (GSS), sda.berkeley.edu, series wrksched; Pofeldt 2014; Weil 2014; Golden 2015; Horowitz 2015; Katz and Krueger 2016; Kalleberg 2018; Mishel 2018a, 2018b; Collins et al. 2019.
11. Osterman 1999; Uchitelle 2006; Farber 2010; Standing 2011.
12. Manning and Mazeine 2020.
13. Schor 1991; Hermann 2015; McCallum 2020.

14. BBC News 2021; Sawhill and Guyot 2020.
15. Boushey and Ansel 2016.
16. General Social Survey, sda.berkeley.edu, series knowschd. The question asks: "How far in advance do you usually know what days and hours you will need to work?" As of 2018, 43 percent said one week or less in advance, 13 percent said one to two weeks, 6 percent said three to four weeks, and 38 percent said four weeks or more.
17. Boushey and Ansel 2016; Carre and Tilly 2017, ch. 5; Schneider and Harknett 2018, table 2.
18. Carre and Tilly 2017, ch. 5.
19. Kenworthy 2022b, "Job Quality" chapter.

Chapter 6

1. Harrington 1982, p. 282.
2. Chapter 16 ("A Livable Planet").
3. Friedman 2005; Inglehart 2018; Kenworthy 2022b, "Progress" and "Happiness" chapters.
4. Hayek 1945; Nove 1983.
5. Acemoglu and Robinson 2012, pp. 75–76.
6. "The capitalistic economy of the present day is an immense cosmos into which the individual is born, and which presents itself to him, at least as an individual, as an unalterable order of things in which he must live. It forces the individual, in so far as he is involved in the system of market relationships, to conform to capitalistic rules of action. The manufacturer who in the long run acts counter to these norms, will . . . inevitably be eliminated from the economic scene." Weber 1905.
7. Kenworthy 2022b, "Economic Growth" chapter. I focus on the period since the late 1970s because this is the era of globalization, central bank independence and tight money, and neoliberalism; because growth in the 1940s, 1950s, and 1960s was heavily influenced by post–World War II rebuilding; because the 1970s were an odd decade dominated economically by two oil shocks and stagflation; and because Portugal and Spain didn't become democratic until the mid-to-late 1970s.
8. Kenworthy 2010, 2022b, "Economic Growth" chapter. Another potential cause is industry concentration. But Thomas Philippon notes that "Even if one argues that the lack of competition is also bad for innovation—and indeed, I believe this is the case— that effect by itself does not predict permanent differences in growth rates between regions such as Europe and the US that trade and share ideas. In a globalized world, technology flows across countries, and the average growth rates of productivity tend to be similar among advanced economies. As a result, the long-run growth rate of GDP per capita in a particular country may not depend much on the degree of competition in that country" (2019, p. 102).
9. Krugman 1994, p. 24; 2013. See also Deaton 2013, p. 237; Avent 2018.

10. Shonfield 1965; Johnson 1982; Magaziner and Reich 1983; Zysman 1983; Thurow 1984; Hall 1986; Dore 1987; Amsden 1989; Stiglitz 1989; Rodrik 2007; Mazzucato 2013, 2021; IPPR Commission on Economic Justice 2018; Tucker 2019; Kuttner 2021a.
11. Kenworthy 2022b, "Economic Growth" chapter.
12. Chapter 16 ("A Livable Planet").
13. Kenworthy 2004; Voitchovsky 2009; Stiglitz 2012; Palley 2015; Boushey 2019. Another possibility is that income shortfalls, whether absolute or relative to others, may encourage people to borrow more, increasing the likelihood of financial crises that reduce economic growth in the short- or long-run. See chapter 10 ("Helpful Finance").
14. Kenworthy 2022b, "Economic Growth" and "Is Income Inequality Harmful?" chapters.
15. Kenworthy 2022b, "Economic Growth" chapter.

Chapter 7

1. Nolan 2018, p. 1.
2. Varoufakis 2018.
3. Gordon 2016.
4. Kenworthy 2011c, figure 2; Nolan, Thewissen, and Lazzati 2018. For those at the bottom, government transfers tend to be the key; see chapter 2 ("An End to Poverty in Rich Countries").
5. Wright 2010, ch. 3; Varghese 2018.
6. OECD 2019b; Kenworthy 2022b, "A Decent and Rising Income Floor" and "Shared Prosperity" chapters.
7. The following draws from Kenworthy 2021.
8. Compensation includes wages plus benefits paid by employers, such as contributions to pensions and workers' health insurance.
9. Kristal 2017.
10. Rogers 1990.
11. See also OECD 2019a, section 2.2.
12. Bosch and Weinkopf 2008; Kelly and Tomlinson 2017; IPPR Commission on Economic Justice 2018.
13. Pollin 2011; Baker and Bernstein 2013; Bernstein 2016; Bernstein, Spielberg, and Bentele 2017; Bernstein and Bentele 2019.
14. Bernstein 2019.
15. Kenworthy 2013.
16. Gautie and Schmitt 2010.
17. In some countries the statutory minimum wage is indexed to prices or wages, so in practice policy makers tend to have limited influence. See Arpaia et al. 2017.
18. Dube 2019, p. 5.

19. Australian Government, Fair Work Ombudsman, "Minimum Wages" and "List of Awards"; Australian Government, Fair Work Commission, "Annual Wage Reviews."
20. Australian Bureau of Statistics, "Employee Hours and Earnings, Australia, May 2018."
21. Madland 2018; Andrias 2019; Dube 2019.
22. Kenworthy 2022b, "How Do We Know?" chapter.
23. Card and Krueger 1995; Dube, Lester, and Reich 2010; Schmitt 2013; Cengiz et al. 2019.
24. Kruse, Freeman, and Blasi 2008.
25. Weitzman 1984.
26. Chozick 2015.
27. Kenworthy 2015; Nichols and Rothstein 2016; Schanzenbach and Strain 2020.
28. Kenworthy 2020, ch. 7.
29. Kenworthy 2015.
30. Luce et al. 2014; Mishel and Bivens 2021.

Chapter 8

1. Wright 2019, p. 9.
2. Robinson 2019, ch. 5.
3. Sen 1999; Nussbaum 2011; Partanen 2016; Hemerijck 2017; Gough 2019; Coote and Percy 2020; Kenworthy 2020, ch. 2; Kishimoto, Steinfort, and Petitjean 2020; Kenworthy 2022b, "Stable Income and Expenses," "Early Education," "Equality of Opportunity," and "Work-Family-Leisure Balance" chapters.
4. Kenworthy 2022b, "Public Insurance and the Least Well-Off" chapter.
5. Braga, Papachristos, and Hureau 2014; Chalfin and McCrary 2018; Mello 2019; Chalfin, Hansen, Weisburst, and Williams 2021; Weisburd 2021.
6. Béland et al. 2021; Kenworthy 2022b.
7. In the United States, the Social Security tax and the Medicare tax are examples of an earmarked tax.
8. For more discussion, see Hacker 2002; Hills 2011; Morgan and Campbell 2011; Konczal 2012.
9. Judt 2010.
10. Dionne, Drogosz, and Litan 2003; New York Times Editorial Board 2021.

Chapter 9

1. Sanders 2013.
2. Kenworthy 2022b, "Health Care" and "Stable Income and Expenses" chapters.
3. Helland and Tabarrok 2019.
4. Kenworthy 2022b, "Health Care" chapter.

5. The following two sections draw from Reid 2009 and Mossialos et al. 2017.
6. Hacker 2016, 2018; Matthews 2016; Kliff and Klein 2017; Starr 2017, 2018; Sparer 2018.
7. Klein 2012.
8. South Korea isn't included in the following comparison because it switched from one type to the other in 2000.

Chapter 10

1. Bello 2018.
2. Malleson 2014, p. 137.
3. Block 2019, p. 531.
4. Kahn 2010; Oreopoulos, von Wachter, and Heisz 2012; Giuliano and Spilimbergo 2014; Tooze 2018.
5. See also Atkinson and Morelli 2010; Morelli and Atkinson 2015.
6. Rodrik 2009; Krugman 2010; Blinder 2013; Johnson 2015; Konczal 2015; Tooze 2018; Hynes, Love, and Stuart 2020.
7. Milanovic 2009; Stiglitz 2009; Rajan 2010; Reich 2010; Thaker and Williamson 2012; Cynamon and Fazzari 2014; Kumhof, Ranciere, and Winant 2015.
8. Atkinson and Morelli 2010; Morelli and Atkinson 2015. See also Bordo and Meissner 2012.
9. Glaeser 2010; Bordo and Meissner 2012; Mian and Sufi 2014.
10. Jacobs and King 2016, p. 22.
11. Block 1977; Lindblom 1977; Therborn 1978; Przeworski and Wallerstein 1988; Panitch 2014, 2020.
12. Krugman 2009, 2012; Blyth 2013.
13. Carville 1993.
14. Hall 1986; Genschel 2002; Rodrik 2010; Young, Banerjee, and Schwartz 2020.
15. Block 1992; Malleson 2014.
16. Iversen and Soskice 2019, Preface. See also Rogers and Rhodes-Conway 2014; Andersen et al. 2015, ch. 5; Calnitsky 2021.
17. Mann and Ornstein 2012; Prasad 2018.
18. Malleson 2014, chs. 6–7. See also Cohen and Rogers 1983; Block 1996; Hann 2018.
19. Malleson 2014, p. 165.
20. Levine 2011; Cowen 2019.
21. There is plenty of experience with local public, community, and cooperative banks in capitalist economies. See Deeg 1999; Schneiberg 2011.

Chapter 11

1. Cited in Campbell 2013.
2. Wright 2010, p. 84.

3. Przeworski et al. 2000; Treisman 2018; Boix 2019.
4. Bartels 2021.
5. Dahl 1989, 2006; Rawls 2001; Cohen 2009.
6. The following draws from Kenworthy 2022a.
7. Chapter 13 ("Less Economic Inequality").
8. Center for Responsive Politics 2020a.
9. Bonica et al. 2014.
10. Evers-Hillstrom 2020.
11. Center for Responsive Politics 2020b.
12. Krugman 2011; Hacker and Pierson 2020, p. 1; Page and Gilens 2017; Reich 2020; Young, Banerjee, and Schwartz 2020.
13. Bartels 2016.
14. Gilens 2012.
15. Ansolabehere, de Figueiredo, and Snyder 2003; Jacobs et al. 2004; Baumgartner et al. 2009; Burstein 2014; Drutman 2015; Bartels 2016, pp. 263–265; Cao et al. 2018.
16. Burstein 2014.
17. Bartels 2016, p. 253.
18. Chapter 13 ("Less Economic Inequality").
19. Hacker and Pierson 2010.
20. Gilens 2012, ch. 7.
21. Wlezien and Stuart Soroka 2011.
22. Chapter 13 ("Less Economic Inequality").
23. Rosset 2016; Persson and Gilljam 2018; Elsässer, Hense, and Schäfer 2021; Schakel 2021.
24. Bartels 2017.
25. Hicks 1999; Huber and Stephens 2001; Alesina and Glaeser 2004.
26. Piketty, Saez, and Stantcheva 2014; OECD 2020; Kenworthy 2022b, "Taxes" chapter.
27. Piketty, Saez, and Zucman 2018, figure 9; Congressional Budget Office 2020, exhibit 11.
28. Philippon and Reshef 2013; Tooze 2018; Kenworthy 2022b, "Finance: Additional Data" appendix.
29. Chapter 7 ("Inclusive Growth").
30. Page, Bartels, and Seawright 2013.
31. Page, Seawright, and Lacombe 2019.
32. Center for Responsive Politics 2020a.
33. Rodden 2019; Kenworthy 2022b, "Democracy" chapter.
34. Page and Gilens 2017, p. 19.
35. Lindert and Williamson 2016.
36. Gordon 2016.
37. Sommeiller and Price 2018.
38. Kenworthy 2022b, "Democracy" chapter, "Finance: Additional Data" appendix, and "Taxes: Additional Data" appendix.
39. Bächtiger et al. 2018; Dryzek et al. 2019.

Chapter 12

1. Chomsky, interviewed in Witkowsky et al. 2015, minute 49–50.
2. Dahl 1985, p. 111.
3. Walzer 1978, p. 328.
4. Fleurbaey 2018, ch. 7.
5. Walzer 1978. Dahl 1985; Ellerman 1990; Archer 2010; Malleson 2014; Witkowsky et al. 2015; Ferreras 2017; Ferreras, Meda, and Battilana 2020.
6. A 2017 survey found that 36–38 percent of employees feel they have "a lot" of say in how to do their job and in the organization of the work schedule. See Kochan et al. 2019.
7. Levine and Tyson 1990; Wilkinson and Dundon 2010; Gallie 2013.
8. Freeman and Medoff 1984; Rosenfeld 2014; Farber et al. 2018. During the period of peak union membership and power, which in many countries was in the 1960s and 1970s, there was a danger that unions might be *too* successful in increasing wages, resulting in high inflation or high unemployment or both. Coordination of wage setting, via centralized bargaining, extension of wage agreements from unionized to nonunionized firms, or government intervention, tended to encourage moderate wage increases. Wage-setting coordination thereby contributed to healthy macroeconomic performance—low unemployment together with low inflation. Since then, however, with the advent of independent central banks and restrictive monetary policy, coordinated wage bargaining hasn't been needed to achieve wage restraint. See Kenworthy 1995, ch. 5; 2002. Now the tables have turned. Technological advance, globalization, heightened product market competition, the shareholder value revolution in corporate governance, looser labor markets, and other developments have increased firms' incentive to resist wage increases and enhanced their leverage vis-à-vis workers. In this new context, the major challenge facing unions, as we saw in chapter 7, is to ensure that wages increase.
9. Freeman and Medoff 1984; Swenson 1989; Card 1996; Wallerstein 1999.
10. Wallerstein 1999; Rueda and Pontusson 2000; Blau and Kahn 2002; Devroye and Freeman 2002; Card, Lemieux, and Riddell 2003; DiPrete 2005; Lucifora, McKnight, and Salverda 2005; Oskarsson 2005; Koeniger, Leonardi, and Nunziata 2007; Baccaro 2008; Kenworthy 2008; Bosch, Mayhew, and Gautie 2010; OECD 2018, ch. 3.
11. Kenworthy 2022b, "Income Distribution" chapter.
12. Volscho and Kelley 2012; Jaumotte and Buitron 2015; Huber, Huo, and Stephens 2019.
13. Unions may block the introduction of new technology in an attempt to preserve jobs. High wages might reduce investment by limiting firms' profits. Unions can reduce the labor market's effectiveness in allocating workers to firms. They may hinder efficiency in the workplace by limiting managerial discretion. Strikes and work slowdowns reduce production. On the other hand, unions may improve communication among workers and between workers and management, and they may contribute to efforts to boost, rather than impede, productivity. Simons 1948, ch. 6; Hayek 1960, ch. 18; Friedman and Friedman 1979; Hirsch 1992.

14. Kenworthy 2022b, "Economic Growth" and "Employee Voice" chapters.
15. Freeman and Rogers 1999; Kochan et al. 2019.
16. Rogers 1995; Kahlenberg and Marvit 2012; Ahlquist and Levi 2013; Meyerson 2014; Bernstein 2015.
17. Rothstein 1992; Western 1997; Scruggs 2002; Dimick 2012; Western and Rosenfeld 2012; Freeman and Hilbrich 2013; Avdagic and Baccaro 2014; Usmani 2018.
18. Rogers and Streek 1995; Gumbrell-McCormick and Hyman 2010.
19. Since 1996, the European Union has required works councils in firms that have more than 1,000 employees in total and more than 150 in each of two or more EU countries.
20. The 1935 National Labor Relations Act forbids nonunion workplace bodies such as works councils in the United States. See Kaufman and Taras 2010.
21. Gumbrell-McCormick and Hyman 2010, p. 293.
22. Rogers and Streeck 1995.
23. Hübler 2015; Jirjahn and Smith 2018.
24. Markey, Balnave, and Patmore 2010; Conchon, Kluge, and Stillt 2015.
25. Sigurt Vitols, personal communication.
26. This is an estimate. As of 2015, the 1,000 companies in the "Fortune 1000" had 34 million employees in total, and the firm at the bottom of the list had revenue of $1.8 billion.
27. A number of studies conclude that firms in countries such as Germany have tended to have longer time horizons than their American and British counterparts, but this may be a product of long-term-oriented owners rather than employee election of part of the board of directors. See Porter 1992; Barton et al. 2017.
28. Holmberg 2017; Warren 2018; Yglesias 2018.
29. A recent study uses within-country variation in Germany to assess the impact of board-level employee representation on wage increases. Beginning in the early 1950s, "stock companies" in Germany—companies not fully owned by a single family—were required to have one-third of their board elected by workers regardless of how many employees they had. In 1994, the German government eliminated this requirement for newly created stock firms with 500 or fewer employees. The authors of the study compare wage developments in stock firms created just before this change with those in stock firms created just after the change. The firms with employee board-level representation didn't have faster wage growth. See Jäger, Schoefer, and Heining 2020. A study of Norwegian firms suggests the same conclusion. Employee board-level representation doesn't seem to have contributed to higher wages or faster growth in wages. Blandhol et al. 2020.

   We also can compare across countries. To do so, it would help to have a country in which labor unions aren't especially strong but board-level representation is. Germany fits the bill. While German unions and collective bargaining remain powerful in some manufacturing industries, they have weakened considerably in much of the rest of the economy. But board-level employee representation has remained quite prevalent (despite the 1994 change mentioned in the previous paragraph). So has Germany had healthy wage growth? No, it hasn't. In fact, Germany's record has been similar to that of the United States: growth of median compensation has been much slower than growth of the economy, and it has lagged well behind compensation growth in most other affluent democratic countries. Kenworthy 2020, ch. 3. (This is true for household income as well. See Kenworthy 2022b, "Shared Prosperity: Additional Data" appendix.) Germany's slow wage growth owes partly to its reunification with the former East Germany in 1990 and its intentional creation of a low-wage ("mini-jobs") segment of the labor market in the early 2000s. Still, its wage performance gives us little cause for optimism about board-level employee representation's ability to boost wages.

30. Vitols 2010; Forcillo 2017; Fox 2018; Jäger, Schoefer, and Heining 2020.
31. National Center for Employee Ownership 2019. About 20 percent of adults employed in the private sector own some kind of stock in the firm they work for, according to the General Social Survey (series ownstock).
32. Dudley 2017.
33. Democracy Collaborative, "Worker Cooperatives."
34. U.K. Labour Party 2017, p. 12.
35. Kaarsemaker, Pendleton, and Poutsma 2010; Blasi 2015.
36. Malleson 2014, pp. 42, 67; Bruni, De Rosa, and Ferri 2019, table 1.
37. Pontusson and Kuruvilla 1992.
38. Putterman 2009; Pencavel 2012; Blasi, Freeman, and Kruse 2013; Malleson 2014, ch. 3; National Center for Employee Ownership, "Research on Employee Ownership."
39. Elster 1989; Block 1992; Bowles and Gintis 1993; Artz and Kim 2011; Ownership Commission 2012; U.K. Labour Party 2017; Trickey 2020.
40. Blasi, Freeman, and Kruse 2013; Groot and van der Linde 2017; U.K. Labour Party; Dow 2018; Gowan 2019; FitzRoy and Nolan 2020.
41. Blasi, Freeman, and Kruse 2013.
42. Harrington 1989, pp. 204–205; Gallie et al. 2017.
43. For additional considerations, see Brighouse 1996.
44. Malleson 2014, p. 39.
45. Malleson 2014, pp. 42, 87; Gowan 2019.
46. Witkowsky et al. 2015.
47. Aisch and Parlapiano 2017.
48. Streeck and Kenworthy 2005. Concertation is one form of "associative democracy"; see Cohen and Rogers 1992.
49. Goldthorpe 1984; Katzenstein 1985; Lange and Garrett 1985; Wilensky 2002.
50. Kenworthy 2022b, "Economic Growth" chapter.
51. Aiginger and Rodrik 2020; Kenworthy 2022b, "Economic Growth" chapter.
52. Malleson 2014.

Chapter 13

1. Quoted in Dreier and Kazin 2020, p. 35.
2. Piketty 2020, p. 966.

3. Kenworthy 2022b, "Income Distribution" chapter.

4. Kenworthy 2022b, "Income Distribution" chapter.

5. Kenworthy 2022b, "Income Distribution" chapter.

6. Kenworthy 2022b, "Income Distribution" chapter.

7. Wilkinson and Pickett 2009; Reich 2010; Stiglitz 2012; IPPR Commission on Economic Justice 2018; Boushey 2019; Sachs 2020.

8. Kenworthy 2022b, "Is Income Inequality Harmful?" chapter.

9. Kenworthy 2022b, "Wealth Distribution" chapter.

10. Data in Atkinson and Morelli 2014 suggest Switzerland is similar or possibly more unequal.

11. Balestra and Tonkin 2018; Causa, Woloszko, and Leite 2019; Pfeffer and Waitkus 2021.

12. Pfeffer and Waitkus 2021.

13. Roemer 2017a.

14. Blanchflower and Oswald 2013; Causa, Woloszko, and Leite 2019.

15. Wilkinson and Pickett 2009; Reich 2010; Obama 2012; Stiglitz 2012; Therborn 2013; Piketty 2020; Pierson 2021.

16. Kenworthy 2022b, "Is Income Inequality Harmful?" chapter.

17. Baker 2021.

18. Bernie Sanders, *Twitter*, September 24, 2019: "There should be no billionaires. We are going to tax their extreme wealth and invest in working people." Number of billionaires per capita is from Andersen et al. 2015, ch. 11.

19. Partanen 2017; Kenworthy 2020.

20. Even skeptics tend to reach this conclusion. See, for example, *The Economist* 2013; Booth 2014.

Chapter 14

1. Taylor 2016, pp. 72–73.

2. Aschoff 2016, pp. 89–90.

3. Kenworthy 2022b, "Inclusion: Women" chapter.

4. Kenworthy 2022b, "Work-Family-Leisure Balance" chapter.

5. Mensi-Klarbach and Seierstad 2020.

6. Stewart 2018.

7. In his detailed study of African Americans in Philadelphia at the end of the 1800s, W.E.B. Du Bois concluded that "the condition of the Negro cannot be considered apart from the great fact of race prejudice—indefinite and shadowy as that phrase may be. It is certain that, while industrial cooperation among the groups of a great city population is very difficult under ordinary circumstances, that here it is rendered more difficult and in some respects almost impossible by the fact that nineteen-twentieths of the population have in many cases refused to co-operate with the other twentieth, even when the co-operation means life to the latter and great advantage to

the former. In other words, one of the great postulates of the science of economics—that men will seek their economic advantage—is in this case untrue, because in many cases men will not do this if it involves association, even in a casual and business way, with Negroes." Du Bois 1899, ch. 9.

8. Myrdal 1944.
9. National Advisory Commission on Civil Disorders 1968.
10. Thernstrom and Thernstrom 1997, pp. 18–19.
11. Kenworthy 2022b, "Inclusion: African Americans" chapter.
12. Kenworthy 2022b, "A Decent and Rising Income Floor" and "Shared Prosperity" chapters.
13. Thompson and Suarez 2019; Wolff 2021; Kenworthy 2022b, "Inclusion: African Americans" and "Wealth Distribution" chapters.
14. Kenworthy 2022b, "Longevity" chapter.

Chapter 15

1. Einstein 1949.
2. Wright 2017.
3. Becker 1957.
4. Edwards, Reich, and Gordon 1975; Roemer 1979.
5. The story is similar in the United Kingdom. Miliband 2021, pp. 61–62.
6. Abrajano and Hajnal 2017; Polakow-Suransky 2017.
7. Kenworthy 2022b, "Migration" chapter.
8. Friedman 2005; Inglehart 2008, 2018; Welzel 2013; Kenworthy 2022b, "Progress" chapter.
9. Hawkley and Cacioppo 2010; Holt-Lunstad et al. 2015; Ortiz-Ospina 2019.
10. Riesman 1950; Packard 1972; Putnam 2000; Brooks 2018. See also Levin 2015; Murthy 2017; Twenge 2017.
11. Kenworthy 1995; Bernstein 2006.
12. Fischer 2011.
13. Kenworthy 2022b, "Social Connections" chapter.
14. Smith 1776.
15. Levine 1996, pp. 232–233.
16. Veenhoven 1999.
17. Cohen 2009, pp. 39–41.
18. Cohen admitted as much, though he remained hopeful: "We socialists don't now know how to replicate camping trip procedures on a nationwide scale, amid the complexity and variety that comes with nationwide size.... But I do not think that we now know that we will never know how to do these things." Cohen 2009, pp. 75–76. See also Arneson 2015.

Chapter 16

1. Klein 2014, p. 21.
2. Smith 2021, p. 175.
3. Carbon Dioxide Information Analysis Center, "800,000-Year Ice-Core Records of Atmospheric Carbon Dioxide"; Earth System Research Laboratory, National Oceanic and Atmospheric Administration, "Trends in Atmospheric Carbon Dioxide"; Intergovernmental Panel on Climate Change 2013, p. 7; *Wikipedia*, "Carbon Dioxide in Earth's Atmosphere."
4. Gerber et al. 2013. See also Gilbert 2012; Bailey, Froggatt, and Wellesley 2014; Poore and Nemecek 2018; Ecofys, "World Greenhouse Gas Emissions Flow Chart."
5. Moskin et al. 2019.
6. *Wikipedia*, "Atmospheric Methane."
7. Because the historical temperature records are incomplete, scientists introduce corrections. Are these corrections biased? This was the concern at the heart of the 2009 "climategate" controversy. However, the Berkeley Earth Surface Temperature (BEST) project has gathered together all existing temperature measures, and the data, even with no corrections, show a similar trend. Rohde et al. 2013. Is this a "heat island" effect? In other words, do these measurements show warming simply because a number of the temperature stations are near towns that have been growing? No. We know this for three reasons: a heat island effect would be strongest on still nights, yet trends from data recorded on still nights are similar to those on windy nights; temperature readings from non-heat-island stations show a similar trend to those from heat-island stations; and the temperature of water at the surface of oceans shows a similar trend to that on land. *The Economist* 2010; Wickham et al. 2013.
8. Berkeley Earth Surface Temperature Project 2013. Also, as Joseph Romm has noted, "if the warming is caused by an increase in greenhouse gases, we expect the lower atmosphere (troposphere) to warm, the upper atmosphere (stratosphere) to cool, and the boundary between them (tropopause) to rise. All of this has been observed. If, for instance, recent warming were due to increases in the intensity of radiation from the sun, then in addition to the troposphere, the stratosphere should be warming, too, which is not happening." Romm 2016, p. 10.
9. Intergovernmental Panel on Climate Change 2013, p. 12; Gillis 2013. William Nordhaus points out that "Scientists are increasingly confident that the basic results of climate modeling are accurate. Climate models calculate that past emissions have contributed to warming of almost one degree centigrade over the last century, with rapid continued warming projected over the present century and beyond. In its 2001 report, the Intergovernmental Panel on Climate Change reported that human activity was 'likely' to be the source of this warming. The IPCC upgraded this evaluation to 'very likely' in its 2007 report and to 'extremely likely' in its 2013 report." Nordhaus 2015. How much consensus is there among climate scientists? In 2010, the *Proceedings of the National Academy of Sciences* reported the findings of a survey of 1,372 climate researchers. It found that 97–98 percent of those publishing in the field believe humans are causing climate change. And "The relative climate expertise and

scientific prominence of the unconvinced researchers . . . are substantially below that of the convinced researchers." Anderegg et al. 2010. A more recent study also found 97 percent agreement. Cook et al. 2013. A 2014 report by the Climate Change Panel of the American Association for the Advancement of Science described the scientific consensus this way: "The science linking human activities to climate change is analogous to the science linking smoking to lung and cardiovascular diseases. Physicians, cardiovascular scientists, public health experts, and others all agree smoking causes cancer. And this consensus among the health community has convinced most Americans that the health risks from smoking are real. A similar consensus now exists among climate scientists, a consensus that maintains climate change is happening, and human activity is the cause." Climate Change Panel 2014, p. 2.

10. Romm 2016.
11. Cullen 2016, using projections by the World Climate Research Program.
12. World Health Organization 2014, p. 21.
13. International Organization for Migration 2014, p. 38.
14. Intergovernmental Panel on Climate Change 2013, pp. 18, 21; Potsdam Institute for Climate Impact Research and Climate Analytics 2012; Romm 2016, p. 94.
15. Wagner and Weitzman 2015, ch. 3. See also Sherwood and Huber 2010.
16. Wallace-Wells 2019, pp. 3–4.
17. Romm 2016, p. 154.
18. Jenkins and Thernstrom 2017; Intergovernmental Panel on Climate Change 2018; Griffith 2019c.
19. Marris 2020; Griffith 2019c.
20. Aronoff et al. 2019.
21. Nordhaus 2015.
22. Jacobson et al. 2017; Griffith 2019b.
23. Griffith 2019a.
24. National Research Council, Committee on Geoengineering Climate 2015.
25. Norhaus and Shellenberger 2007; Manzi 2008; Romm 2016; Drum 2020.
26. Gore 2020; *Nikkei Asia* 2020.
27. *Wikipedia*, "Paris Agreement"; *Wikipedia*, "Carbon Neutrality"; Darby 2019; NRDC 2019.
28. Climate Action Tracker 2020.
29. See also Next System Project 2018.
30. Friedman 2005; Scruggs and Benegal 2012; Cassidy 2020; Irwin 2021.
31. Adler 2019, p. 38.
32. Next System Project 2018.
33. Rich 2018.
34.. See also Driscoll 2022.
35. Sunkara 2019, p. 241.

Chapter 17

1. But even then, perhaps no. See International Panel on Social Progress 2018, ch. 8.
2. Wilkinson 2017.
3. Boldizzoni 2020.
4. Streeck 2016. See also Streeck 2014.
5. Polanyi 1944.
6. Streeck 2016, ch. 1.
7. International Panel on Social Progress 2018, pp. 17–18.
8. Wallerstein et al. 2013.
9. Streeck 2016, ch. 1.
10. Kenworthy 2020, 2022b.
11. Wallerstein et al. 2013, ch. 5; Milanovic 2019.
12. Wright 2010, 2019.
13. Meidner 1981; Pontusson and Kuruvilla 1992; Gowan and Lawrence 2019.
14. Matthews 2019b.
15. Kenworthy 2020.
16. Palier 2010; Hemerijck 2013, 2017; Andersen et al. 2015; Birnbaum et al. 2017; Kenworthy 2020.

References

Abrajano, Marisa and Zoltan L. Hajnal. 2017. *White Backlash: Immigration, Race, and American Politics*. Princeton University Press.

Acemoglu, Daron and James Robinson. 2012. *Why Nations Fail: The Origins of Power, Prosperity, and Poverty*. Crown.

Adler, Paul S. 2019. *The 99 Percent Economy: How Democratic Socialism Can Overcome the Crises of Capitalism*. Oxford University Press.

Ahlquist, John and Margaret Levi. 2013. *In the Interest of Others: Organizations and Social Activism*. Princeton University Press.

Aiginger, Karl and Dani Rodrik. 2020. "Rebirth of Industrial Policy and an Agenda for the Twenty-First Century." *Journal of Industry, Competition, and Trade* 20, 189–207.

Aisch, Gregor and Alicia Parlapiano. 2017. "What Do You Think Is the Most Important Problem Facing This Country Today?" *New York Times*, February 27.

Alesina, Alberto and Edward L. Glaeser. 2004. *Fighting Poverty in the US and Europe*. Oxford University Press.

Amsden, Alice. 1989. *Asia's Next Giant: South Korea and Late Industrialization*. Oxford University Press.

Anderegg, William R.L., James W. Prall, Jacob Harold, and Stephen H. Schneider. 2010. "Expert Credibility in Climate Change." *Proceedings of the National Academy of Sciences* 107, 12107–12109.

Andersen, Torben M., Jesper Roine, Bernt Bratsberg, Knut Roed, Michael Svarer, Michael Rosholm, Tuomas Takalo, Otto Toivanen, Guttorm Schjelderup, Julian V. Johnsen, Katrine V. Løken, Helena Holmlund, Nabanita Datta Gupta, Bent Jesper Christensen, Andreas Bergh, Johanna Mollerstrom, and Kalle Moene. 2015. *Nordic Economic Policy Review: Whither the Nordic Welfare Model?* Norden.

Andrias, Kate. 2019. "An American Approach to Social Democracy: The Forgotten Promise of the Fair Labor Standards Act." *Yale Law Journal* 128, 616–709.

Ansolabehere, Stephen, John de Figueiredo, and James M. Snyder Jr. 2003. "Why Is There So Little Money in U.S. Politics?" *Journal of Economic Perspectives* 17(1), 105–130.

Archer, Robin. 2010. "Freedom, Democracy, and Capitalism: Ethics and Employee Participation." In *Oxford Handbook of Participation in Organizations*, edited by Adrian Wilkinson, Paul J. Gollan, Mick Marchington, and David Lewin, Oxford University Press, 590–608.

Arneson, Richard J. 2015. "Why Not Capitalism?" In *Distributive Justice and Access to Advantage*, edited by Alexander Kaufman, Oxford University Press, 207–234.

Aronoff, Kate, Alyssa Battistoni, Daniel Aldana Cohen, and Thea Riofrancos. 2019. *A Planet to Win: Why We Need a Green New Deal*. Verso.

Aronoff, Kate, Peter Dreier, and Michael Kazin. 2020. "Introduction." In *We Own the Future: Democratic Socialism—American Style*, edited by Kate Aronoff, Peter Dreier, and Michael Kazin, New Press, 5–14.

Arpaia, Alfonso, Pedro Cardoso, Aron Kiss, Kristine Van Herck, and Anneleen Vandeplas. 2017. "Statutory Minimum Wages in the EU: Institutional Settings and Macroeconomic Implications." Policy Paper 124, Institute for Labor Economics (IZA).

Artz, Georgeanne M. and Younjun Kim. 2011. "Business Ownership by Workers: Are Worker Cooperatives a Viable Option?" Economics Working Paper 99, Iowa State University.

Aschoff, Nicole. 2016. "Aren't Socialism and Feminism Sometimes in Conflict?" In *The ABCs of Socialism*, edited by Bhaskar Sunkara, Verso, 82–92.

Atkinson, Anthony B. 2015. *Inequality: What Can Be Done?* Harvard University Press.

Atkinson, Anthony and Salvatore Morelli. 2010. "Inequality and Banking Crises: A First Look." Report for the International Labour Organization (ILO).

Atkinson, Anthony B. and Salvatore Morelli. 2014. "Chartbook of Economic Inequality." Unpublished.

Auerbach, Paul. 2016. *Socialist Optimism*. Palgrave Macmillan.

Autor, David, David Dorn, and Gordon H. Hanson. 2015. "The China Shock: Learning from Labor Market Adjustment to Large Changes in Trade." Working Paper 21906, National Bureau of Economic Research.

Autor, David, David Mindell, and Elisabeth Reynolds. 2021. "The Work of the Future: Building Better Jobs in an Age of Intelligent Machines." Report of the MIT Task Force on the Work of the Future.

Avdagic, Sabina and Lucio Baccaro. 2014. "The Future of Employment Relations in Advanced Capitalism: Inexorable Decline?" In *Oxford Handbook of Employment Relations*, edited by Adrian Wilkinson, Geoffrey Wood, and Richard Deeg, Oxford University Press, 701–726.

Avent, Ryan. 2018. "Economists Understand Little about the Causes of Growth." *The Economist: Free Exchange*, April 14.

Baccaro, Lucio. 2008. "Labour Institutions, Globalization, and Inequality." International Labour Organization.

Bächtiger, Andre, John S. Dryzek, Jane Mansbridge, and Mark Warren, eds. 2018. *Oxford Handbook of Deliberative Democracy*. Oxford University Press.

Bailey, Rob, Antony Froggatt, and Laura Wellesley. 2014. "Livestock: Climate Change's Forgotten Sector." Research Paper, Chatham House.

Baker, Dean. 2021. "Wealth Inequality: Should We Care?" Center for Economic Policy Research, February 8.

Baker, Dean and Jared Bernstein. 2013. *Getting Back to Full Employment*. Center for Economic and Policy Research.

Balestra, Carlotta and Richard Tonkin. 2018. "Inequalities in Household Wealth across OECD Countries: Evidence from the OECD Wealth Distribution Database." Statistics Working Paper 2018/01, OECD.

Bartels, Larry M. 2016. *Unequal Democracy*. 2nd edition. Princeton University Press.

Bartels, Larry M. 2017. "Political Inequality in Affluent Democracies: The Social Welfare Deficit." Working Paper 5-2017, Center for the Study of Democratic Institutions, Vanderbilt University.

Bartels, Larry M. 2021. *Public Opinion and the Crisis of Democracy in Europe*. Unpublished book draft.

Barton, Dominic, et al. 2017. "Measuring the Economic Impact of Short-Termism." McKinsey Global Institute.

Bastani, Aaron. 2019. *Fully Automated Luxury Communism*. Verso.

Baumgartner, Frank R., Jeffrey M. Berry, Marie Hojnacki, David C. Kimball, and Beth L. Leech. 2009. *Lobbying and Public Policy*. University of Chicago Press.

BBC News. 2021. "Four-Day Week 'An Overwhelming Success' in Iceland." July 6.

Becker, Gary. 1957. *The Economics of Discrimination*. University of Chicago Press.

Bello, Walden. 2018. "Ten Years after 2008 Crisis, There's No 'Reforming' Global Capitalism." *Business Standard*, September 21.

Bentham, Jeremy. 1843. *The Complete Works of Jeremy Bentham*. Volume 10. Online Library of Liberty.

Berkeley Earth Surface Temperature Project (BEST). 2013. "Summary of Results."

Béland, Daniel, Stephan Liebfried, Kimberly J. Morgan, Herbert Obinger, and Christopher Pierson, eds. 2021. *Oxford Handbook of the Welfare State*. 2nd edition. Oxford University Press.

Berlin, Isaiah. 1958. "Two Concepts of Liberty." Oxford University Press.

Berman, Sheri. 2006. *The Primacy of Politics*. Cambridge University Press.

Bernard, Tara Siegel, and Ron Lieber. 2020. "FAQs on Stimulus Checks, Unemployment, and the Coronavirus Bill." *New York Times*, March 27.

Bernstein, Jared. 2006. *All Together Now*. Berrett-Koehler.

Bernstein, Jared. 2015. "Realistic Ways Policymakers Could Strengthen Collective Bargaining." *Washington Post: Post Everything*, June 23.

Bernstein, Jared. 2016. *The Reconnection Agenda: Reuniting Growth and Prosperity*. http://jaredbernsteinblog.com/wp-content/uploads/2015/04/The-Reconnection-Agenda_Jared-Bernstein.pdf.

Bernstein, Jared. 2019. "Recent Wage Trends Are Impressive. Their Levels . . . Not So Much." *Washington Post: Post Everything*, May 8.

Bernstein, Jared and Keith Bentele. 2019. "The Increasing Benefits and Diminished Costs of Running a High-Pressure Labor Market." Center on Budget and Policy Priorities.

Bernstein, Jared, Ben Spielberg, and Keith Bentele. 2017. "The Relationship between Tight Labor Markets and the Earnings of Low-Income Households." Yankelovich Center for Social Science Research, University of California-San Diego.

Birnbaum, Simon, Tommy Ferrarini, Kenneth Nelson, and Joakim Palme. 2017. *The Generational Welfare Contract*. Edward Elgar.

Blakeley, Grace. 2019. *Stolen: How to Save the World from Financialisation*. Repeater.

Blanchflower, David and Andrew J. Oswald. 2013. "Does High Homeownership Impair the Labor Market?" Working Paper 19079, National Bureau of Economic Research.

Blandhol, Christine, Magne Mogstad, Peter Nilsson, and Ola L Vestad. 2020. "Do Employees Benefit from Worker Representation on Corporate Boards?" Working Paper 28269, National Bureau of Economic Research.

Blasi, Joseph R. 2015. "Tipping the Scale of Employee Ownership." Morgan Stanley.

Blasi, Joseph R., Richard B. Freeman, and Douglas L. Kruse. 2013. *The Citizen's Share*. Yale University Press.

Blau, Francine D. and Lawrence M. Kahn. 2002. *At Home and Abroad: US Labor Market Performance in International Perspective*. Russell Sage Foundation.

Blinder, Alan. 2013. "Financial Collapse: A Twelve-Step Recovery Plan." *New York Times*, January 19.

Block, Fred. 1977. "The Ruling Class Does Not Rule: Notes on the Marxist Theory of the State." *Socialist Revolution* 33, 6-28.

Block, Fred. 1992. "Capitalism without Class Power." *Politics and Society* 20, 277-303.

Block, Fred. 1996. "Finance and Market Socialism." In *Equal Shares: Making Market Socialism Work*, edited by Erik Olin Wright, Verso, 159-169.

Block, Fred. 2018. *Capitalism: The Future of an Illusion*. University of California Press.

Block, Fred. 2019. "Financial Democratization and the Transition to Socialism." *Politics and Society* 47, 529–556.

Blyth, Mark. 2013. *Austerity: The History of a Dangerous Idea*. Oxford University Press.

Boix, Carles. 1998. "Partisan Governments, the International Economy, and Macroeconomic Policies in Advanced Nations, 1960–93." *World Politics* 53, 38–73.

Boix, Carles. 2019. *Democratic Capitalism at the Crossroads*. Princeton University Press.

Boldizzoni, Francesco. 2020. *Foretelling the End of Capitalism: Intellectual Misadventures since Karl Marx*. Harvard University Press.

Bonica, Adam, Nolan McCarty, Keith T. Poole, and Howard Rosenthal. 2014. "Why Hasn't Democracy Slowed Rising Inequality?" *Journal of Economic Perspectives* 27(3), 103–124.

Booth, Michael. 2014. *The Almost Nearly Perfect People*. Jonathan Cape.

Bordo, Michael D. and Christopher M. Meissner. 2012. "Does Inequality Lead to a Financial Crisis?" Working Paper 17896, National Bureau of Economic Research.

Bosch, Gerhard, Ken Mayhew, and Jerome Gautié. 2010. "Industrial Relations, Legal Regulations, and Wage Setting." In *Low-Wage Work in the Wealthy World*, edited by Jerome Gautié and John Schmitt, Russell Sage Foundation, 91–146.

Bosch, Gerhard and Claudia Weinkopf, eds. 2008. *Low-Wage Work in Germany*. Russell Sage Foundation.

Boushey, Heather. 2019. *Unbound: How Inequality Constricts Our Economy and What We Can Do about It*. Harvard University Press.

Boushey, Heather and Bridget Ansel. 2016. "Working by the Hour: The Economic Consequences of Unpredictable Scheduling Practices." Washington Center on Equitable Growth.

Bowles, Samuel and Herbert Gintis. 1993. "A Political and Economic Case for the Democratic Enterprise." *Economics and Philosophy* 9, 75–100.

Braga, Anthony A., Andrew V. Papachristos, and David M. Hureau. 2014. "The Effects of Hot Spots Policing on Crime: An Updated Systematic Review and Meta-Analysis." *Justice Quarterly* 31, 633–663.

Bridge, Yael. 2021. The Big Scary "S" Word. Wayland Productions.

Brighouse, Harry. 1996. "Transitional and Utopian Market Socialism." In *Equal Shares: Making Market Socialism Work*, edited by Erik Olin Wright, Verso, 187–208.

Brooks, David. 2018. "Where American Renewal Begins." *New York Times*, July 26.

Bruenig, Elizabeth. 2018. "It's Time to Give Socialism a Try." *Washington Post*, March 6.

Bruenig, Matt. 2017. "Capitalism and Poverty." *Jacobin*, September.

Bruni, Luigino, Dalila De Rosa, and Giovanni Ferri. 2019. "Cooperatives and Happiness: Cross-Country Evidence on the Role of Relational Capital." *Journal of Applied Economics* 51, 3325–3343.

Burczak, Theodore A. 2006. *Socialism after Hayek*. University of Michigan Press.

Burstein, Paul. 2014. *American Public Opinion, Advocacy, and Policy in Congress: What the Public Wants and What It Gets*. Cambridge University Press.

Calnitsky, David. 2017. "Debating Basic Income." *Catalyst*, Fall.

Calnitsky, David. 2020. "There Is a Fully Socialist Economy for the 20th Century." YouTube, https://www.youtube.com/watch?v=_hBal2J0QU8.

Calnitsky, David. 2021. "The Policy Road to Socialism." *Critical Sociology*. doi/10.1177/08969205211031624.

Campbell, Peter Scott. 2013. "Democracy v. Concentrated Wealth: In Search of a Louis D. Brandeis Quote." *Green Bag* 16, 251–256.

Cao, Zhiyan, Guy D. Fernando, Arindam Tripathy, and Arun Upadhyay. 2018. "The Economics of Corporate Lobbying." *Journal of Corporate Finance* 49, 54–80.

Caplan, Bryan and Vipul Naik. 2014. "A Radical Case for Open Borders." Unpublished.

Caplan, Bryan and Zach Weinersmith. 2019. *Open Borders*. First Second.

Card, David. 1996. "The Effect of Unions on the Structure of Wages: A Longitudinal Analysis." *Econometrica* 64, 957–979.

Card, David and Alan B. Krueger. 1995. *Myth and Measurement: The New Economics of the Minimum Wage*. Princeton University Press.

Card, David, Thomas Lemieux, and W. Craig Riddell. 2003. "Unionization and Wage Inequality: A Comparative Study of the US, the UK, and Canada." Working Paper 9473, National Bureau of Economic Research.

Cardoso, F.H. and E. Faletto. 1979. *Dependency and Development in Latin America*. University of California Press.

Carre, Francoise and Chris Tilly. 2017. *Where Bad Jobs Are Better: Retail Jobs across Countries and Companies*. Russell Sage Foundation.

Carville, James. 1993. "The Bond Vigilantes." *Wall Street Journal*, February 25.

Cassidy, John. 2020. "Can We Have Prosperity without Growth?" *The New Yorker*, February 10.

Causa, Orsetta, Nicolas Woloszko, and David Leite. 2019. "Housing, Wealth Accumulation, and Wealth Distribution: Evidence and Stylized Facts." Economics Department Working Paper 1588, OECD.

Cengiz, Doruk, Arindrajit Dube, Attila Lindner, and Ben Zipperer. 2019. "The Effect of Minimum Wages on Low-Wage Jobs." *Quarterly Journal of Economics* 134, 1405–1454.

Center for Responsive Politics. 2020a. "Cost of Election." Opensecrets.org.

Center for Responsive Politics. 2020b. "Lobbying Data Summary." Opensecrets.org.

Chalfin, Aaron, Benjamin Hansen, Emily K. Weisburst, and Morgan C. Williams Jr. 2021. "Police Force Size and Civilian Race."

Chalfin, Aaron and Justin McCrary. 2018. "Are US Cities Underpoliced? Theory and Evidence." *Review of Economics and Statistics* 100, 167–186.

Chibber, Vivek. 2019. "Understanding Capitalism." In *The ABCs of Capitalism*, Jacobin Foundation, 4–41.

Chomsky, Noam. 2019. "'There Are Reasons for Optimism': Interview with John Nichols." *Catalyst*, Spring.

Chozick, Amy. 2015. "Hillary Clinton Proposes Tax Credit for Businesses That Share Profits." *New York Times*, July 16.

Clemens, Michael A. 2007. "Smart Samaritans." *Foreign Affairs*, September–October.

Clemens, Michael A., Claudio E. Montenegro, and Lant Pritchett. 2008. "The Place Premium: Wage Differences for Identical Workers across the US Border." Policy Research Working Paper 4671, World Bank.

Climate Action Tracker. 2020. "Warming Projections Global Update." December.

Climate Change Panel. 2014. *What We Know: The Reality, Risks, and Response to Climate Change*. American Association for the Advancement of Science.

Cohen, G.A. 2009. *Why Not Socialism?* Princeton University Press.

Cohen, Joshua. 2009. "Money, Politics, Political Equality." In Cohen, *Philosophy, Politics, Democracy*, Harvard University Press, 268–302.

Cohen, Joshua and Joel Rogers. 1983. *On Democracy*. Penguin.

Cohen, Joshua and Joel Rogers. 1992. "Secondary Associations and Democratic Governance." *Politics and Society* 20, 393–472.

Collier, Paul. 2007. *The Bottom Billion*. Oxford University Press.

Collins, Brett, Andrew Garin, Emilie Jackson, Dmitri Koustas, and Mark Payne. 2019. "Is Gig Work Replacing Traditional Employment? Evidence from Two Decades of Tax Returns."

Conchon, Aline, Norbert Kluge, and Michael Stollt. 2015. "Worker Board-Level Participation in the 31 European Economic Area Countries." European Trade Union Institute.

Congressional Budget Office. 2020. "The Distribution of Household Income, 2017."

Cook, John, et al. 2013. "Quantifying the Consensus on Anthropogenic Global Warming in the Scientific Literature." *Environmental Research Letters* 8, 1–7.

Coote, Anna and Andrew Percy. 2020. *The Case for Universal Basic Services*. Polity Press.

Cowen, Tyler. 2019. *Big Business: A Love Letter to an American Anti-Hero*. St. Martin's Press.

Cullen, Heidi. 2016. "Think It's Hot Now? Just Wait." *New York Times*, August 20.

Cumbers, Andrew. 2012. *Reclaiming Public Ownership*. Zed Books.

Cumbers, Andrew. 2020. *The Case for Economic Democracy*. Polity Press.

Cynamon, Barry Z. and Steven M. Fazzari. 2014. "Inequality, the Great Recession, and Slow Recovery." Unpublished.

Dahl, Robert A. 1985. *A Preface to Economic Democracy*. University of California Press.

Dahl, Robert A. 1989. *Democracy and Its Critics*. Yale University Press.

Dahl, Robert A. 2006. *On Political Equality*. Yale University Press.

Damaske, Sarah, Joshua M. Smyth, and Matthew J. Zawadzki. 2014. "Has Work Replaced Home as a Haven? Re-examining Arlie Hochschild's Time Bind Proposition with Objective Stress Data." *Social Science and Medicine* 115, 130–138.

Damaske, Sarah, Joshua M. Smyth, and Matthew J. Zawadzki. 2016. "Stress at Work: Differential Experiences of High versus Low SES Workers." *Social Science and Medicine* 156, 125–133.

Darby, Megan. 2019. "Which Countries Have a Net Zero Carbon Goal?" *Climate Home News*, June 14.

Day, Meagan. 2018. "Democratic Socialism, Explained by a Democratic Socialist." *Vox*, August 1.

Deaton, Angus. 2013. *The Great Escape*. Princeton University Press.

Deeg, Richard. 1999. *Finance Capital Unveiled*. University of Michigan Press.

DeLong, J. Bradford. 2020. *An Economic History of the Twentieth Century*. Unpublished.

Democratic Socialists of America. 2021. "What Is Democratic Socialism?" https://www.dsausa.org/about-us/what-is-democratic-socialism.

Devine, Pat, Xiaoqin Ding, Peihua Mao, Xing Yin, Robin Hahnel, Marta Harnecker, David Laibman, Paul Cockshott, and Allin Cottrell. 2012. "Feasibility and Coordination." *Science and Society* 76, 172–198.

Devroye, Dan and Richard B. Freeman. 2002. "Does Inequality in Skills Explain Inequality of Earnings across Advanced Countries?" Discussion Paper 0552, Centre for Economic Performance.

Dimick, Matthew. 2012. "Labor Law, New Governance, and the Ghent System." *North Carolina Law Review* 90, 319–378.

Dionne, E.J., Kayla Meltzer Drogosz, and Robert E. Litan, eds. 2003. *United We Serve: National Service and the Future of Citizenship*. Brookings Institution Press.

DiPrete, Thomas A. 2005. "Labor Markets, Inequality, and Change." *Work and Occupations* 32, 119–139.

Dollar, David, Tatjana Kleineberg, and Aart Kraay. 2016. "Growth Still Is Good for the Poor." *European Economic Review* 81, 68–85.

Dore, Ronald. 1987. *Taking Japan Seriously*. Stanford University Press.

Dow, Gregory K. 2018. *The Labor-Managed Firm*. Cambridge University Press.

Dreier, Peter and Michael Kazin. 2020. "How Socialists Changed America." In *We Own the Future: Democratic Socialism—American Style*, edited by Kate Aronoff, Peter Dreier, and Michael Kazin, New Press, 15–45.

Driscoll, Daniel. 2022. *National Carbon Prices*. PhD dissertation. Department of Sociology, University of California-San Diego.

Drum, Kevin. 2020. "We Need a Massive Climate War Effort—Now." *Mother Jones*, January–February.

Drutman, Lee. 2015. *The Business of America Is Lobbying*. Oxford University Press.

Dryzek, John S., et al. 2019. "The Crisis of Democracy and the Science of Deliberation." *Science* 363, 1144–1146.

Du Bois, W.E.B. 1899. *The Philadelphia Negro: A Social Study*. University of Pennsylvania Press.

Dube, Arindrajit. 2018. "Using Wage Boards to Raise Pay." Research Brief, Economists for Inclusive Prosperity.

Dube, Arindrajit, T. William Lester, and Michael Reich. 2010. "Minimum Wage Effects across State Borders: Estimates Using Contiguous Counties." *Review of Economics and Statistics* 92, 945–964.

Dudley, Thomas. 2017. "How Big Is America's Employee-Owned Economy?" *Medium*, June 22.

Easterly, William. 2009. "Can the West Save Africa?" *Journal of Economic Literature* 47, 373–447.

Edwards, Richard, Michael Reich, and David Gordon. 1975. *Labor Market Segmentation*. D.C. Heath.

Ehrenreich, Barbara. 2001. *Nickel and Dimed: On (Not) Getting by in America*. Henry Holt and Company.

Einstein, Albert. 1949. "Why Socialism?" *Monthly Review*, May.

Ellerman, David P. 1990. *The Democratic Worker-Owned Firm*. Unwin Hyman.

Elsässer, Lea, Svenja Hense, and Armin Schäfer. 2021. "Not Just Money: Unequal Responsiveness in Egalitarian Democracies." *Journal of European Public Policy* 28, 1890–1908.

Elster, Jon. 1989. "From Here to There; or, If Cooperative Ownership Is So Desirable, Why Are There So Few Cooperatives?" *Social Philosophy and Policy* 6(2), 93–111.

Engels, Friedrich. 1845. *The Condition of the Working Class in England*.

Esping-Andersen, Gøsta. 1985. *Politics against Markets: The Social Democratic Road to Power*. Princeton University Press.

Esping-Andersen, Gøsta, with Duncan Gallie, Anton Hemerijck, and John Myles. 2002. *Why We Need a New Welfare State*. Oxford University Press.

Eurostat. 2017. "Material Deprivation Statistics."

Evers-Hillstrom, Karl. 2020. "Majority of Lawmakers in 116th Congress Are Millionaires." Center for Responsive Politics, Opensecrets.org, April 23.

Farber, Henry S. 2010. "Job Loss and the Decline in Job Security in the United States." In *Labor in the New Economy*, edited by Katharine G. Abraham, James R. Spletzer, and Michael Harper, University of Chicago Press, 223–266.

Farber, Henry S., Daniel Herbst, Ilyana Kuziemko, and Suresh Naidu. 2018. "Unions and Inequality over the Twentieth Century: New Evidence from Survey Data." Working Paper 24587, National Bureau of Economic Research.

Ferreras, Isabelle. 2017. *Firms as Political Entities: Saving Democracy through Economic Bicameralism*. Translated and edited by Miranda Richmond Mouillot. Cambridge University Press.

Ferreras, Isabelle, Dominique Meda, and Julie Battilana. 2020. "Work: Democratize, Decommodify, Remediate." https://democratizingwork.org.

Fischer, Claude. 2011. *Still Connected: Family and Friends in America since 1970*. Russell Sage Foundation.

FitzRoy, Felix and Michael A. Nolan. 2020. "Towards Economic Democracy and Social Justice: Profit Sharing, Co-Determination, and Employee Ownership." Discussion Papers 13238, Institute of Labor Economics (IZA).

Fleurbaey, Marc, with Olivier Bouin, Marie-Laure Salles-Djelic, Ravi Kanbur, Helga Nowotny, and Elisa Reis. 2018. *A Manifesto for Social Progress*. Cambridge University Press.

Forcillo, Donato. 2017. "Codetermination: the Presence of Workers on the Board." University of Cagliari and Sassari.

Fox, Justin. 2018. "Why German Corporate Boards Include Workers." *Bloomberg Opinion*, August 24.

Freeman, Richard B. and Kelsey Hilbrich. 2013. "Do Labor Unions Have a Future in the United States?" In *The Economics of Inequality, Poverty, and Discrimination in the 21st Century*, volume 2, edited by Robert S. Rycroft, Praeger.

Freeman, Richard B. and Morris M. Kleiner. 2000. "Who Benefits Most from Employee Involvement: Firms or Workers?" *American Economic Review* (Papers and Proceedings) 90, 219–223.

Freeman, Richard B. and James L. Medoff. 1984. *What Do Unions Do?* Basic Books.

Freeman, Richard B. and Joel Rogers. 1999. *What Workers Want*. ILR Press and Russell Sage Foundation.

Friedman, Benjamin M. 2005. *The Moral Consequences of Economic Growth*. Knopf.

Friedman, Milton and Rose Friedman. 1979. *Free to Choose*. Harcourt Brace Jovanovich.

Galbraith, John Kenneth. 1998 (1958). *The Affluent Society*. 40th anniversary edition. Houghton Mifflin.

Gallie, Duncan. 2013. "Direct Participation and the Quality of Work." *Human Relations* 66, 453–473.

Gallie, Duncan, Ying Zhou, Alan Felstead, Francis Green, and Golo Henseke. 2017. "The Implications of Direct Participation for Organisational Commitment, Job Satisfaction and Affective Psychological Well-Being: A Longitudinal Analysis." *Industrial Relations Journal* 48, 174–191.

Gardner, Bradley M. 2017. *China's Great Migration*. Independent Institute.

Garritzmann, Julian L., Silja Häusermann, and Bruno Palier. 2021. "Social Investment." In *Oxford Handbook of the Welfare State*, edited by Daniel Beland, Kimberly J. Morgan, Herbert Obinger, and Christopher Pierson, Oxford University Press, 188–205.

Garson, Barbara. 1994. *All the Livelong Day: The Meaning and Demeaning of Routine Work*, updated edition. Penguin.

Gautié, Jerome and John Schmitt, eds. 2010. *Low-Wage Work in the Wealthy World*. Russell Sage Foundation.

Genschel, Philipp. 2002. "Globalization, Tax Competition, and the Welfare State." *Politics and Society* 30, 245–275.

Gerber, P.J., et al. 2013. *Tackling Climate Change through Livestock: A Global Assessment of Emissions and Mitigation Opportunities.* Food and Agriculture Organization of the United Nations.

Gilbert, Natasha. 2012. "One-Third of Our Greenhouse Gas Emissions Come from Agriculture." *Nature*, October 31.

Gilens, Martin. 2012. *Affluence and Influence.* Princeton University Press.

Gilens, Martin and Benjamin I. Page. 2014. "Testing Theories of American Politics: Elites, Interest Groups, and Average Citizens." *Perspectives on Politics* 12, 564–581.

Gillis, Justin. 2013. "Climate Panel Cites Near Certainty on Warming." *New York Times*, August 20.

Gindin, Sam. 2018. "Socialism for Realists." *Catalyst*, Fall.

Giuliano, Paola and Antonio Spilimbergo. 2014. "Growing Up in a Recession." *Review of Economic Studies* 81, 787–817.

Glaeser, Edward. 2010. "Does Economic Inequality Cause Crises?" *New York Times: Economix*, December 14.

Golden, Lonnie. 2015. "Irregular Work Scheduling and Its Consequences." Briefing Paper 394, Economic Policy Institute.

Goldthorpe, John H., ed. 1984. *Order and Conflict in Contemporary Capitalism.* Clarendon Press.

Gordon, Robert G. 2016. *The Rise and Fall of American Growth.* Princeton University Press.

Gore, Al. 2020. "Where I Find Hope." *New York Times*, December 1.

Gough, Ian. 2019. "Universal Basic Services: A Theoretical and Moral Framework." *Political Quarterly* 90, 534–542.

Gowan, Peter. 2019. "Right to Own: A Policy Framework to Catalyze Worker Ownership Transitions." Next System Project.

Gowan, Peter and Mathew Lawrence. 2019. "Democratic Ownership Funds: Creating Shared Wealth and Power." Next System Project.

Griffith, Saul. 2019a. "The Green New Deal: The Enormous Opportunity in Shooting for the Moon." *Medium*, February 20.

Griffith, Saul. 2019b. "How Do We Decarbonize?" *Medium*, May 23.

Griffith, Saul. 2019c. "Interview." *The Ezra Klein Show*, December.

Groot, Loek and Daan van der Linde. 2017. "The Labor-Managed Firm: Permanent or Start-Up Subsidies?" *Journal of Economic Issues* 51, 1074–1093.

Guendelsberger, Emily. 2019. *On the Clock: What Low-Wage Work Did to Me and How It Drives America Insane.* Little, Brown, and Company.

Gumbrell-McCormick, Rebecca and Richard Hyman. 2010. "Works Councils: The European Model of Industrial Democracy?" In *Oxford Handbook of Participation in Organizations*, edited by Adrian Wilkinson, Paul J. Gollan, Mick Marchington, and David Lewin, Oxford University Press, 286–314.

Hacker, Jacob S. 2002. *The Divided Welfare State.* Cambridge University Press.

Hacker, Jacob S. 2016. "Stronger Policy, Stronger Politics." *The American Prospect,* Fall.

Hacker, Jacob S. 2018. "The Road to Medicare for Everyone." *The American Prospect,* January 3.

Hacker, Jacob S. and Paul Pierson. 2010. *Winner-Take-All Politics.* Simon and Schuster.

Hacker, Jacob S. and Paul Pierson. 2020. *Let Them Eat Tweets: How the Right Rules in an Age of Extreme Inequality.* Liveright.

Hahnel, Robin. 2012. *Of the People, By the People: The Case for a Participatory Economy.* Soapbox.

Hahnel, Robin. 2021. *Democratic Economic Planning*. Routledge.

Hall, Peter A. 1986. *Governing the Economy*. Oxford University Press.

Hanna, Mark. 2018. "The Crisis Next Time: Planning for Public Ownership as an Alternative to Corporate Bank Bailouts." The Democracy Collaborative.

Harrington, Michael. 1978. "What Socialists Would Do in America—If They Could." *Dissent*, Fall, 440–452.

Harrington, Michael, 1982. "Is Capitalism Still Viable?" *Journal of Business Ethics* 1, 281–284.

Harrington, Michael. 1989. *Socialism, Past and Future*. Arcade Publishing.

Hartig, Hannah. 2019. "Stark Partisan Divisions in Americans' Views of 'Socialism,' 'Capitalism.'" Pew Research Center, June 25.

Hawkley, L.C. and J.T. Cacioppo. 2010. "Loneliness Matters: A Theoretical and Empirical Review of Consequences and Mechanisms." *Annals of Behavioral Medicine* 40, 218–227.

Hayek, Friedrich. 1945. "The Price System as a Mechanism for Using Knowledge." *American Economic Review* 35, 519–530.

Hayek, Friedrich A. 1960. *The Constitution of Liberty*. University of Chicago Press.

Hayek, Friedrich A. 1979. *Law, Legislation, and Liberty*. Volume 3. University of Chicago Press.

Helland, Eric and Alex Tabarrok. 2019. *Why Are the Prices So Damn High? Health, Education, and the Baumol Effect*. Mercatus Center.

Hemerijck, Anton. 2013. *Changing Welfare States*. Oxford University Press.

Hemerijck, Anton, ed. 2017. *The Uses of Social Investment*. Oxford University Press.

Hermann, Christoph. 2015. *Capitalism and the Political Economy of Work Time*. Routledge.

Hick, Rod and Tania Burchardt. 2016. "Capability Deprivation." In *Oxford Handbook of the Social Science of Poverty*, edited by David Brady and Linda M. Burton, Oxford University Press, 75–92.

Hicks, Alexander. 1999. *Social Democracy and Welfare Capitalism*. Cornell University Press.

Hickel, Jason. 2018a. *The Divide: Global Inequality from Conquest to Free Markets*. W.W. Norton.

Hickel, Jason. 2018b. "The Moral Egregiousness of Poverty Is Worse Than Ever Before in History." Jason Hickel blog, August 30.

Hills, John. 2011. "The Changing Architecture of the UK Welfare State." *Oxford Review of Economic Policy* 4, 589–607.

Hirsch, Barry T. 1992. "Firm Investment Behavior and Collective Bargaining Strategy." In *Labor Market Institutions and the Future Role of Unions*, edited by M.F. Bognanno and M.M. Kleiner, Blackwell.

Hochschild, Arlie Russell. 1997. *The Time Bind: When Work Becomes Home and Home Becomes Work*. Metropolitan Books.

Holmberg, Susan R. 2017. "Fighting Short-Termism with Worker Power." Roosevelt Institute.

Holt-Lunstad, Julianne, Timothy B. Smith, Mark Baker, Tyler Harris, and David Stephenson. 2015. "Loneliness and Social Isolation as Risk Factors for Mortality: A Meta-Analytic Review." *Perspectives on Psychological Science* 10, 227–237.

Horowitz, Sara. 2015. "Help for the Way We Work Now." *New York Times*, September 7.

Huber, Evelyne, Jingjing Huo, and John D. Stephens. 2019. "Power, Policy, and Top Income Shares." *Socio-Economic Review* 17, 231–253.

Huber, Evelyn and John D. Stephens. 2001. *Development and Crisis of the Welfare State*. University of Chicago Press.

Hübler, Olaf. 2015. "Do Works Councils Raise or Lower Firm Productivity?" IZA World of Labor.

Huo, Jingjing, Moira Nelson, and John D. Stephens. 2008. "Decommodification and Activation in Social Democratic Policy: Resolving the Paradox." *Journal of European Social Policy* 18, 5–20.

Hynes, William, Patrick Love, and Angela Stuart, eds. 2020. *The Financial System.* OECD Publishing.

Inglehart, Ronald F. 2008. "Changing Values among Western Publics from 1970 to 2006." *West European Politics* 31, 130–146.

Inglehart, Ronald F. 2018. *Cultural Evolution.* Cambridge University Press.

Intergovernmental Panel on Climate Change (IPCC). 2013. "Working Group 1 Summary for Policymakers." *Fifth Assessment Report.*

Intergovernmental Panel on Climate Change (IPCC). 2018. "Summary for Policymakers of IPCC Special Report on Global Warming of 1.5C."

International Organization for Migration. 2014. "IOM Outlook on Migration, Environment, and Climate Change."

International Panel on Social Progress. 2018. *Rethinking Society for the 21st Century.* 3 vols. Cambridge University Press.

IPPR Commission on Economic Justice. 2018. *Prosperity and Justice: A Plan for the New Economy.* Polity Press.

Irwin, Neil. 2021. "How Should the Fed Deal with Climate Change?" *New York Times,* August 26.

Iversen, Torben and David Soskice. 2019. *Democracy and Prosperity.* Princeton University Press.

Jacobs, Lawrence, et al. 2004. "American Democracy in an Age of Rising Inequality." Report of the American Political Science Association Task Force on Inequality and American Democracy. *Perspectives on Politics* 2, 651–666.

Jacobs, Lawrence R. and Desmond King. 2016. *Fed Power: How Finance Wins.* Oxford University Press.

Jacobson, Mark Z., et al. 2017. "100% Clean and Renewable Wind, Water, and Sunlight All-Sector Energy Roadmaps for 139 Countries of the World." *Joule* 1, 108–121.

Jackson, Andrew. 2021. *The Fire and the Ashes: Rekindling Democratic Socialism.* Between the Lines.

Jäger, Simon, Benjamin Schoefer, and Jörg Heining. 2020. "Labor in the Board Room." NBER Conference Paper.

Jahoda, Marie. 1982. *Employment and Unemployment: A Social Psychological Analysis.* Cambridge University Press.

Jaumotte, Florence and Carolina Osorio Buitron. 2015. "Inequality and Labor Market Institutions." Staff Discussion Note 15/14, International Monetary Fund.

Jencks, Christopher. 2009. "The Poor Die Young: What's Killing Them?" Unpublished.

Jenkins, Jesse D. and Samuel Thernstrom. 2017. "Deep Decarbonization of the Electric Power Sector: Insights from Recent Literature." Energy Information Reform Project.

Jetter, Michael, Sabine Laudage, and David Stadelmann. 2019. "The Intimate Link between Income Levels and Life Expectancy: Global Evidence from 213 Years." *Social Science Quarterly* 100, 1387–1403.

Jirjahn, Uwe and Stephen C. Smith. 2016. "Nonunion Employee Representation: Theory and the German Experience with Mandated Works Councils." *Annals of Public and Cooperative Economics* 89, 201–234.

Johnson, Chalmers. 1982. *MITI and the Japanese Miracle*. Stanford University Press.

Johnson, Simon. 2015. "Resurrecting Glass-Steagall." *Project Syndicate*, October 29.

Judis, John B. 2020. *The Socialist Awakening*. Columbia Global Reports.

Judt, Tony. 2010. *Ill Fares the Land*. Penguin.

Kaarsemaker, Eric, Andrew Pendleton, and Erik Poutsma. 2010. "Employee Share Ownership." In *Oxford Handbook of Participation in Organizations*, edited by Adrian Wilkinson, Paul J. Gollan, Mick Marchington, and David Lewin, Oxford University Press, 315–337.

Kahlenberg, Richard D. and Moshe Z. Marvit. 2012. "Why the Right to Form a Union Should Be a Civil Right." *Washington Post*, August 31.

Kahn, Lisa. 2010. "The Long-Term Labor Market Consequences of Graduating from College in a Bad Economy." *Labour Economics* 17, 303–316.

Kalecki, Michal. 1943. "Political Aspects of Full Employment." *Political Quarterly* 14, 322–330.

Kalleberg, Arne L. 2018. *Precarious Lives: Job Insecurity and Well-Being in Rich Democracies*. Polity Press.

Karma, Roge. 2019. "Five Myths about Global Poverty." *Current Affairs*, July 26.

Katz, Lawrence F. and Alan B. Krueger. 2016. "The Rise and Nature of Alternative Work Arrangements in the United States, 1999–2015."

Katzenstein, Peter J. 1985. *Small States in World Markets*. Cornell University Press.

Kaufman, Bruce E. and Daphne G. Taras. 2010. "Employee Participation through Non-Union Forms of Employee Representation." In *Oxford Handbook of Participation in Organizations*, edited by Adrian Wilkinson, Paul J. Gollan, Mick Marchington, and David Lewin, Oxford University Press, 258–285.

Kautto, Mikko and Kati Kuitto. 2021. "The Nordic Countries." In *Oxford Handbook of the Welfare State*, edited by Daniel Beland, Kimberly J. Morgan, Herbert Obinger, and Christopher Pierson, Oxford University Press, 803–825.

Keith-Jennings, Brynne. 2018. "Millions Still Struggling to Afford Food." Center on Budget and Policy Priorities.

Kelly, Gavin and Daniel Tomlinson. 2017. "Putting Tech to Work: The Urgent Need for Innovation in How the Low-Wage Workforce Is Supported." Resolution Trust.

Kenworthy, Lane. 1990. "What Kind of Economic System? A Leftist's Guide." *Socialist Review* 20(2), 102–124.

Kenworthy, Lane. 1995. *In Search of National Economic Success*. Sage.

Kenworthy, Lane. 2002. "Corporatism and Unemployment in the 1980s and 1990s." *American Sociological Review* 67, 367–388.

Kenworthy, Lane. 2004. *Egalitarian Capitalism*. Russell Sage Foundation.

Kenworthy, Lane. 2008. *Jobs with Equality*. Oxford University Press.

Kenworthy, Lane. 2010. "Institutions, Wealth, and Inequality." In *Oxford Handbook of Comparative Institutional Analysis*, edited by Glenn Morgan, John L. Campbell, Colin Crouch, Ove Kaj Pedersen, and Richard Whitley, Oxford University Press, 399–420.

Kenworthy, Lane. 2011a. "How Should We Measure the Poverty Rate?" *Consider the Evidence*, August 14.

Kenworthy, Lane. 2011b. *Progress for the Poor*. Oxford University Press.

Kenworthy, Lane. 2011c. "When Does Economic Growth Benefit People on Low to Middle Incomes—and Why?" Commission on Living Standards, Resolution Foundation.

Kenworthy, Lane. 2013. "What's Wrong with Predistribution?" *Juncture* 20, 111–117.

Kenworthy, Lane. 2015. "Do Employment-Conditional Earnings Subsidies Work?" ImPRovE Working Paper 15-10, Herman Deleeck Centre for Social Policy, University of Antwerp.

Kenworthy, Lane. 2020. *Social Democratic Capitalism*. Oxford University Press.

Kenworthy, Lane. 2021. "Is There a Solution to America's Mobility Failure?" Yankelovich Center for Social Research, University of California-San Diego.

Kenworthy, Lane. 2022a. "Economic Inequality and Plutocracy." *Contemporary Sociology* 51, 6–15.

Kenworthy, Lane. 2022b. *The Good Society*. https://lanekenworthy.net.

Kishimoto, Satoko, Lavinia Steinfort, and Olivier Petitjean, eds. 2020. *The Future Is Public: Towards Democratic Ownership of Public Services*. Transnational Institute.

Klein, Ezra. 2012. "Our Corrupt Politics—It's Not All Money." *New York Review of Books*, March 22.

Klein, Naomi. 2014. *This Changes Everything: Capitalism versus the Climate*. Simon and Schuster.

Kleven, Henrik Jacobsen. 2014. "How Can Scandinavians Tax So Much?" *Journal of Economic Perspectives* 28, 77–98.

Kliff, Sarah and Ezra Klein. 2017. "The Lessons of Obamacare." *Vox*, March 15.

Knight, Jack and Ramani Gunatilaka. 2018. "Rural-Urban Migration and Happiness in China." In *World Happiness Report 2018*, edited by John F. Helliwell, Richard Layard, and Jeffrey D. Sachs, 66–87.

Kochan, Thomas A., Duanyi Yang, William T. Kimball, and Erin L. Kelly. 2019. "Worker Voice in America: Is There a Gap between What Workers Expect and What They Experience?" *ILR Review* 72, 3–38.

Kochnar, Rakesh. 2015. "A Global Middle Class Is More Promise Than Reality." Pew Research Center.

Koeniger, Winfried, Marco Leonardi, and Luca Nunziata. 2007. "Labor Market Institutions and Wage Inequality." *Industrial and Labor Relations Review* 60, 340–356.

Konczal, Mike. 2012. "No Discount: Comparing the Public Option to the Coupon Welfare State." New America Foundation.

Konczal, Mike. 2015. "Structural Reform Beyond Glass-Steagall." *Next New Deal*, October 13.

Kornai, Janos. 1983. *Contradictions and Dilemmas: Studies on the Socialist Economy and Society*. MIT Press.

Korpi, Walter. 1982. *The Democratic Class Struggle*. Routledge and Kegan Paul.

Kristal, Tali. 2017. "What Can Unions Do? An Impact Estimate for an Increase in the Private-Sector Unionization Rate on Workers' Earnings." Yankelovich Center for Social Science Research, University of California-San Diego.

Krueger, Alan B. 2016. "Where Have All the Workers Gone?"

Krugman, Paul. 1994. *Peddling Prosperity*. W.W. Norton.

Krugman, Paul. 2009. *The Return of Depression Economics and the Crisis of 2008*. W.W. Norton.

Krugman, Paul. 2010. "Six Doctrines in Search of a Policy Regime." *New York Times: The Conscience of a Liberal*, April 18.

Krugman, Paul. 2011. "Oligarchy, American Style." *New York Times*, November 4.

Krugman, Paul. 2012. *End This Depression Now!* W.W. Norton.

Krugman, Paul. 2013. "The New Growth Fizzle." *New York Times: The Conscience of a Liberal*, April 18.

Krugman, Paul. 2018. "The Fraudulence of the Fiscal Hawks." *New York Times*, February 9.

Krugman, Paul. 2021a. "Globalization: An Ambiguous Good." *Econofact Chats*, February 21.

Krugman, Paul. 2021b. "Honey, Who Shrunk the World?" *New York Times: Newsletter*, August 20.

Kruse, Douglas, Richard Freeman, and Joseph Blasi. 2008. "Do Workers Gain by Sharing? Employee Outcomes under Employee Ownership, Profit Sharing, and Broad-Based Stock Options." Working Paper 14233, National Bureau of Economic Research.

Kumhof, Michael, Romain Ranciere, and Pablo Winant. 2015. "Inequality, Leverage, and Crises." *American Economic Review* 105, 1217–1245.

Kuttner, Robert. 2011. "Simplify Banks and Bank Regulation." *Huffington Post*, October 16.

Kuttner, Robert. 2021a. "Bringing the Supply Chain Back Home." *New York Review of Books*, November 18.

Kuttner, Robert. 2021b. "Capitalism vs. Liberty." *The American Prospect*, December 1.

Kuttner, Robert. 2021c. "The Agony of Social Democratic Europe." *The American Prospect*, August 4.

Lampman, Robert J. 1971. *Ends and Means of Reducing Income Poverty*. Markham.

Lange, Peter and Geoffrey Garrett. 1985. "The Politics of Growth." *Journal of Politics* 47, 792–827.

Layard, Richard. 2005. *Happiness*. Penguin.

Lee, Ronald, et al. 2015. *The Growing Gap in Life Expectancy by Income*. National Academies Press.

Levin, Yuval. 2015. *The Fractured Republic*. Basic Books.

Levine, Andrew. 1996. "Saving Socialism and/or Abandoning It." In *Equal Shares: Making Market Socialism Work*, edited by Erik Olin Wright, Verso, 231–249.

Levine, David I. and Laura D'Andrea Tyson. 1990. "Participation, Productivity, and the Firm's Environment." In *Paying for Productivity*, edited by Alan S. Blinder, Brookings Institution, 183–237.

Levine, Ross. 2011. "Finance, Long-Run Growth, and Economic Opportunity." *VoxEU*, October 25.

Lindblom, Charles E. 1977. "The Privileged Position of Business." In *Politics and Markets*, Basic Books, 170–188.

Lindert, Peter H. and Jeffrey G. Williamson. 2016. *Unequal Gains: American Growth and Inequality since 1700*. Princeton University Press.

Lowrey, Annie. 2014. "Income Gap, Meet the Longevity Gap." *New York Times*, May 15.

Lowrey, Annie. 2018. *Give People Money: How a Universal Basic Income Would End Poverty, Revolutionize Work, and Remake the World*. Crown.

Lucas, Robert. 2003. Presidential Address to the American Economic Association.

Luce, Stephanie, Jennifer Luff, Joseph A. McCartin, and Ruth Milkman, eds. 2014. *What Works for Workers? Public Policies and Innovative Strategies for Low-Wage Workers*. Russell Sage Foundation.

Lucifora, Claudio, Abigail McKnight, and Wiemer Salverda. 2005. "Low-Wage Employment in Europe: A Review of the Evidence." *Socio-Economic Review* 3, 259–292.

Mackenbach, Johan P. 2016. "Changes in Mortality Inequalities over Two Decades: Register Based Study of European Countries." *BMJ*. dx.doi.org/10.1136/bmj.i1732.

Maddison, Angus. 2007. *Contours of the World Economy, 1-2030 AD*. Oxford University Press.

Madland, David. 2018. "Wage Boards for American Workers." Center for American Progress.

Magaziner, Ira C. and Robert B. Reich. 1983. *Minding America's Business*. Vintage.

Malleson, Tom. 2014. *After Occupy: Economic Democracy for the 21st Century*. Oxford University Press.

Mann, Thomas E. and Norman J. Ornstein. 2012. *It's Even Worse Than It Looks*. Basic Books.

Manning, Alan and Graham Mazeine. 2020. "Subjective Job Insecurity and the Rise of the Precariat: Evidence from the UK, Germany, and the United States." Discussion Paper 1712, London School of Economics and Political Science.

Manzi, Jim. 2008. "Keeping Our Cool: What to Do about Global Warming." *Cato Unbound*, August 11.

Markey, Raymond, Nicola Balnave, and Greg Patmore. 2010. "Worker Directors and Worker Ownership/Cooperatives." In *Oxford Handbook of Participation in Organizations*, edited by Adrian Wilkinson, Paul J. Gollan, Mick Marchington, and David Lewin, Oxford University Press, 237–257.

Marmor, Theodore R., Jerry L. Mashaw, and John Pakutka. 2014. *Social Insurance*. CQ Press.

Marris, Emma. 2020. "How to Stop Freaking Out and Tackle Climate Change." *New York Times*, January 10.

Marx, Karl. 1867. *Capital*, volume 1.

Massey, Douglas S. 2008. "Caution, NAFTA at Work: How Europe's Trade Model Could Solve America's Immigration Problem." *Pacific Standard*, March 4.

Matthews, Dylan. 2014. "A Guaranteed Income for Every American Would Eliminate Poverty—and It Wouldn't Destroy the Economy." *Vox*, July 23.

Matthews, Dylan. 2016. "Donald Trump Promised 'Insurance for Everybody'. Here's How He Can Do It." *Vox*, May 24.

Matthews, Dylan. 2019a. "Bill Gates Tweeted Out a Chart and Sparked a Huge Debate about Global Poverty." *Vox*, February 12.

Matthews, Dylan. 2019b. "Bernie Sanders's Most Socialist Idea Yet, Explained." *Vox*, May 29.

Matthews, Dylan. 2021. "How the US Won the Economic Recovery." *Vox*, April 30.

Mazzucato, Mariana. 2013. *The Entrepreneurial State: Debunking Public vs. Private Sector Myths*. Anthem Press.

Mazzucato, Mariana. 2021. *Mission Economy: A Moonshot Guide to Changing Capitalism*. Harper Business.

McCallum, Jamie K. 2020. *Worked Over: How Round-the-Clock Work Is Killing the American Dream*. Basic Books.

McCarthy, Mike. 2020. "Our First 100 Days Could Be a Nightmare." *Jacobin*, Winter, 68–80.

Meidner, Rudolf. 1981. "Collective Asset Formation through Wage-Earner Funds." *International Labour Review* 120, 303–317.

Mello, Steven. 2019. "More Cops, Less Crime." *Journal of Public Economics* 172, 174–200.

Mensi-Klarbach, Heike and Cathrine Seierstad. 2020. "Gender Quotas on Corporate Boards: Similarities and Differences in Quota Scenarios." *European Management Review* 17, 615–631.

Meyerson, Harold. 2014. "The Seeds of a New Labor Movement." *The American Prospect*, December 29.

Meyerson, Harold. 2020. "How Socialism Surged, and How It Can Go Further." In *We Own the Future: Democratic Socialism—American Style*, edited by Kate Aronoff, Peter Dreier, and Michael Kazin, New Press, 290–304.

Mian, Atif and Amir Sufi. 2014. *House of Debt*. University of Chicago Press.

Milanovic, Branko. 2009. "Income Inequality and Speculative Investment by the Rich and Poor in America Led to the Financial Meltdown." *Yale Global Online*, May 4.

Milanovic, Branko. 2016. *Global Inequality*. Harvard University Press.

Milanovic, Branko. 2019. *Capitalism, Alone*. Harvard University Press.

Miliband, Ed. 2021. *Go Big: How to Fix Our World*. Bodley Head.

Miliband, Ralph. 1994. *Socialism for a Skeptical Age*. Verso.

Mishel, Lawrence. 2018a. "Contingent Worker Survey Is Further Evidence That We Are Not Becoming a Nation of Freelancers." Economic Policy Institute.

Mishel, Lawrence. 2018b. "Self-Employment Headcount Has Risen but Economic Impact Remains Small." Economic Policy Institute.

Mishel, Lawrence and Josh Bivens. 2021. "Identifying the Policy Levers Generating Wage Suppression and Wage Inequality." Economic Policy Institute.

Morel, Nathalie, Bruno Palier, and Joakim Palme, eds. 2012. *Towards a Social Investment Welfare State?* Policy Press.

Morelli, Salvatore and Anthony Atkinson. 2015. "Inequality and Crises Revisited." *Economia Politica* 32, 31–51.

Morgan, Kimberly J. and Andrea Louise Campbell. 2011. *The Delegated Welfare State*. Oxford University Press.

Moskin, Julia, Brad Plumer, Rebecca Lieberman, and Eden Weingart. 2019. "Your Questions about Food and Climate Change, Answered." *New York Times*, April 30.

Mossialos, Elias, Ana Djordjevic, Robin Osborn, and Dana Sarnak, eds. 2017. *International Profiles of Health Care Systems*. Commonwealth Fund.

Murray, Charles. 2006. *In Our Hands: A Plan to Replace the Welfare State*. AEI Press.

Murray, Charles 2008. "Guaranteed Income as a Replacement for the Welfare State." *Basic Income Studies* 3, 1–12.

Murray, Charles. 2012. *Coming Apart: The State of White America, 1960–2010*. Crown Forum.

Murthy, Vivek. 2017. "Work and the Loneliness Epidemic." *Harvard Business Review*, September 26.

Myrdal, Gunnar. 1944. *An American Dilemma: The Negro Problem and Modern Democracy*. Harper and Brothers.

National Advisory Commission on Civil Disorders. 1968. *The Kerner Report*.

National Center for Employee Ownership. 2019. "Employee Ownership by the Numbers." July.

National Research Council, Committee on Geoengineering Climate. 2015. "News Release."

Newport, Frank. 2018. "Democrats More Positive about Socialism Than Capitalism." Gallup, August 13.

Next System Project. 2018. "The Systemic Roadblocks to Climate Action." November 5.

New York Times Editorial Board. 2021. "Should Young Americans Be Required to Give a Year of Service?" *New York Times*, May 1.

Nichols, A. and J. Rothstein. 2016. "The Earned Income Tax Credit." In *Economics of Means-Tested Transfer Programs in the United States*, vol. 1, edited by R. Moffitt, University of Chicago Press, 137–218.

Nikkei Asia. 2020. "Toyota's Game-Changing Solid-State Battery En Route for 2021 Debut." December 10.

Nolan, Brian. 2018. "Introduction." In *Inequality and Inclusive Growth in Rich Countries*, edited by Brian Nolan, Oxford University Press, 1–10.

Nolan, Brian, Stefan Thewissen, and Alice Lazzati. 2018. "Sources of Household Income Growth in Rich Countries." In *Generating Prosperity for Working Families in Affluent Countries*, edited by Brian Nolan, Oxford University Press, 111–133.

Nordhaus, William. 2015. "A New Solution: The Climate Club." *New York Review of Books*, June 4.

Norhaus, Ted and Michael Shellenberger. 2007. *Break Through*. Houghton Mifflin.

Nove, Alec. 1983. *The Economics of Feasible Socialism*. George Allen and Unwin.

NRDC. 2019. "Unpacking New York's Big New Climate Bill: A Primer." June 20.

Nussbaum, Martha C. 2011. *Creating Capabilities*. Harvard University Press.

Obama, Barack. 2012. "State of the Union Address."

OECD (Organization for Economic Cooperation and Development). 2008. *Growing Unequal?* OECD Publishing.

OECD. 2018. *OECD Employment Outlook 2018*. OECD Publishing.

OECD. 2019a. *Negotiating Our Way Up: Collective Bargaining in a Changing World of Work*. OECD Publishing.

OECD. 2019b. *Under Pressure: The Squeezed Middle Class*. OECD Publishing.

OECD. 2020. "Top Statutory Personal Income Tax Rates."

Oesch, Daniel and Giorgio Piccitto. 2019. "The Polarization Myth: Occupational Upgrading in Germany, Spain, Sweden, and the UK, 1992–2015." *Work and Occupations* 46, 441–469.

Olsen, Gregg M. 2021. *Poverty and Austerity amid Prosperity*. University of Toronto Press.

Olshansky, S. Jay, et al. 2012. "Differences in Life Expectancy Due to Race and Educational Differences Are Widening, and Many May Not Catch Up." *Health Affairs* 8, 1803–1813.

O'Neill, Martin and Thad Williamson, eds. 2012. *Property-Owning Democracy: Rawls and Beyond*. Wiley-Blackwell.

Oreopoulos, Philip, Till von Wachter, and Andrew Heisz. 2012. "The Short- and Long-Term Career Effects of Graduating in a Recession: Hysteresis and Heterogeneity in the Market for College Graduates." *American Economic Journal: Applied Economics* 4, 1–29.

Ortiz-Ospina, Esteban. 2019. "How Important Are Social Relations for Our Health and Well-Being?" *Our World in Data*.

Oskarsson, Sven. 2005. "Divergent Trends and Different Causal Logics: The Importance of Bargaining Centralization When Explaining Earnings Inequality across Advanced Democratic Societies." *Politics and Society* 33, 359–385.

Osterman, Paul. 1999. *Securing Prosperity*. Princeton University Press.

Ownership Commission. 2012. *Plurality, Stewardship, and Engagement: The Report of the Ownership Commission*. Muto.

Packard, Vance. 1972. *A Nation of Strangers*. David McKay Co.

Page, Benjamin I., Larry M. Bartels, and Jason Seawright. 2013. "Democracy and the Policy Preferences of Wealthy Americans." *Perspectives on Politics* 11, 51–73.

Page, Benjamin and Martin Gilens. 2017. *Democracy in America? What Has Gone Wrong and What We Can Do about It*. University of Chicago Press.

Page, Benjamin I, Jason Seawright, and Matthew J. Lacombe. 2019. *Billionaires and Stealth Politics*. University of Chicago Press.

Palier, Bruno, ed. 2010. *A Long Goodbye to Bismarck? The Politics of Welfare Reform in Continental Europe*. University of Chicago Press.

Palley, Thomas I. 2015. "Inequality, the Financial Crisis, and Stagnation: Competing Stories and Why They Matter." Working Paper 151, Macroeconomic Policy Institute.

Panitch, Leo. 2014. "Europe's Left Has Seen How Capitalism Can Bite Back." *The Guardian*, January 12.

Panitch, Leo. 2020. "The Long Shot of Democratic Socialism Is Our Only Shot." Interview with Bhaskar Sunkara. *Jacobin*, January 15.

Panitch, Leo and Sam Gindin. 2018. *The Socialist Challenge Today*. Merlin Press.

Partanen, Anu. 2016. *The Nordic Theory of Everything*. Harper.

Pencavel, John. 2012. "Worker Cooperatives and Democratic Governance." Discussion Paper 12-003, Stanford Institute for Economic Policy Research.

Persson, Mikael and Mikael Gilljam. 2018. "Who Got What They Wanted? The Opinion-Policy Link in Sweden 1956–2014."

Pfeffer, Fabian T., and Nora Waitkus. 2021. "The Wealth Inequality of Nations." *American Sociological Review*, doi.org/10.1177/00031224211027800.

Philippon, Thomas. 2019. *The Great Reversal: How America Gave Up on Markets*. Harvard University Press.

Philippon, Thomas and Ariell Reshef. 2013. "An International Look at the Growth of Modern Finance." *Journal of Economic Perspectives* 27(2), 73–96.

Pickard, Jim and Robert Shrimsley. 2019. "Jeremy Corbyn's Plan to Rewrite the Rules of the UK Economy." *Financial Times*, August 31.

Pierson, Christopher. 2021. *The Next Welfare State?* Polity Press.

Piketty, Thomas. 2020. *Capital and Ideology*. Translated by Arthur Goldhammer. Harvard University Press.

Piketty, Thomas. 2021. *Time for Socialism*. Yale University Press.

Piketty, Thomas, Emmanuel Saez, and Stefanie Stantcheva. 2014. "Optimal Taxation of Top Labor Incomes: A Tale of Three Elasticities." *American Economic Journal: Economic Policy* 6, 230–271.

Piketty, Thomas, Emmanuel Saez, and Gabriel Zucman. 2018. "Distributional National Accounts: Methods and Estimates for the United States." *Quarterly Journal of Economics* 133, 553–609.

Pofeldt, Elaine. 2014. "Is the Job of the Future a Freelance One?" CNBC, January 29.

Polakow-Suransky, Sasha. 2017. *Go Back to Where You Came From: The Backlash against Immigration and the Fate of Western Democracy*. Bold Type Books.

Polanyi, Karl. (1944) 1957. *The Great Transformation*. Beacon Press.

Pollin, Robert. 2011. "Back to Full Employment." *Boston Review*.

Pontusson, Jonas. 1987. "Radicalism and Retreat in Swedish Social Democracy." *New Left Review* 165, 5–33.

Pontusson, Jonas. 2011. "Once Again a Model: Nordic Social Democracy in a Globalized World." In *What's Left of the Left?*, edited by James Cronin, George Ross, and James Shoch, Duke University Press, 89–115.

Pontusson, Jonas and Sarosh Kuruvilla. 1992. "Swedish Wage-Earner Funds: An Experiment in Economic Democracy." *Industrial and Labor Relations Review* 45, 779–791.

Potsdam Institute for Climate Impact Research and Climate Analytics. 2012. "Turn Down the Heat: Why a 4°C Warmer World Must Be Avoided." World Bank.

Poore, J. and T. Nemecek. 2018. "Reducing Food's Environmental Impacts through Producers and Consumers." *Science* 360, 987–992.

Porter, Michael E. 1992. *Capital Choices: Changing the Way America Invests in Industry.* Council on Competitiveness.

Prasad, Monica. 2018. *Starving the Beast: Ronald Reagan and the Tax Cut Revolution.* Russell Sage Foundation.

Pritchett, Lant. 2006. *Let Their People Come.* Center for Global Development.

Pritchett, Lant. 2018. "Alleviating Global Poverty: Labor Mobility, Direct Assistance, and Economic Growth." Working Paper 479, Center for Global Development.

Pritchett, Lant. 2020. "Poverty Reduction and Economic Growth." *EconoFact*, February 2.

Przeworski, Adam. 1985. *Capitalism and Social Democracy.* Cambridge University Press.

Przeworski, Adam, Michael E. Alvarez, Jose Antonio Cheibub, and Fernando Limongi. 2000. *Democracy and Development.* Cambridge University Press.

Przeworski, Adam and Michael Wallerstein. 1988. "Structural Dependence of the State on Capital." *American Political Science Review* 82, 1–29.

Putnam, Robert D. 2000. *Bowling Alone: The Collapse and Revival of American Community.* Simon and Schuster.

Putterman, Louis. 2009. "Labour-Managed Firms." In *The New Palgrave Dictionary of Economics*, Palgrave Macmillan.

Rajan, Raghuram G. 2010. *Fault Lines.* Princeton University Press.

Rawls, John. 2001. *Justice as Fairness: A Restatement.* Harvard University Press.

Reich, Robert B. 2010. *Aftershock.* Knopf.

Reich, Robert B. 2015. *Saving Capitalism.* Knopf.

Reich, Robert B. 2020. *The System: Who Rigged It, How We Fix It.* Knopf.

Reid, T.R. 2009. *The Healing of America: A Global Quest for Better, Cheaper, Fairer Health Care.* Penguin.

Renwick, Chris. 2017. *Bread for All: The Origins of the Welfare State.* Allen Lane.

Reuters. 2020. "German Parliament Suspends Debt Brake to Fight Coronavirus Outbreak." *New York Times*, March 28.

Rich, Nathaniel. 2018. "Losing Earth: The Decade We Almost Stopped Climate Change." *New York Times*, April 18.

Riesman, David. 1950. *The Lonely Crowd.*

Robeyns, Ingrid. 2018. *Well-Being, Freedom, and Social Justice: The Capabilities Approach Reexamined.* Open Book Publishers.

Robin, Corey. 2018. "The New Socialists." *New York Times*, August 24.

Robinson, Joan and Frank Wilkinson. 1977. "What Has Become of Employment Policy?" *Cambridge Journal of Economics* 1, 5–14.

Robinson, Nathan J. 2019. *Why You Should Be a Socialist.* All Points Books.

Robinson, William I. 2014. *Global Capitalism and the Crisis of Humanity.* Cambridge University Press.

Rodden, Jonathan. 2019. *Why Cities Lose: The Deep Roots of the Urban–Rural Political Divide.* Basic Books.

Rodney, Walter. 1972. *How Europe Underdeveloped Africa.* Bogle-L'Ouverture Publications.

Rodrik, Dani. 2007. *One Economics, Many Recipes.* Princeton University Press.

Rodrik, Dani. 2009. "The Tobin Tax Lives Again." *Project Syndicate*, September 11.

Rodrik, Dani. 2010. *The Globalization Paradox.* W.W. Norton.

Rodrik, Dani. 2013. "The Past, Present, and Future of Economic Growth." Global Citizen Foundation.

Roemer, John E. 1979. "Divide and Conquer: Microfoundations of a Marxian Theory of Wage Discrimination." *Bell Journal of Economics* 10, 695–705.

Roemer, John E. 1994. *A Future for Socialism*. Harvard University Press.

Roemer, John E. 2017a. "Socialism Now?" Janus Lecture Series, Brown University.

Roemer, John E. 2017b. "Socialism Revised." *Philosophy and Public Affairs* 45, 261–315.

Roemer, John E., et al. 1996. *Equal Shares: Making Market Socialism Work*. Verso.

Rogers, Joel. 1990. "Divide and Conquer: Further 'Reflections on the Distinctive Character of American Labor Laws.'" *Wisconsin Law Review* 1, 1–7.

Rogers, Joel. 1995. "A Strategy for Labor." *Industrial Relations* 34, 367–381.

Rogers, Joel and Satya Rhodes-Conway. 2014. *Cities at Work: Progressive Local Policies to Rebuild the Middle Class*. Center for American Progress Action Fund.

Rogers, Joel and Wolfgang Streeck, eds. 1995. *Works Councils*. University of Chicago Press.

Rohde, R., R.A. Muller, R. Jacobsen, E. Muller, S. Perlmutter, et al. 2013. "A New Estimate of the Average Earth Surface Land Temperature Spanning 1753 to 2011." *Geoinformatics and Geostatistics: An Overview*.

Romm, Joseph. 2016. *Climate Change: What Everyone Needs to Know*. Oxford University Press.

Rosenfeld, Jake. 2014. *What Unions No Longer Do*. Harvard University Press.

Rosset, Jan. 2016. *Economic Inequality and Political Representation in Switzerland*. Springer.

Rothstein, Bo. 1992. "Labor Market Institutions and Working-Class Strength." In *Structuring Politics: Historical Institutionalism in Comparative Analysis*, edited by Sven Steinmo, Kathleen Thelen, and Frank Longstreth, Cambridge University Press, 33–56.

Rothstein, Bo. 2015. "The Moral, Economic, and Political Logic of the Swedish Welfare State." In *Oxford Handbook of Swedish Politics*, edited by Jon Pierre, Oxford University Press, 69–84.

Rueda, David and Jonas Pontusson. 2000. "Wage Inequality and Varieties of Capitalism." *World Politics* 52, 350–383.

Sachs, Jeffrey D. 2005. *The End of Poverty*. Penguin.

Sachs, Jeffrey D. 2020. "How Inequality Fuels Covid-19 Deaths." *Projective Syndicate*, June 29.

Sanders, Bernie. 2013. "A Single-Payer System Makes Economic Sense." *The Hill*, September 10.

Sawhill, Isabel V. and Katherine Guyot. 2020. "The Middle Class Time Squeeze." Brookings Institution.

Schakel, Wouter. 2021. "Unequal Policy Responsiveness in the Netherlands." *Socio-Economic Review* 19, 37–57.

Schall, Carly Elizabeth. 2016. *The Rise and Fall of the Miraculous Welfare Machine: Immigration and Social Democracy in Twentieth-Century Sweden*. ILR University Press.

Schanzenbach, Diane Whitmore and Michael R. Strain. 2020. "Employment Effects of the Earned Income Tax Credit: Taking the Long View." Working Paper 28041, National Bureau of Economic Research.

Schmitt, John. 2013. "Why Does the Minimum Wage Have No Discernible Effect on Employment?" Center for Economic and Policy Research.

Schneiberg, Marc. 2011. "Toward an Organizationally Diverse American Capitalism? Cooperative, Mutual, and Local, State-Owned Enterprise." *Seattle University Law Review* 34, 1409–1434.

Schneider, Daniel and Kristen Harknett. 2018. "Consequences of Routine Work Schedule Instability for Worker Health and Wellbeing." Washington Center on Equitable Growth.

Schor, Juliet B. 1991. *The Overworked American*. Basic Books.

Schweickart, David. 2011. *After Capitalism*. 2nd edition. Rowman and Littlefield.

Scruggs, Lyle. 2002. "The Ghent System and Union Membership in Europe, 1970–1996." *Political Research Quarterly* 55, 275–297.

Scruggs, Lyle and Salil Benegal. 2012. "Declining Public Concern about Climate Change: Can We Blame the Great Recession?" *Global Environmental Change* 22, 505–515.

Sen, Amartya. 1999. *Development as Freedom.* Oxford University Press.

Sen, Amartya. 2009. *The Idea of Justice.* Harvard University Press.

Settle, Michael. 2015. "Corbyn: I'm a Socialist Not a Unionist." *The Herald*, August 17.

Sherwood, Steven C. and Matthew Huber. 2010. "An Adaptability Limit to Global Warming Due to Heat Stress." *Proceedings of the National Academy of Sciences.*

Shonfield, Andrew. 1965. *Modern Capitalism.* Oxford University Press.

Simons, Henry C. 1948. *Economic Policy for a Free Society.* University of Chicago Press.

Sinclair, Upton. 1906. *The Jungle.*

Smith, Adam. 1776. *The Wealth of Nations.*

Smith, Richard. 2021. "Six Theses on Saving the Planet." In *The New Systems Reader*, edited by James Gustave Speth and Kathleen Courrier, Routledge, 173–192.

Sommeiller, Estelle and Mark Price. 2018. "The New Gilded Age: Income Inequality in the U.S. by State, Metropolitan Area, and County." Economic Policy Institute.

Sparer, Michael S. 2018. "Buying into Medicaid: A Viable Path for Universal Coverage." *The American Prospect*, January 10.

Speth, James Gustave, and Kathleen Courrier, eds. 2021. *The New Systems Reader.* Routledge.

Standing, Guy. 2011. *The Precariat.* Bloomsbury.

Standing, Guy. 2017. *Basic Income: A Guide for the Open-Minded.* Yale University Press.

Starr, Paul. 2017. "The Next Progressive Health Agenda." *The American Prospect*, March 23.

Steinmo, Sven. 1988. "Social Democracy vs. Socialism: Goal Adaptation in Social Democratic Sweden." *Politics and Society* 16, 403–446.

Stern, Andy with Lee Kravitz. 2016. *Raising the Floor: How a Universal Basic Income Can Renew Our Economy and Rebuild the American Dream.* PublicAffairs.

Stevenson, Betsey and Justin Wolfers. 2008. "Economic Growth and Subjective Well-Being: Reassessing the Easterlin Paradox." *Brookings Papers on Economic Activity*, Spring, 1–87.

Stewart, Emily. 2018. "California Just Passed a Law Requiring More Women on Boards. It Matters, Even if It Fails." *Vox*, October 3.

Stiglitz, Joseph E. 1989. "On the Economic Role of the State." In *The Economic Role of the State*, edited by Arnold Heertje, Basil Blackwell.

Stiglitz, Joseph E. 2006. *Making Globalization Work.* W.W. Norton.

Stiglitz, Joseph E. 2009. "Drunk Driving on the US's Road to Recovery." *Real Clear Politics*, January 9.

Stiglitz, Joseph E. 2012. *The Price of Inequality.* W.W. Norton.

Streeck, Wolfgang. 2014. *Buying Time: The Delayed Crisis of Democratic Capitalism.* Verso.

Streeck, Wolfgang. 2016. *How Will Capitalism End? Essays on a Failing System.* Verso.

Streeck, Wolfgang and Lane Kenworthy. 2005. "Theories and Practices of Neo-Corporatism." In *The Handbook of Political Sociology*, edited by Thomas Janoski, Robert Alford, Alexander Hicks, and Mildred A. Schwartz, Cambridge University Press, 441–460.

Sunkara, Bhaskar, ed. 2016. *The ABCs of Socialism.* Verso.

Sunkara, Bhaskar. 2019. *The Socialist Manifesto*. Basic Books.

Swenson, Peter. 1989. *Fair Shares: Unions, Pay, and Politics in Sweden and West Germany*. Cornell University Press.

Tabarrok, Alex. 2015. "The Case for Getting Rid of Borders—Completely." *The Atlantic*, October 10.

Tanner, Michael. 2015. "The Pros and Cons of a Guaranteed National Income." Policy Analysis 773. Cato Institute.

Taylor, Keeanga-Yamahtta. 2016. "What about Racism?" In *The ABCs of Socialism*, edited by Bhaskar Sunkara, Verso, 70–81.

Terkel, Studs. 1974. *Working: People Talk about What They Do All Day and How They Feel about What They Do*. Pantheon.

Thaker, Anant C. and Elizabeth C. Williamson. 2012. "Unequal and Unstable: The Relationship between Inequality and Financial Crises." New America Foundation.

The Economist. 2010. "The Science of Climate Change." March 18.

The Economist. 2013. "Special Report: The Nordic Countries." February 2.

Thernstrom, Stephen and Abigail Thernstrom. 1997. *America in Black and White: One Nation, Indivisible*. Harvard University Press.

Therborn, Goran. 1978. *What Does the Ruling Class Do When It Rules?* Verso.

Therborn, Goran. 2013. *The Killing Fields of Inequality*. Polity Press.

Thier, Hadas. 2021. *A People's Guide to Capitalism*. Haymarket Books.

Thomas, Norman. 1953. *Democratic Socialism: A New Appraisal*. League for Industrial Democracy.

Thompson, Jeffrey P. and Gustavo A. Suarez. 2019. "Accounting for Racial Wealth Disparities in the United States." Working Paper 19-13, Federal Reserve Bank of Boston.

Thurow, Lester C. 1984. "Building a World-Class Economy." *Society* 22, 16–29.

Tooze, Adam. 2018. *Crashed: How a Decade of Financial Crises Changed the World*. Penguin.

Trickey, Erick. 2020. "How Boston Is Becoming the City Where Workers Rule." *Politico*, March 12.

Triesman, Daniel. 2018. "Is Democracy in Danger? A Quick Look at the Data."

Truesdale, Beth C. and Christopher Jencks. 2016. "The Health Effects of Income Inequality: Averages and Disparities." *Annual Review of Sociology* 37, 413–430.

Tucker, Todd. 2019. "Industrial Policy and Planning." Roosevelt Institute.

Tversky, Amos and Daniel Kahneman. 1992. "Advances in Prospect Theory: Cumulative Representation of Uncertainty." *Journal of Risk and Uncertainty* 5: 297–323.

Twenge, Jean M. 2017. *iGen: Why Today's Super-Connected Kids Are Growing Up Less Rebellious, More Tolerant, Less Happy—and Completely Unprepared for Adulthood*. Atria Books.

Uchitelle, Louis. 2006. *The Disposable American*. Knopf.

UK Labour Party. 2017. "Alternative Models of Ownership."

US Congressional Budget Office. 2008. "Growing Disparities in Life Expectancy." Economic and Budget Issue Brief.

Usmani, Adaner. 2018. "The Rise and Fall of Labor."

Van Parijs, Philippe. 2001. "A Basic Income for All." In *What's Wrong with a Free Lunch?* edited by Joshua Cohen and Joel Rogers, Beacon Press, 3–26.

Van Parijs, Philippe and Yannick Vanderborght. 2017. *Basic Income*. Harvard University Press.

Varghese, Robin. 2018. "What Did You Expect from Capitalism?" *Foreign Affairs*, July–August, 34–42.

Varoufakis, Yanis. 2018. "Marx Predicted Our Present Crisis—and Points the Way Out." *The Guardian*, April 20.

Veenhoven, Ruut. 1999. "Quality-of-Life in Individualistic Society: A Comparison in 43 Nations in the Early 1990s." *Social indicators Research* 48, 157–186.

Vitols, Sigurt. 2010. "Board Level Employee Representation, Executive Remuneration, and Firm Performance in Large European Companies." Hans Böckler Foundation.

Voitchovsky, Sarah. 2009. "Inequality and Economic Growth." In *The Oxford Handbook of Economic Inequality*, edited by Wiemer Salverda, Brian Nolan, and Timothy M. Smeeding, Oxford University Press, 549–574.

Volscho, Thomas W. and Nathan J. Kelley. 2012. "The Rise of the Super-Rich: Power Resources, Taxes, Financial Markets, and the Dynamics of the Top 1 Percent, 1949 to 2008." *American Sociological Review* 77, 679–699.

Wagner, Gernot and Martin L. Weitzman. 2015. *Climate Shock: The Economic Consequences of a Hotter Planet*. Princeton University Press.

Wagner, John. 2018. "'No Person in America Should Be Too Poor to Live': Ocasio-Cortez Explains Democratic Socialism to Colbert." *Washington Post*, June 29.

Wallace-Wells, David. 2019. *The Uninhabitable Earth*. Duggan Books.

Wallerstein, Immanuel. 1974. *The Modern World-System I: Capitalist Agriculture and the Origins of the European World-Economy in the Sixteenth Century*. Academic Press.

Wallerstein, Immanuel, Randall Collins, Michael Mann, Georgi Derluguian, and Craig Calhoun. 2013. *Does Capitalism Have a Future?* Oxford University Press.

Wallerstein, Michael. 1999. "Wage-Setting Institutions and Pay Inequality in Advanced Industrial Societies." *American Journal of Political Science* 43, 649–680.

Walzer, Michael. 1978. "Town Meetings and Workers' Control." *Dissent*, Summer, 325–333.

Walzer, Michael. 1990. "A Credo for This Moment." *Dissent*, Spring, 160.

Walzer, Michael. 2010. "Which Socialism?" *Dissent*, Summer.

Warren, Elizabeth. 2018. "Companies Shouldn't Be Accountable Only to Shareholders." *Wall Street Journal*, August 14.

Weber, Max. 1905. *The Protestant Ethic and the Spirit of Capitalism*.

Weil, David. 2014. *The Fissured Workplace*. Harvard University Press.

Weisburd, Sarit. 2021. "Police Presence, Rapid Response Rates, and Crime Prevention." *Review of Economics and Statistics* 103(2), 280–293.

Weitzman, Martin L. 1984. *The Share Economy*. Harvard University Press.

Welzel, Christian. 2013. *Freedom Rising: Human Empowerment and the Quest for Emancipation*. Cambridge University Press.

Western, Bruce. 1997. *Between Class and Market: Postwar Unionization in the Capitalist Democracies*. Princeton University Press.

Western, Bruce and Jake Rosenfeld. 2012. "Workers of the World Divide: The Decline of Labor and the Future of the Middle Class." *Foreign Affairs*, May-June.

Wickham, C., R. Rohde, R.A. Muller, J. Wurtele, J. Curry, et al. 2013. "Influence of Urban Heating on the Global Temperature Land Average using Rural Sites Identified from MODIS Classifications." *Geoinformatics and Geostatistics: An Overview*.

Wilensky, Harold. 2002. *Rich Democracies*. University of California Press.

Wilkinson, Adrian and Tony Dundon. 2010. "Direct Employee Participation." *Oxford Handbook of Participation in Organizations*, edited by Adrian Wilkinson, Paul J. Gollan, Mick Marchington, and David Lewin, Oxford University Press, 167–185.

Wilkinson, Richard and Kate Pickett. 2009. *The Spirit Level: Why Greater Equality Makes Societies Stronger*. Bloomsbury Press.

Wilkinson, Will. 2017. "Public Policy after Utopia." Niskanen Center, October 24.

Witkowsky, Patrik, Jesper Lundgren, André Nyström, and Nils Säfström. 2015. *Can We Do It Ourselves? A Film about Economic Democracy*. https://www.youtube.com/watch?v=ZfaFriFAz1k.

Wlezien, Christopher and Stuart N. Soroka. 2011. "Inequality in Policy Responsiveness?" In *Who Gets Represented?*, edited by Peter K. Enns and Christopher Wlezien, Russell Sage Foundation, 285–310.

Wolff, Edward D. 2021. "African-American and Hispanic Income, Wealth, and Homeownership Since 1989." *Review of Income and Wealth*, doi: 10.1111/roiw.12518.

Wolff, Richard D. 2012. *Democracy at Work: A Cure for Capitalism*. Haymarket Books.

World Health Organization. 2014. "Quantitative Risk Assessment of the Effects of Climate Change on Selected Causes of Death, 2030s and 2050s."

Wright, Erik Olin. 2010. *Envisioning Real Utopias*. Verso.

Wright, Erik Olin. 2017. "What Is Socialism?" Lecture notes, Sociology 621, University of Wisconsin.

Wright, Erik Olin. 2019. *How to Be an Anticapitalist in the Twenty-First Century*. Verso.

Wright, Erik Olin and Joel Rogers. 2015. *American Society: How It Really Works*. 2nd edition. W.W. Norton.

Yang, Yao. 2020. "China's Economic Growth in Retrospect." In *China 2049: Economic Challenges of a Rising Global Power*, edited by David Dollar, Yiping Huang, and Yang Yao, Brookings Institution Press, 3–28.

Yglesias, Matthew. 2018. "Elizabeth Warren Has a Plan to Save Capitalism." *Vox*, August 15.

Young, Kevin A., Tarun Banerjee, and Michael Schwartz. 2020. *Levers of Power: How the 1% Rules and What the 99% Can Do about It*. Verso.

Younis, Mohamed. 2019. "Four in Ten Americans Embrace Some Form of Socialism." Gallup, May 10.

Zwolinski, Matt. 2015. "Property Rights, Coercion, and the Welfare State: The Libertarian Case for a Basic Income for All." *Independent Review* 19, 515–529.

Zysman, John. 1983. *Governments, Markets, and Growth*. Cornell University Press.

Index

Figures are indicated by *f* following the page number

Accountable Capitalism Act (United States), 112
Acemoglu, Daron, 56
Adler, Paul, 162
African Americans. *See* Black Americans
Alaska, 23
altruism, 153
Ansel, Bridget, 54
Aschoff, Nicole, 131
Atkinson, Anthony, 93–94
Australia, 59*f*, 71, 84, 89
Austria, 9, 59*f*, 85, 112, 117

Bartels, Larry, 100–103
Belgium
  concertation in, 117
  economic growth in, 59*f*
  healthcare in, 85
  minimum wage in, 70
  public sector employment and, 42
  unions in, 66–67
  wage levels in, 65–66
Bello, Walden, 91
Berlin, Isaiah, 5
Biden, Joe, 104
Black Americans. *See also* racial equality
  civil rights movement and, 138
  corporate leadership positions held by, 138, 140, 143, 166
  education among, 138–139, 143, 166
  happiness levels among, 141–143, 166
  income inequality and, 131, 139–141
  labor markets and, 138–139, 143
  life expectancy among, 141, 143
  political inequality and, 141–143
  poverty among, 138
  slavery and segregation's legacies among, 137
  wages among, 138–140, 143
  white Americans' public opinion regarding, 146*f*
Blair, Tony, 9
Block, Fred, 91
Bloomberg, Michael, 99
Botswana, 28, 32

Boushey, Heather, 54
Brandeis, Louis, 97
Brazil, 24, 25*f*, 28, 32
Brooks, David, 151
Brown, Gordon, 9
Burstein, Paul, 101
Bush, George H.W., 104
Bush, George W., 104–105, 123

California, 71, 106–107, 134, 161, 166
Calvinism, 57
Canada
  economic growth in, 59*f*
  greenhouse gas emissions in, 161
  healthcare in, 84–85
  life expectancy and, 20
  minimum wage in, 70
  universal basic income programs in, 23
capitalism. *See also* social democratic capitalism
  altruism and, 153
  automation and, 17, 20, 36, 44, 49, 64
  climate change and, 162
  democracy and, 97–98
  economic democracy and, 115–116, 118, 165
  economic growth and, 15–16, 56–62, 64, 167
  financial crises and, 91–93
  gender inequality and, 131–137, 143, 145, 165–166
  globalization and, 16–17, 20, 27, 28*f*, 36, 44, 49, 64, 167
  income inequality and, 93, 97–98, 120–121, 131, 167
  income redistribution programs and, 22–23
  job regularity and security under, 48–51, 55, 163
  job satisfaction levels under, 54–55, 163
  labor markets and, 36–37, 39–40, 44, 64, 163
  low-end household income and, 16, 20, 22
  political equality and, 165
  poverty and, 15, 17, 24, 163
  predicted collapse of, 167–168
  private property and, 56
  public goods and, 79–81, 164
  public opinion regarding, 1

capitalism (*cont.*)
   racial equality and, 131, 143
   recessions and, 40
   social cohesion and, 144, 151–152
   social support under, 152–153, 166
   tolerance and inclusion under, 144–148, 166, 168
   trust levels under, 148–150, 166
   unions and, 16, 44
   wages and, 16, 64–74, 128, 164, 167
   welfare state programs and, 22, 64, 117
   work hours under, 51–54
   working conditions under, 44–48, 55, 163
Caplan, Brian, 34
Card, David, 71–72
Carville, James, 94
Chibber, Vivek, 15
childcare programs
   gender equality and, 133
   as a public good, 75–76, 78
   social democratic capitalism and, 2, 4, 22
China
   economic growth in, 28, 30–31, 57–58
   global trade and, 28, 31
   greenhouse gas emissions in, 161
   migration within, 33–34
   nondemocratic capitalism in, 168
   poverty in, 24, 30
Chomsky, Noam, 108
Citizens United v. FEC, 104
Civil Rights Act of 1964 (United States), 138
Civil War (United States), 105, 137
Clemens, Michael, 32
climate change
   capitalism and, 162
   clean energy sources as means of combating, 63, 118, 159–160, 162, 166
   democratic socialism and, 161–162, 166
   economic growth and, 56, 162, 166
   geoengineering as a means of combating, 160
   global warming and, 155, 157–159
   greenhouse gas emissions and, 155–157, 159–162
   human health and, 158
   Intergovernmental Panel on Climate Change and, 157–158
   mass extinctions and, 158–159
   melting of Greenland and West Antarctic ice sheets and, 158
   Paris Climate Accord and, 159, 161
Clinton, Bill, 104–105
Clinton, Hillary, 72
Cohen, G.A., 153–154

community, 154, 166
concertation, 117–119, 165
Conservative Party (United Kingdom), 9
Corbyn, Jeremy, 11
coupon socialism, 12–13, 74, 127
Covid-19 pandemic, 40, 69
Cuba, 1

Dahl, Robert, 108
democracy
   campaign finance and, 99, 104–105, 165
   capitalism and, 97–98
   far-right parties and, 98
   income inequality and, 97–107, 129
   majority rule in, 98
   political equality and, 97–98, 164–165
   public opinion regarding, 98
   voting rights and, 165
Democratic Party (United States), 1, 13–14, 104–105
democratic socialism. *See also* socialism
   climate change and, 161–162, 166
   community cohesion under, 154, 166
   coupon socialism and, 12–13, 74, 127
   economic democracy and, 13–14, 115–119, 165–167
   economic equality and, 1, 11, 13–14, 63, 107, 120, 127–129, 165–167
   economic growth and, 14, 62–63, 164
   finance sector and, 96
   financial crises and, 63, 164
   gender equality and, 14, 141–143, 165–166
   government steering of investment to specific sectors under, 62–63, 118, 164
   healthcare and, 14, 87–90, 164
   immigration policies and, 34–35
   labor markets and, 14, 37, 42–43, 55, 163
   political equality and, 107, 164–165
   poverty and, 14–15, 24, 163
   profit sharing and, 42, 74, 164, 167
   public goods and, 75, 81, 164
   public ownership of businesses and, 11–13, 62–63, 128, 168
   racial equality and, 14, 141–143, 166
   Sanders and, 1, 14
   wages and, 74, 164
   wealth inequality and, 128
   worker cooperatives and, 13, 42–43, 128, 163
Democratic Socialists of America (DSA), 1
Denmark
   board-level employee representation in, 112
   concertation in, 117
   economic growth in, 59*f*
   economic insecurity levels in, 19

happiness levels in, 8
healthcare in, 84–85
income inequality in, 127, 129
public sector employment in, 42
social democratic capitalism and, 7
unions in, 67
work scheduling in, 54
Dube, Arindrajit, 71–72
Du Bois, W.E.B., 186–187n7
Durkheim, Émile, 151

Earned Income Tax Credit (EITC, United
    States), 72–73, 106
economic democracy
    board-level employee representation and,
        112, 165
    capitalism and, 115–116, 118, 165
    concertation and, 117–119, 165
    democratic polities and, 116–117
    democratic socialism and, 13–14, 115–119,
        165–167
    employee share ownership plans and, 113–114
    poverty and, 15
    unions and, 109–110, 116, 165
    worker participation in decision-making,
        109, 165
    works councils and, 110–112, 165
economic growth
    capitalism and, 15–16, 56–62, 64, 167
    climate change and, 56, 162, 166
    cultural foundations of, 57
    democratic socialism and, 14, 62–63, 164
    effective government and, 57
    financial crises and, 63
    greenhouse gas emissions and, 162, 166
    income inequality and, 63–64, 125, 129, 164–165
    life expectancy and, 16
    living standards and, 56
    low-end household income and, 17, 18f, 20
    markets and, 56–57
    property rights and, 15, 60
    public services and, 60
    scientific research and, 57
    social democratic capitalism and, 2, 14
    unions and, 110
economic insecurity, 5–6, 19, 75
economic stability, 91–94
education
    apprenticeship programs and, 77
    early childhood education programs and, 4
    gender equality and, 132–133, 142, 165
    income inequality and, 121, 124–125, 129
    public colleges and, 76–77
    as a public good, 75–77, 80

public sector employment in, 168
    racial equality and, 138–139, 143, 146, 166
    social democratic capitalism and, 2, 10
Einstein, Albert, 144
eldercare, 4, 22, 79, 133
electric vehicles, 160
employee share ownership plans, 113–114
employment. See labor markets
European Convention on Human Rights, 161
European Union, 34

family leave programs, 4, 76, 78, 106
Federal Reserve (United States), 40, 69, 94
financial sector
    automation and, 122
    biases in, 95–96
    capital movement and, 94–95
    capital requirements and, 92
    climate change and, 96
    democratic socialism and, 96, 164
    financial crises and, 91–92, 164
    income inequality and, 122
    necessary role of, 91
    political influence of, 94
    public investment and, 96
    regulation of, 92–93
    transaction taxes and, 93
Finland
    board-level employee representation in, 112
    economic growth in, 59f
    economic security in, 5
    happiness levels in, 8
    healthcare in, 84
    life expectancy in, 19
    public sector employment and, 42
    social democratic capitalism and, 7
    unions in, 67
    universal basic income programs in, 23
Fischer, Claude, 151–152
Fleurbaey, Marc, 108
France
    board-level employee representation in, 112
    economic growth in, 15, 16f, 59f, 63
    European Union immigration policy and, 34
    greenhouse gas emissions in, 161
    healthcare in, 85–86, 89
    life expectancy in, 19
    minimum wage in, 70
    public sector employment and, 42
    state guidance of the economy in, 63, 118
    unions in, 66–67
    wage levels in, 66
    wealth inequality in, 125–126
    work hours in, 51

freedom
    affluence and, 27
    democratic socialism and, 1
    employment and, 23, 109
    of movement, 33
    positive liberty and, 5
    property rights and, 56
    public goods and, 75
    social democratic capitalism and, 5–6, 169

gay rights, 147–148
gender equality
    capitalism and, 131–137, 143, 145, 165–166
    childcare and, 133
    democratic socialism and, 14, 141–143,
        165–166
    education and, 132–133, 142, 165
    employment rates and, 38–39, 133, 143, 145
    family leave programs and, 133
    happiness and, 135–136, 142, 165–166
    life expectancy and, 135–136, 142, 165
    political equality and, 97, 135, 137
    public opinion regarding, 145
    unions and, 134
    United States and, 132, 134
    wages and, 134–135, 143, 166
    women in corporate leadership roles and,
        133–134, 166
Germany
    board-level employee representation in, 112,
        112n29
    Covid-19 fiscal policies and, 40
    economic growth in, 15–17, 58–59
    European Union immigration policy
        and, 34
    greenhouse gas emissions in, 161
    healthcare in, 85–86, 89
    link between income inequality and political
        inequality in, 103
    low-end household income in, 17
    pension programs in, 26
    public sector employment and, 42
    reunification (1990) of, 17, 112n29
    social democratic capitalism and, 9
    unions in, 68
    work scheduling in, 54
Gilded Age (United States), 106
Gilens, Martin, 100–102, 105–106
Glass-Steagall Law (United States), 93
Global Financial Crisis (2008-9), 20, 40, 94. See
    also Great Recession
global warming, 155, 157–159. See also climate
    change
Great Depression, 26, 105, 126
Great Recession, 40, 64, 94, 125. See also Global
    Financial Crisis (2008-9)

greenhouse gas emissions, 155–157, 159–162
Greenspan, Alan, 69, 94

Hacker Jacob, 99, 102
happiness
    gender equality and, 135–136, 142, 165–166
    income inequality and, 125, 129, 165
    racial inequality and, 141–143, 166
    social democratic capitalism and, 7, 169
Harrington, Michael, 56
Hayek, Friedrich, 167
healthcare
    avoidable death rates and, 87, 88f
    copayments and, 84–86
    democratic socialism and, 14, 87–90, 164
    employers' role in providing, 85–86
    income inequality and, 19
    insurance fund healthcare systems and,
        85–89, 164
    life expectancy and, 82, 87, 164
    markets and, 83
    Medicaid and, 84–85, 106
    Medicare and, 84–85
    Military Health System (US) and, 84
    National Health Service (United Kingdom)
        and, 84
    patient choice and, 83
    as public good, 75–76, 78–80
    public sector employment in, 168
    single-payer model of, 82–85, 87–90, 164
    spending on, 82–83, 87, 88f, 164
    United States and, 19, 84–85, 88–89
    Veterans Administration (US) and, 84
Hochschild, Arlie, 48

income inequality. See also poverty
    automation and, 122–124
    bottom 99 percent of incomes and, 123–124,
        126, 128
    capitalism and, 93, 97–98, 120–121, 131, 167
    corporate governance and, 122
    democracy and, 97–107, 129
    democratic socialism and, 1, 11, 13–14, 63,
        107, 120, 127–129, 165–167
    economic growth and, 63–64, 125, 129, 164–165
    education and, 121, 124–125, 129
    financial crises and, 93–94
    financial sector and, 122
    globalization and, 122–124
    government transfers and, 21
    happiness and, 125, 129, 165
    healthcare and, 19
    home equity and, 129, 139–140
    immigration and, 121–122
    large firms' dominant market positions
        and, 123

life expectancy and, 125
minimum wages and, 121
Nordic countries and, 121, 123, 128–129, 165
normative arguments regarding, 129, 165
one-adult households and, 124
political inequality and, 99–103, 107, 165
public goods and, 75
racial inequality and, 131, 139–141
stock prices and, 122
taxes and, 103–104, 123, 126
top 1 percent of incomes and, 121–123, 126
unions and, 109, 123–124, 126
wage inequality and, 123–124
wealth inequality and, 125–128
women's employment and, 124
India, 24, 25*f*, 30–32, 34
Inglehart, Ronald, 26, 147
insurance fund healthcare systems, 85–89, 164
Intergovernmental Panel on Climate Change
    (IPCC), 157–158
International Monetary Fund (IMF), 31
Ireland, 58, 60*f*, 70, 84, 112
Italy, 19, 60*f*, 84, 133
Iversen, Torben, 95

Japan
    economic growth in, 58, 60*f*, 63
    gender pay inequality in, 134
    greenhouse gas emissions in, 161
    healthcare in, 85–86
    income inequality in, 103
    public sector employment and, 41–42
    state guidance of the economy in, 63, 118
    taxes in, 103
    work hours in, 51
jobs. *See* labor markets
job satisfaction, 54–55, 163
Johnson, Lyndon B., 137

Kerner Commission, 137
Keynes, John Maynard, 36, 40–41, 167
King Jr., Martin Luther, 120
Klein, Naomi, 155, 162
Korea. *See* South Korea
Krueger, Alan, 72
Krugman, Paul, 31, 62, 99

labor markets
    automation and, 36, 39
    capitalism and, 36–37, 39–40, 44, 64, 163
    democratic socialism and, 14, 37, 42–43,
        55, 163
    employment-promoting government
        services and, 2–4, 10
    employment rates and, 37–39, 163
    fiscal policy and, 40

gender equality and, 38–39, 133, 143, 145
globalization and, 36
job placement and retraining programs'
    impact on, 4
manufacturing sector and, 39
minimum wages and, 71
monetary policy and, 40, 68–69
Nordic countries and, 7–8
public sector employment and, 41–42
racial equality and, 138–139
recessions and, 40
service sector and, 39
social democratic capitalism and, 2–5, 10, 43
unemployment rates and, 20, 37, 69, 71
universal basic income programs and, 23
wages and, 68–69
worker cooperatives and, 42–43, 163
Labour Party (United Kingdom), 9
Levine, Andrew, 153
life expectancy
    economic growth and, 16
    gender equality and, 135–136, 142, 165
    healthcare and, 82, 87, 164
    income inequality and, 125
    poverty and, 19–20, 26
    racial inequality and, 141, 143
life satisfaction. *See* happiness
living standards
    democratic socialism and, 163–164
    economic growth and, 56
    economic inequality and, 64
    the least well-off and, 8*f*, 17
    in the nineteenth-century United States, 106
    ordinary workers and, 16
    public goods and, 75
    social democratic capitalism and, 2–3, 168
Lucas, Robert, 40

Malleson, Tom, 13, 91, 96, 115–116
markets, 2–4, 10, 56–57, 83
Marx, Karl, 2, 15, 94, 167
Mauritius, 28, 32
Medicaid, 84–85, 106
Medicare, 84–85
Meidner Plan (Sweden), 113
methane emissions, 156–157
Mill, John Stuart, 5
minimum wages
    economic redistribution and, 16
    global minimum wage proposal and, 31
    income inequality and, 121
    policymakers' role in setting, 70–71
    sector-specific minimum wages and, 71, 164, 167
    subnational variations in, 71–72, 106
    unemployment levels and, 71
    unions and, 69

Mitterrand, François, 94
Morelli, Salvatore, 93–94
Myrdal, Gunnar, 137

Naik, Vipul, 34
National Health Service (NHS, United Kingdom), 84
National Labor Relations Act (United States, 1935), 66–67
The Netherlands
    board-level employee representation in, 112
    concertation in, 117
    economic growth in, 58, 60f
    greenhouse gas emissions in, 161
    healthcare in, 85–86, 89
    income inequality in, 127
    minimum wage in, 70
    public sector employment in, 42
    relationship between income inequality and political inequality in, 103
    social democratic capitalism in, 9
    unions in, 66–67
    wage levels in, 66
    works councils in, 111
New York State, 71, 106, 161
New Zealand, 60f, 70, 84, 89, 161
Nolan, Brian, 64
Nordhaus, William, 159
Nordic countries. See also specific countries
    balanced public budgets in, 40
    clean energy programs and, 166
    economic democracy and, 165
    economic security in, 129
    happiness levels in, 8
    healthcare and, 164
    income inequality in, 121, 123, 128–129, 165
    labor markets in, 7–8
    life expectancy in, 22
    low-end household income in, 7–8, 17, 22
    public goods and, 81, 164
    public sector employment and, 42
    social democratic capitalism and, 2–3, 9, 14, 128, 168–169
    unions in, 66, 74, 164
    wages in, 66, 74, 164
    welfare state programs in, 10, 22, 141
Norway
    board-level employee representation in, 112
    concertation in, 117
    economic growth in, 60f
    greenhouse gas emissions and, 161
    happiness levels in, 8
    healthcare in, 84, 89
    income inequality in, 103, 127, 129

life expectancy in, 19
public sector employment and, 42
social democratic capitalism and, 7
taxes in, 103
unions in, 67
women in corporate leadership roles in, 134

Obama, Barack, 104–105, 138
Ocasio-Cortez, Alexandria, 15
Olsen, Gregg, 15
open border immigration policies, 32–35, 163
opportunity, 2, 5–6, 169

Packard, Vance, 151
Page, Benjamin, 105–106
Paris Climate Accord, 159, 161
Partanen, Anu, 5–6
Pierson, Paul, 99, 102
Piketty, Thomas, 120
plutocracy, 99–106
populist parties, 167
Portugal, 60f, 84
postmaterialism, 26–27, 147
poverty. See also income inequality
    Black Americans and, 138
    "the bottom billion" and, 32
    capitalism and, 15, 17, 24, 163
    China and, 24, 30
    democratic socialism and, 14–15, 24, 163
    economic democracy and, 15
    foreign aid to poor countries and, 31
    global dimensions of, 24–31, 163
    globalization and, 27–28, 31
    immigration policies and, 32–35, 163
    life expectancy and, 19–20, 26
    negative income tax programs and, 22
    social democratic capitalism and, 14, 32, 163, 169
    United States and, 17, 19–20
    universal basic income programs and, 22, 163
profit sharing, 42, 72, 74, 164, 167
The Protestant Ethic and the Spirit of Capitalism (Weber), 57
public goods
    banking services and, 78
    capitalism and, 79–81, 164
    child allowance programs and, 76, 78
    childcare and, 75–76, 78
    democratic socialism and, 75, 81
    disability services and, 76
    economic insecurity and, 75
    education and, 75–77, 80
    family leave programs and, 4, 76, 78
    government-provider model and, 79–80
    healthcare and, 75–76, 78–80

housing and, 77
job training and placement services and, 77
legal services and, 78
pensions and, 78–79
policing and, 78–79
private-provider model and, 80
social division and, 80
transportation and, 78–80
utilities and, 79–80
Puerto Rico, 34
Putnam, Robert, 151
racial equality. *See also* Black Americans
  capitalism and, 131, 143
  corporate leadership positions and, 138, 140,
    143, 166
  democratic socialism and, 14, 141–143, 166
  education and, 138–139, 143, 146, 166
  financial sector and, 96
  happiness levels and, 141–143, 166
  income inequality and, 131, 139–141
  Kerner Commission and, 137
  labor markets and, 138–139
  life expectancy and, 141, 143
  political equality and, 97, 141–143
  public opinion regarding, 146
  wages and, 138–140, 143
Reagan, Ronald, 104–105, 123
recessions, 40, 64, 94, 125
Reconstruction (United States), 105
Republican Party (United States), 95, 104–106,
  110
Riesman, David, 151
Robinson, James, 56
Robinson, Joan, 36
Robinson, Nathan, 44, 75, 174n30
Roemer, John, 12–13, 74, 127–128

Sachs, Jeffrey, 31
Sanders, Bernie, 1, 13–14, 82, 129, 169
San Francisco (California), 54
Schengen Agreement, 34
Schor, Juliet, 44
Sen, Amartya, 5
Singapore, 28, 32
single-payer healthcare
  avoidable death rates and, 87, 88*f*
  copayments and, 84–85
  expenditures under, 87, 88*f*, 164
  government decisions about healthcare costs
    and delivery under, 83–85
  healthcare system performance under, 89–90
  life expectancy and, 87
  referral system under, 84–85
  supplemental insurance and, 84

tax-based funding of, 84
uncovered treatments under, 84
US options regarding, 85
Smith, Richard, 155
social cohesion, 144, 151–152
social democratic capitalism
  economic democracy and, 170
  economic growth and, 2, 14
  economic security and, 2, 4–7, 92–93, 169
  education programs under, 2, 10
  employment-promoting public services and,
    2–4, 10
  equality of opportunity and, 2, 5–6, 169
  finance sector and, 164
  gender equality and, 14, 166
  globalization and, 7
  global poverty and, 32, 163
  happiness and, 7, 169
  healthcare and, 14, 169
  income inequality and, 7, 14
  labor markets and, 2–5, 10, 43
  low-end household income and, 2–4, 7–8
  Nordic model and, 2–3, 9, 14, 128, 168–169
  poverty and, 14, 32, 163, 169
  product market regulation and, 2–4, 10
  public ownership of businesses and, 170
  racial equality and, 14
  welfare state programs and, 2–4, 9–10, 14
socialism. *See also* democratic socialism
  communal reciprocity and, 153
  economic growth and, 62
  global poverty and, 31–32
  government ownership of businesses under, 1
  healthcare and, 83
  public opinion regarding, 1
  "transition trough" regarding, 2
Social policy, 100, 117. *See also* welfare state
Social Security (US pension system), 21
social support, 152–153, 166
solar energy, 159–160
Soroka, Stuart, 102
Soskice, David, 95
South Korea
  economic growth in, 27–28, 60*f*
  economic insecurity levels in, 19
  gender pay inequality in, 134
  government steering of investment to specific
    sectors in, 118
  greenhouse gas emissions in, 161
  healthcare in, 84
  social support levels in, 152*f*, 153
  work hours in, 51
Soviet Union, 1, 120
Spain, 19, 60*f*, 84

Standing, Guy, 44
Steyer, Tom, 99
Streeck, Wolfgang, 36, 167–168
Sunkara, Bhaskar, 24, 162
Sweden
    board-level employee representation in, 112
    concertation in, 117
    earnings subsidies in, 73
    economic growth in, 60*f*
    employment rate in, 37
    greenhouse gas emissions in, 161
    happiness levels in, 8
    healthcare in, 84–85, 89
    income inequality in, 127, 129
    life expectancy in, 19
    public sector employment and, 42
    relationship between income inequality and
        political inequality in, 103
    social democratic capitalism and, 7
    unions in, 67
    wage-earner fund scheme in, 113, 168–169
    wealth inequality in, 125–126
Switzerland
    concertation in, 117
    economic growth in, 60*f*
    healthcare in, 85–86, 89
    life expectancy in, 19
    public sector employment and, 41–42
    relationship between income inequality and
        political inequality in, 103
    universal basic income program proposal in, 23

Taft-Hartley Act (United States, 1949), 110
Taiwan, 28, 32
Taylor, Keeanga-Yamahtta, 131
Temporary Assistance for Needy Families
    (TANF), 106
Thernstrom, Stephen and Abigail, 138
tolerance, 144–148, 166, 168
Tonnies, Fernand, 151
Toyota, 160
trade, 28, 31
"transition trough," 2
Trump, Donald, 99, 104, 123
trust, 148–150, 166

unemployment, 20, 37, 69, 71
unions
    collective bargaining and, 16, 67–68
    concertation and, 117
    decline of, 17, 20, 44, 66–67, 74, 123–124, 167
    economic democracy and, 109–110, 116, 165
    economic growth and, 110

gender inequality and, 134
income inequality and, 109, 123–124, 126
National Labor Relations Act (United States,
    1935) and, 66–67
public ownership of businesses and, 12
strikes and, 16
Taft-Hartley Act (1949) and, 110
in the United States, 66–67, 103, 110
wages and, 66–69, 109, 128, 164
United Kingdom
    earnings subsidies in, 72
    economic growth in, 57–58, 61*f*
    employee share ownership plans in, 113
    European Union immigration policy and, 34
    greenhouse gas emissions in, 161
    healthcare in, 84, 89
    labor markets in, 69
    life expectancy in, 19
    minimum wage in, 70–71
    social democratic capitalism and, 9
    unions in, 68
    wage levels in, 69
    wealth inequality in, 125–126
United States
    campaign finance in, 104–105
    climate change and, 158
    Covid-19 fiscal policies and, 40
    distribution of employment by industry in, 11–12
    economic growth in, 15–17, 58, 61*f*
    economic insecurity in, 5–6, 19
    election (2020) in, 99, 104
    employee share ownership plans
        in, 113–114
    financial sector in, 93
    gay rights and, 147–148
    gender inequality in, 132, 134
    happiness levels in, 8
    healthcare in, 19, 84–85, 88–89
    households with zero earners in, 20–21
    immigrant workers and immigration policy
        in, 32–35, 146–147
    income inequality in, 121, 123, 125
    labor markets in, 8, 20, 68–69
    life expectancy in, 19–20, 87*f*
    low-end household income in, 17, 20–22
    minimum wage in, 70–71
    poverty in, 17, 19–20
    relationship between income inequality and
        political inequality in, 99–103
    social cohesion in, 151–152
    social democratic capitalism and, 9, 169
    taxes in, 103–104, 123
    tolerance and inclusion in, 144–148

trust levels in, 148–149
unemployment in, 20
unions in, 66–67, 103, 110
universal basic income programs in, 23
wage levels in, 64–66, 68–69
wealth inequality in, 125–126
welfare state programs in, 10, 141
winner-take-all election system in, 103
work hours in, 51
universal basic income (UBI), 22–23, 163
unselfishness, 144, 153–15

Vanderborght, Yannick, 22
Van Parijs, Philippe, 22
Varoufakis, Yanis, 64
Vietnam War, 149
Voting Rights Act of 1965, 138

wages
    capitalism and, 16, 64–74, 128, 164, 167
    democratic socialism and, 74, 164
    earnings subsidies and, 72–73
    gender inequality and, 134–135, 143, 166
    profit sharing and, 72
    racial inequality and, 138–140, 143
    unions and, 66–69, 109, 128, 164
Wagner, Gernot, 158
Wallace-Wells, David, 158–159

Walzer, Michael, 108
Watergate scandal (1972-74), 149
wealth inequality, 125–128
Weber, Max, 57, 151
Weitzman, Martin, 158
welfare state
    capitalism and, 22, 64, 117
    in Nordic countries, 10, 22, 141
    social democratic capitalism and, 2–4,
        9–10, 14
    in the United States, 10, 141
Welzel, Christian, 26, 147
Wilkinson, Frank, 36
wind energy, 159–160
Wlezien, Christopher, 102
worker cooperatives
    as defining feature of democratic socialism,
        13, 42
    economic democracy and, 113
    economic equality and, 128
    labor markets and, 42–43, 163
    normative case for, 165
works councils, 110–112, 165
World Bank, 31
World Trade Organization (WTO), 31
World War I, 126
World War II, 105, 126
Wright, Erik Olin, 36, 44, 75, 97, 144